Lay Ecclesial Ministry

Pathways Toward the Future

Edited by
Zeni Fox

A SHEED & WARD BOOK

ROWMAN & LITTLEFIELD PUBLISHERS, INC.
Lanham • New York • Toronto • Plymouth, UK

A Sheed & Ward Book

Rowman & Littlefield Publishers, Inc.

Published by Rowman & Littlefield Publishers, Inc.
A wholly owned subsidary of The Rowman & Littlefield Publishing Group, Inc.
4501 Forbes Boulevard, Suite 200, Lanham, Maryland 20706
http://www.rowmanlittlefield.com

Estover Road, Plymouth PL6 7PY, United Kingdom

British Library Cataloguing in Publication Information Available

Library of Congress Cataloging-in-Publication Data

Lay ecclesial ministry : pathways toward the future / edited by Zeni Fox.
    p. cm.
 Includes index.
 ISBN 978-1-4422-0184-2 (cloth : alk. paper) — ISBN 978-1-4422-0185-9 (pbk. : alk. paper) — ISBN 978-1-4422-0186-6 (electronic)
 1. Lay ministry–United States. 2. Lay ministry–Catholic Church. 3. Catholic Church–United States. 4. Co-workers in the vineyard of the Lord. I. Fox, Zeni.
 BX1920.L38 2010
 262'.152–dc22

                                                     2010009090

Printed in the United States of America

Contents

Foreword

The ten years during which the U.S. Conference of Catholic Bishops (USCCB) Subcommittee on Lay Ministry focused its attention on the issues around lay ecclesial ministry brought many questions to the bishop members of the subcommittee, their advisors and consultants, their staff, and the many persons with whom they dialogued. Those persons came from a wide variety of roles within the church. There were many other bishops from the "related committees" (Canonical Affairs, Diaconate, Doctrine, Laity, Priestly Formation, Vocations) as well as the entire USCCB and bishop representatives from the Conference of Latin American Bishops and the Canadian Conference of Catholic Bishops. There were a number of theologians, directors of ministry formation programs, canon and civil lawyers, priests and deacons, human resource specialists, diocesan officers responsible for staffing parishes, seminary rectors, and many lay ecclesial ministers themselves, from a variety of ethnic backgrounds, who were serving in a wide range of settings. The style of the subcommittee, from its very beginning, was dialogic and consultative.

Some of the persistent questions were how much the subcommittee could say about the phenomenon of lay ecclesial ministry, which the church had witnessed for at least thirty years, as well as how this new phenomenon fit into the theological self-understanding of the church: questions of terminology that required careful nuancing; questions of whether their document should be prescriptive or descriptive; questions of how to say anything, particularly about formation goals, that would be helpful for their brother bishops, given the wide diversity of resources within the U.S. church.

As the document that resulted from the subcommittee's consultations and deliberations, *Co-Workers in the Vineyard of the Lord*, began to assume what would be its final shape, but the bishops realized that whatever they said about this new phenomenon would not be the final word. The subtitle makes that understanding explicit: *A Resource for Guiding the Development of Lay Ecclesial Ministry*. What the bishops finally agreed to call lay ecclesial ministry is a living reality; it is not static but will change and develop in the years to come.

Immediately after its publication, *Co-Workers* was the subject of many articles in various journals and in the newsletters of ministerial associations. It also served as a topic for many ministerial associations during their annual gatherings as well as the principal agenda for several diocesan assemblies involving both laity and clergy. When the document was first published, the general response was deep gratitude for its clarity in acknowledging that lay ecclesial ministry is the work of the Holy Spirit in the church, thus continuing statements the bishops had made about the reality since 1980.

There were also those who expressed disappointment that it was what they described as tentative and modest. That tentativeness and modesty sprang from the bishops' understanding that the work of the Holy Spirit continues. Particularly in the conclusion of *Co-Workers*, the bishops call for continued reflection and examination of lay ecclesial ministry. That is not the perfunctory "implications for further research" that concludes most scholarly work. It is a sincere call for continued theological study and writing about the topic. The bishops acknowledge that they cannot do this work by themselves; they are dependent on the whole church in their task of discerning where the Holy Spirit is leading.

Lay Ecclesial Ministry: Pathways toward the Future is a significant response to that call. Coming five years after the publication of *Co-Workers*, it enjoys a maturity of thought and reflection that only time can bring. The chapters here reflect a range of knowledge and experience similar to that which informed *Co-Workers*. Chapters by lay theologians are side by side with one by a bishop theologian; the writers who contributed to this volume are lay and clerical, vowed religious and married. Several of the writers here contributed to the work of the subcommittee; others bring a fresh perspective from their own areas of study and experience. Canonical and human resource perspectives are side by side with the perspective of spirituality and prayer. The publication of this collection continues well the tradition of dialogue and consultation that was started by the subcommittee.

Zeni Fox, the editor of this book, is well positioned for the task and deserves the gratitude of the entire church for taking it on. The bishops on the subcommittee were limited by USCCB rules to three-year terms, and each of them made significant contributions to the work of the subcommittee during his term. Invited by each succeeding subcommittee chairman to continue to serve as an advisor, Zeni participated throughout its entire history, often providing its institutional memory and always, in her gentle and cogent way, offering insights and observations grounded in her own experiences as theologian, teacher of seminarians and prospective lay ecclesial ministers, and parish minister. For this great expenditure of time and energy, Zeni never received—nor did she ever seek—any compensation beyond travel expenses, but how could one ever repay waiting in airports as flights are delayed and then canceled, rescheduling classes, and postponing family gatherings? It was an extraordinarily generous commitment—and that commitment continues.

The opening of the theological section of *Co-Workers* contains two short, but profound sentences: "God calls. We respond."[1] In many ways, *Co-Workers* itself was a call to the entire church, and the chapters here can surely be considered a response. Each of them is in its own way also a call for further reflection. We are grateful to Zeni and to each of the writers for ensuring that the dialogue continues.

Amy Hoey, RSM

NOTE

1. U.S. Conference of Catholic Bishops, *Co-Workers in the Vineyard of the Lord: A Resource for Guiding the Development of Lay Ecclesial Ministry* (Washington, DC: United States Conference of Catholic Bishops, 2005), 7.

Preface

The future. Certainly, we cannot predict it. But just as certainly, we can contribute to its unfolding. The purpose of this volume is to foster the ongoing development of lay ecclesial ministry, and lay ecclesial ministers, in the Catholic Church in the United States in the years ahead. It builds on work already done, particularly *Co-Workers in the Vineyard of the Lord: A Resource for Guiding the Development of Lay Ecclesial Ministry.* This document, published in 2005, represented a culmination of over ten years of reflection by the bishops of the United States; it in turn built upon the reflection that had been ongoing in the larger Catholic community for about forty years.

Lay ecclesial ministry has arisen as a significant reality in ministerial leadership today through the agency of great numbers of women and men, from a wide diversity of disciplines and roles in the ecclesial community. At the beginning, individual pastors called forth particular persons to lead areas of ministry in their parishes; the early pioneers accepted the invitation to set forth on a path not yet formally named. Colleges and universities, dioceses, and seminaries developed programs designed to form these new leaders for their roles in ministry. Theologians—biblical scholars, canonists, historians, liturgists, systematicians—reflected on this sign of the times and sought the wisdom of the tradition to assess it. Professional organizations of ministers fostered conversation and education about this new ecclesial ministry, and foundations funded studies of the new reality. In the birthing of lay ecclesial ministry, "midwives" were many, and those who fostered its life and growth innumerable. And most important, as *Co-Workers* asserts, "Lay ecclesial ministry has emerged and taken shape in our country through the working of the Holy Spirit."[1] In building on this history, this volume follows a similar pattern, seeking the wisdom of persons with diverse experience, who hold different roles in the church. Through these multiple perspectives we seek to further elucidate this new reality and suggest paths toward the future. Individually and collectively, they chronicle here the ongoing development of lay ecclesial ministry, giving ample evidence of the dynamism of the church, a dynamism that is surely the work of the Spirit, who blows where she will.

Part I examines the response to *Co-Workers* by the church in the United States. In chapter 1 H. Richard McCord, Jr., who has long followed pastoral developments in ministry and who directed the project of the bishops that developed *Co-Workers*, notes that the document has been warmly welcomed by lay ecclesial ministers and assesses the multiple and varied ways it is used in dioceses, colleges, and universities. Richard Gaillardetz, a systematic theologian whose writing and lecturing has influenced many lay ecclesial ministers, analyzes the theological import of this reception in chapter 2. He explores both the theology of ministry the bishops present and what this ecclesial reception represents.

Part II explores the ways in which our theological tradition can further elucidate and support lay ecclesial ministry. In chapter 3, Emil Wcela, a bishop and biblical scholar who served on the committee that developed the document, probes various examples of ministry described in the New Testament and elucidates their value for our understanding of ministry today. The extensive work on the history and theology of ministry by church historian Thomas O'Meara has shaped the conversation for several decades, and in chapter 4 he contributes fresh insights into lay ecclesial ministry by exploring various historical developments in the light of our present reality, reminding us that history is our helper. Systematic theologian Edward Hahnenberg's prior influential work on the theology of ministry is furthered here in chapter 5, as he reflects on the contributions of *Co-Workers*, names the yet unanswered questions that the lived reality of lay ecclesial ministers poses, and identifies areas that call for further theological reflection. In chapter 6 Catherine Vincie, a sacramental and liturgical theologian, probes both church liturgical tradition and theories of ritual from the social sciences and ritual studies to explore the important place that rituals of blessing or authorization hold for lay ecclesial ministers and church communities. In chapter 7, canon lawyer Sharon Euart brings her experience of the life of the church in the United States, gained from over ten years as associate general secretary of the USCCB, to her analysis of the role of canon law in the development of lay ecclesial ministry and of the options the law presents for parish leadership now and implications for the future.

Part III draws upon the spiritual tradition of the church, seeking models for the formation of lay leaders and for the faithful and fruitful living of their lives. Vincentian spirituality scholar and poet Regina Bechtle in chapter 8 presents snapshots of several saints, not simply as guides for personal piety, but more precisely as coaches for assistance in addressing the concrete challenges that arise in ministry, as in life. Juliana Casey is a leader in Catholic health care and a pioneer in the formation of lay leaders in health systems. In chapter 9 she charts the evolution of lay formation in this arena of mission and ministry (broadening the focus beyond that of many of the chapters in this volume that emphasize parish ministry).

Part IV focuses on the implications for pastoral practice of some topics presented in *Co-Workers*. William Johnston is a pastoral theologian and former chair of the National Association for Lay Ministry Board. In chapter 10 he draws upon a broad range of research to address the bishops' emphasis on the importance of both formation and cultural diversity, offering strategies to develop a more richly intercultural ministry formation. In chapter 11, Michael O'Loughlin with Michael Brough, both on the National Leadership Roundtable on Church Management, draw on the best practices from church and business settings to outline what can be done to recruit and retain excellent personnel for church ministry. In chapter 12 I draw on systems theory to explore ways of more effectively integrating lay ecclesial ministers into the community of ministerial leadership. (Chapter 12 is a revised version of articles that first appeared in the publication of the National Pastoral Life Center, *The Common Ground Initiative Newsletter,* in March and June 2005. It is used with permission.)

The foreword is written by Amy Hoey, who coordinated the project that resulted in *Co-Workers*. Writing from her over ten years of work with the subcommittee, she gives a glimpse of the complexities the bishops engaged as they sought clarity about what they named "lay ecclesial ministry." Because she lectured extensively about the document after its publication, she is also able to note some of the responses to it.

As editor of this volume, I came to this project with the conviction that *Co-Workers* represents an important step in the evolution of lay ecclesial ministry and with a desire to further strengthen and support both lay ecclesial ministers and the church we serve. As I thought about what would help my goal, I invited the authors of this volume to share in this effort. To my delight, they agreed to lend their expertise and vision to this project. I am grateful to each of them for making the work of compilation so exciting, especially as I read each of their chapters. (They also made the work much less arduous by their kind attention to deadlines and copyediting suggestions.) One morning I wakened thinking of them. I had the image of gardeners tending the beds, nurturing growth, and then thought: no, tending the vines in the vineyard. And as I pondered further, I realized that I have known each of these men and women, most personally, all of them through their service of the church, for many years. I have much evidence of the faithfulness and fruitfulness of their varied ministries, and I am grateful for *them*, as well as their sharing in this project with me.

The shaping of the framework of this volume was influenced by my students at Seton Hall and in the summers at Fordham University, as well as by countless lay ecclesial ministers throughout the country with whom I have been privileged to interact in various venues. Professional colleagues, especially those involved in the work of the Subcommittee on Lay Ministry of the United States Conference of Catholic Bishops and members of the National Association for Lay Ministry, have been of great assistance in clarifying my understandings of lay ecclesial ministry and what is needed as we move toward the future. I am thankful to each one, companions as we are on this journey.

Because of the sabbatical year granted to me for 2009 by Immaculate Conception Seminary, Seton Hall University School of Theology, I was able to give focused attention to this work. This was my third Seton Hall sabbatical, each allowing me to build on prior work that these gifts of time made possible, for each of which I am grateful. This sabbath time allowed me to work with relaxed concentration, which made the work a joy.

In the final stages of this effort, Patricia Noone gave invaluable editorial expertise, as well as most welcome personal encouragement toward completing the tasks of preparing the manuscript and preparing the index. For her help, and friendship, she has my heartfelt thanks. I am also grateful for the expert editorial assistance of Elaine McGarraugh, production editor, Rowman & Littlefield, who offered many helpful suggestions, and Sarah Stanton, associate editor at Rowman & Littlefield, who shephered this volume.

Finally, it is you, the readers of this book, who will walk the pathways toward the future, building what will be by what you do. Just as many trod the paths that are now known and, relatively speaking, established, so now new pilgrims—lay ecclesial ministers, their co-workers in ministry (bishops, brothers, deacons, lay ministers, priests, sisters), theologians, members of national associations, funders—all following the lead of the Holy Spirit will create the ever-renewed community of the church.

> February 13, 2011
> Feast of Aquila and Priscilla
> Eastern Orthodox Calendar

NOTE

1. U.S. Conference of Catholic Bishops, *Co-Workers in the Vineyard of the Lord: A Resource for Guiding the Development of Lay Ecclesial Ministry* (Washington, DC: United States Conference of Catholic Bishops, 2005), 14.

Part I

RESPONSE TO *CO-WORKERS IN THE VINEYARD OF THE LORD*

Co-Workers in the Vineyard of the Lord: A Pastoral Perspective on Its Reception

H. Richard McCord, Jr.

WHAT'S IN A TITLE?

In the choice of both a title and a subtitle for their document on lay ecclesial ministry, the U.S. Catholic bishops make important points about understanding and using this significant publication. The title, *Co-Workers in the Vineyard of the Lord*, is a variation on St. Paul's description of his colleagues, Prisca and Aquila, as "my co-workers in Christ Jesus" (Rom. 16:3). Using this phrase not only connects the contemporary phenomenon of lay ecclesial ministry to an experience in the early church, but it also discloses that the theological framework for understanding this reality will be a relational theology of ministry that is grounded in an ecclesiology of communion. In additional chapters in this volume, other writers will have more to say about that foundational notion and, by extension, about this rationale for the chosen title.

In this chapter I will focus on the subtitle: *A Resource for Guiding the Development of Lay Ecclesial Ministry*. It is the subtitle that indicates how the bishops intend their document to be used and, I would suggest, also to be assessed for its practical value in the life of the church. The subtitle expresses what the bishops saw themselves doing when they wrote the document. Their intent was not primarily doctrinal nor was it juridical. They did not deliberately propose a set of teachings, nor did they establish particular law or a set of norms that would be binding throughout U.S. dioceses.

Instead, the introduction to *Co-Workers in the Vineyard of the Lord* describes the document as "a common frame of reference for ensuring that the development of lay ecclesial ministry continues in ways that are faithful to the Church's theological and doctrinal tradition and that respond to contemporary pastoral needs and situations."[1] This statement is a key to appreciating how *Co-Workers* fits into the historical flow of the U.S. bishops' theological and pastoral reflection on laity and ministry. It also provides a basis for describing and evaluating how, in the course of the past five years, *Co-Workers* has been received and utilized.

In this chapter I will develop both of those points, namely, the consistent theological and pastoral methodology of the bishops as reflected in *Co-Workers* and the nature of the document as practical guidance. Both points are essential to gaining a pastoral perspective on the reception of *Co-Workers in the Vineyard of the Lord*.

CO-WORKERS AS A RESPONSE

The U.S. Catholic bishops, acting as a national body, made their first official statement about lay ministry in 1980. In a brief, disarmingly simple, and highly readable document titled *Called and Gifted: The American Catholic Laity*, the bishops adopted a stance of describing and reflecting on "what we have been experiencing and learning" from the laity about how they are called to participation in the church as the people of God.[2] The bishops acknowledged emerging developments that might require new concepts, terminology, attitudes, and practices. They approached these matters as partners in an ongoing dialogue, both speaking and listening.

Called and Gifted was issued to commemorate the fifteenth anniversary of the Second Vatican Council's *Decree on the Apostolate of the Laity*. This interval gave the bishops more than a decade to observe and listen before summarizing what they had seen and heard. The practical significance—and humility—of this methodology did not go unnoticed. It set a pattern for future activity.

It should also be noted that *Called and Gifted* first introduced the term "ecclesial ministry" when referring to the role and activity of some lay people. It identified as ecclesial ministers those "lay persons who have prepared for professional ministry in the Church."[3] The bishops welcomed their service as a gift to the church. At the same time, they admitted that the roles of lay ecclesial ministers were not clearly spelled out; they showed an awareness of the sacrifices experienced by the ministers and their families; and they pledged to keep working on solutions to the practical matters of job openings, hiring procedures, and providing just wages and benefits.

Fifteen years later, in 1995, the Bishops Conference published another set of reflections, titled *Called and Gifted for the Third Millennium*. This document followed the outline of the 1980 statement and adopted its attitude of observing and commenting on what laypersons were saying and doing in the life of the church. Lay ecclesial ministry was one topic of reflection. The bishops acknowledged that lay ecclesial ministers often spoke of their service as a calling and not merely a job. They identified the need for respectful collaboration between clergy and laity, going so far as to declare that "the new evangelization will become a reality only if ordained and lay members of Christ's faithful understand their roles and ministries as complementary, and their purposes joined to the one mission and ministry of Jesus Christ."[4]

Finally, beginning in 1995 and ending in 2005 with the publication of *Co-Workers in the Vineyard of the Lord*, the U.S. Conference of Catholic Bishops engaged in a ten-year process of research; theological and pastoral inquiry; and consultation with lay ministers, directors of formation programs, bishops and priests, educators, and a variety of other experts, as well as with representatives from other national episcopal conferences. Their process was one of learning through disciplined and respectful listening to experience as well as consulting church teaching and the relevant theological expertise and literature. In the midst of the process the bishops published a report of their work titled *Lay Ecclesial Ministry: The State of the Questions.*[5] Besides continuing the methodology of engaged listening and pastoral reflection that the bishops initiated in 1980, this document set the stage in an immediate sense for *Co-Workers*. It detailed what had been learned in various aspects of the consultation process and offered some tentative conclusions in propositional form.

With these three documents all leading toward *Co-Workers*, the bishops maintained and even refined a methodology of responding to what they saw, heard, and understood to be happening in the life of the church that was contributing to the emergence of lay ecclesial ministry. This very same methodology is at the heart of *Co-Workers*.

This methodology does not produce statements that are meant to end a dialogue or a process of development. It also does not favor statements that proceed in a deductive fashion from abstract principles to concrete applications. It does not force the bishops to speak only in the language of decrees and norms. At the same time, such an approach does not imply that the bishops are merely casual bystanders making random observations. It requires that they speak as informed and responsible leaders whose ministry is one of oversight (*episcopē*) and who take seriously their scriptural charge not to extinguish the Spirit, but to test everything and to retain what is good (1 Thes. 5:19, 21).

In summary, *Co-Workers in the Vineyard of the Lord* is a response by the bishops as a national body to a phenomenon that has become truly national in scope. Lay ecclesial ministers serve in every region of the country and in many arenas of church life. Thus, it made sense for the bishops to give a national response. Although this was necessary, it was not sufficient. Something more was needed because lay ecclesial ministry, as a national phenomenon, is carried out in local circumstances under a wide variety of leaders. With this in mind, the bishops structured their response as a resource for local leaders to use.

CO-WORKERS AS A RESOURCE

What does it mean to "guide the development of lay ecclesial ministry," and what specific kind of resource would do this? The bishops answer the question by making the following points in the introduction to *Co-Workers*. They describe their document as one that:

- Expresses what was learned from the experiences shared by lay ecclesial ministers;
- Suggests concepts, goals, strategies, resources, and ideas to consider;
- Invites local adaptation, application, and implementation to achieve consistency where possible and to encourage diversity where appropriate;
- Calls church leaders, ordained and lay, to become more intentional and effective in ordering and integrating lay ecclesial ministers within the ministerial life of dioceses.

The kind of resource that the bishops envision *Co-Workers* to be is one that addresses three interconnected challenges or tasks. The tasks are: *naming*, *claiming*, and *sustaining* lay ecclesial ministry as a valid and necessary dimension of church ministry today. *Co-Workers* initiates each of these three tasks by what it presents in the text itself. Then, with the textual material as a resource, it enables pastoral leaders to continue implementing the process in their local settings.

When viewed as a single process, the three tasks describe what the ongoing "development of lay ecclesial ministry" entails. Moreover, it is possible to understand this process as the dynamic of practical "reception" by which *Co-Workers* finds its place in the pastoral activity of the church. In my view, the process is not a linear one but a cyclical one in which the three tasks are always being addressed and a momentum is being created.

In the remainder of this chapter I will describe each task, offer examples of how they are actually being undertaken, and then make a final comment on the process of practical reception.

Naming Lay Ecclesial Ministry

Co-Workers carefully explains each of the three elements that compose the term "lay ecclesial ministry." In addition, it also lists four descriptive characteristics of someone who could be considered a lay ecclesial minister, and it mentions a few examples of roles (e.g., pastoral associate, director of cateche-sis, youth ministry leader) that would fit the descriptive definition offered.[6]

Never before have the bishops been so specific in naming this reality. That fact notwithstanding, however, they are quick to say:

> "Lay ecclesial minister" is not itself a specific position title. We do not use the term in order to establish a new rank or order among the laity. Rather, we use the terminology as adjective to identify a developing and growing reality, to describe it more fully, and to seek a deeper understanding of it under the guid-ance of the Holy Spirit.[7]

In the debate that preceded the vote to approve *Co-Workers*, some bishops challenged and disputed the use of this terminology, expressing fears about the "clericalization of the laity" and the possible confusion of lay ministry with ordained ministry. It was an intervention by Cardinal Avery Dulles on the floor of the Bishops' Conference meeting in November 2005 supporting the terminology and its underlying theology that set some minds at rest and paved the way to an affirmative vote.

A few months later Cardinal Dulles delivered his annual McGinley lecture at Fordham University on the topic of the mission of the laity. In the course of his wide-ranging remarks he commented approvingly on lay ecclesial ministry and, using the language of *Co-Workers in the Vineyard of the Lord*, explained how it was to be understood and justified while not being confused with ordained ministry. Referring to the document he said, "While not mak-ing a class out of lay ministers, it does give them the kind of recognition they so richly deserve."[8]

To name something is to recognize its existence and, implicitly at least, to value it. Naming means distinguishing one thing or person from another. Naming is the beginning of a commitment and a relationship. The bishops began to do all these things when they proposed the title lay ecclesial minister to describe a specific category of lay people. In so doing, they meant to offer a resource that would introduce coherence and consistency into our church lan-guage in the United States. Cardinal Dulles helpfully reinforced their intent.

It is one thing, however, for the bishops to propose a name and quite an-other matter for it actually to be used widely. Thus far it seems that the term lay ecclesial ministry is being accepted and utilized in the way the bishops intended. A few examples may serve to demonstrate this.

Cardinal Francis George has specifically designated pastoral associates and directors of religious education as lay ecclesial ministers in the archdio-cese of Chicago and, on two different occasions, has held a public ceremony in which he called them to ecclesial service in the local church. The diocese of Trenton, as one example among others, has a formal lay ecclesial ministry formation program and an annual commissioning ceremony for the graduates. The diocese of Austin recently established an institute for preparing lay ecclesial ministers. The dioceses of Boise and Oakland have each instituted a Lay Ecclesial Ministry Council as one of their advisory bodies for the bishop.

The biannual *Catholic Ministry Formation Directory*, published by the Center for Applied Research in the Apostolate (CARA), now customarily includes a large section on lay ecclesial ministry formation programs in addition to sections on priestly and diaconal formation.[9]

In the extensive work associated with the national project known as Emerging Models of Pastoral Leadership, the term and the reality of lay ecclesial ministry appear frequently.[10] One gets the impression in such instances that lay ecclesial ministry is an identified and accepted facet of church life in the United States.

This impression is further strengthened when a bishop uses the term in reference to his own diocesan experience. In addition to the example of Cardinal George cited earlier, there is Archbishop John Vlazny (Portland, Oregon),[11] who writes in his diocesan newspaper of lay ecclesial ministers being significant partners with the clergy in church ministry, and Bishop Matthew Clark (Rochester, New York),[12] who writes about the broad reality of lay ecclesial ministry, using the lens of his own local pastoral experience.

Finally, there are numerous examples—virtually impossible to document completely—of articles, lectures, workshops, and the like that continue to occur in dioceses, universities, and the meetings of national associations that explain and expound upon the reality of lay ecclesial ministry using the terminology found in *Co-Workers*. In all these instances the naming function begun by the bishops in their document not only is acknowledged but, more importantly, is continued and strengthened. This is a necessary step in the process of pastoral reception.

Claiming Lay Ecclesial Ministry

Claiming goes a step beyond naming. It involves affirming and legitimizing. To claim is to bring something or someone into a firmer relationship, making a connection between it and a larger whole.

There are three ways in which *Co-Workers* carries out the function of claiming lay ecclesial ministry. Each of them has provided the impetus for the activity to continue happening in the life of the church.

First, *Co-Workers* connects lay ecclesial ministry to the contemporary magisterium and theological tradition by showing how it can be understood as consistent with an ecclesiology of communion and mission that is rooted in the Trinitarian mystery of God's love. The bishops do this in a substantive section of the document titled "Understanding the Realities [of lay ecclesial ministry] in Light of Theology and Church Teaching." Including a solid theological rationale and framework for the practice of lay ecclesial ministry in a document originating from the U.S. bishops has provided a new and needed level of legitimacy.

In chapter 2 of this volume Richard Gaillardetz identifies the main concepts contained in the theology of ministry found in *Co-Workers*. This theological vision is grounded in the excellent work of many scholars influential in the Second Vatican Council and in the years following it. The vision adopted by the bishops stands on the shoulders of such giants as Yves Congar and continues to develop in the current work of theologians such as Edward Hahnenberg and Susan Wood—to name just a few. In the few years following its publication, *Co-Workers* has focused attention on what can be considered a theological and practical consensus about ministry and the place of lay ecclesial ministry within it. As this consensus grows, so also does the reception of *Co-Workers*.

The second way in which *Co-Workers* acts as a resource for claiming lay ecclesial ministry is found in the chapter titled "Pathways to Lay Ecclesial Ministry." In this section the bishops discuss such issues as promoting lay ecclesial ministry as a vocational choice (particularly for young people), helping people discern whether they are called to this kind of service, and providing criteria for determining the suitability of candidates. Even to imagine doing these things, much less to actually build them into church structures, shows the desire to claim lay ecclesial ministry by offering it institutional support.

The *National Certification Standards for Lay Ecclesial Ministers* is a collaborative product of three national ministry associations, which was granted the approval of the U.S. Conference of Catholic Bishops' Commission on Certification and Accreditation.[13] These competency-based standards are offered as a resource to dioceses and parishes in order to help persons understand what a particular ministry requires and acquire the necessary knowledge and skills to be qualified for that ministry. The standards were completed before *Co-Workers* was published, but they are now being revised in order to reference more explicitly and completely what the document says should be expected of a lay ecclesial minister. Not only does the existence of the standards point to the value of *Co-Workers* as a resource document, but in addition the utilization of the standards contributes to the ongoing reception of the bishops' document.

The third example of how the claiming of lay ecclesial ministry is taking place can be seen in formation programs. *Co-Workers* devotes its largest chapter to discussing formation for ecclesial ministry, using the very same four

"pillars" found in other church documents that deal with priesthood and diaconate: human, spiritual, intellectual, and pastoral formation. The bishops present
lay ecclesial ministry formation in the same integrated way, regarding it as
necessary for the competent service of God's people. In effect, they are saying
that making a serious effort to offer high-quality formation is a way of laying
claim to lay ecclesial ministry and making it integral to the life of the church.

Current statistics on lay ecclesial ministry formation indicate that there are
234 programs nationwide with a total enrollment of 17,538 persons. Nine
percent of the programs offer only an academic degree, while 42 percent offer either a degree or a certificate and 49 percent offer only a certificate. In
the five-year period beginning in 2004, the number of programs has remained
mostly stable. The same is true of enrollments, which have fluctuated during
that period between a high of 20,240 and a low of 16,037.[14]

Most of these formation programs were begun before *Co-Workers* was
published. However, the programs engage in a continual process of review
and revision in regard to curriculum, methodologies, and requirements. *Co-
Workers* is gradually becoming the reference point for such a process. For
example, it is not uncommon for a university to promote its graduate program
in pastoral ministry as being modeled on the bishops' document. Most often
this modeling refers to the presence of all four pillars of formation. Current
statistics show that between 50 and 70 percent of degree and certificate programs offer both a pastoral formation and a spiritual formation component in
addition to their academic courses.[15]

The *National Certification Standards for Lay Ecclesial Ministers* is
another important guide for designing or revising lay ministry formation
programs. As these standards become more deliberately connected to *Co-
Workers*, it can be expected that the formation programs will also strengthen
that connection.

In the introduction to *Co-Workers* the bishops mention two similar documents that they have already produced that respectively set forth norms for
the formation of candidates for priesthood and for diaconate. They note that
Co-Workers does not have the binding status of the other two documents, but
nonetheless they imply that it can function in an analogous way by proposing
a common approach to lay ecclesial ministry formation. As the elements of
this approach become more commonly used, albeit with certain local adaptations, the practical reception of *Co-Workers* becomes more widespread.

Sustaining Lay Ecclesial Ministry

The sustaining stage of the reception process builds on what has taken place
in the first two stages and seeks to create structures of institutional commit-

ment and practical support that will promote the continuing development of lay ecclesial ministry. In this regard, *Co-Workers* strongly emphasizes the ministerial responsibility of the bishop to "order" all the ministries in his diocese. The task of ordering is a multifaceted one aimed at establishing and preserving a set of right relationships among the ministries that is faithful to our theological tradition and feasible in actual practice.

Co-Workers uses the term "authorization" to identify an activity or set of activities by which the bishop and/or his delegate(s) entrust the lay ecclesial minister with certain responsibilities and with the appropriate amount of authority to perform them. The bishops intended authorization to be a broad term that could encompass several specific activities like certification, commissioning, and various other kinds of recognition such as granting an academic degree or awarding a certificate of program completion. *Co-Workers* sees each of these activities as contributing some necessary element to the overall process of authorization. Moreover, it envisions the bishop ultimately to be in charge of the process, even though he might only be responsible for seeing that it was established and that it continues to function smoothly. When a diocese has a process of authorization for lay ecclesial ministry, including the many structures and systems needed for it to function, this diocese is taking steps to sustain lay ecclesial ministry and is thereby advancing the pastoral reception of *Co-Workers*.

The archdiocese of Chicago has established a "framework that leads to recognition as a lay ecclesial minister."[16] It is a five-step process consisting of:

1. Call from God: experienced as a vocational call by the individual and tested by prayer, reflection, spiritual direction, and discernment with pastors.
2. Training and preparation: academics and spiritual formation utilizing the institutional resources of the archdiocese and the various universities within it.
3. Certification: professional credentialing granted by the appropriate archdiocesan office after reviewing transcripts, interviews, ministerial experience, and so forth.
4. Call by the archbishop: a public "call" to lay ecclesial ministry ritualized in a ceremony with the archbishop that is a onetime event for the individuals involved.
5. Commissioning to a specific ministry: the sending or assigning of a lay ecclesial minister to a particular parish accomplished by means of a letter from the archbishop. Commissioning establishes a relationship between the lay ecclesial minister and the archbishop, making him or her a minister of the archdiocese, not simply a parish employee. Commissioning takes place every time a person takes on a new assignment.

This framework extends beyond what *Co-Workers* considers authorization in a narrow sense. Nonetheless, it is a significant example of a process that seeks to institutionalize lay ecclesial ministry (thereby sustaining it) and that creates an ecclesial relationship between the bishop and the lay ecclesial minister. This process could easily serve as a model for other dioceses and, as it becomes utilized more widely, would deepen the reception of *Co-Workers*.

Another sign that a diocese has taken the need to institutionalize lay ecclesial ministry seriously is the extent to which it publicly promotes the roles in which lay ecclesial ministers can serve and takes practical steps to market and recruit for them. A good example of such an initiative comes from the diocese of Albany, which has produced an attractive booklet of "ministry opportunities for homegrown leaders." The booklet describes such roles as liturgical coordinator, pastoral associate, parish life director, campus minister, school principal, parish youth ministry leader, and parish catechetical leader. It contains a message from Bishop Howard J. Hubbard saying: "The call to lay ecclesial ministry is a profound one, discovered in community, deepened through preparation, and completed by formal confirmation. I invite you to read through these pages prayerfully, seeking ways in which the Spirit of God might work through you."[17]

We all know that "money talks" and, for this reason, financial support is a very important sign that the church is serious about sustaining lay ecclesial ministry. An example of this sort of commitment is found in the diocese of Pittsburgh. Bishop David A. Zubik wrote the following in a pastoral letter to his diocese:

> Recently the Conference of Bishops in our country released a document called *Co-Workers in the Vineyard of the Lord* that describes the necessary and rightful place of lay faithful who are appointed to carry out formal ministry in the Church. In our local Church of Pittsburgh, we are in need of these ministers in order to sustain the quality of ministry that all our faithful expect from the Church. I recently approved a plan that will help finance the training of the non-ordained to prepare for positions needed in so many of our parishes. It will be important for our parishes to discern how lay ecclesial ministry can be of service to the parish community.[18]

National ministry associations and Catholic institutions of higher education have an important part to play in the sustaining of lay ecclesial ministry that supports and extends what any diocese can do. An example of collaboration among Catholic institutions of higher education was initiated by Fordham University's Graduate School of Religion and Religious Education in 2007. The school began with a convocation on *Co-Workers in the Vineyard of the Lord* for pastoral leaders in the New York area, as well as representatives from other Jesuit schools. As a follow-up to the convocation, representatives from Boston College, Creighton, Loyola Maryland, Loyola Chicago, Loyola New Orleans, Santa Clara, the Jesuit School of Theology at Berkeley, Seattle University, Loyola Marymount University, Gonzaga, and Spring Hill took steps to form a consortium of Jesuit schools, which they named the Association of Jesuit Colleges and Universities (ACJU) Consortium for Pastoral and Theological Education. The goals of this consortium are to share resources in order to help the members deliver courses and programs based on *Co-Workers*. This service would also include Jesuit institutions in developing nations.

Among the consortium's initial projects are a proposed Doctor of Ministry program offered in a distance-learning format and a series of four national *Co-Workers* conferences underscoring the Ignatian contribution to lay ecclesial ministry. Two such conferences have been held at Fordham University, in 2008 and 2009. Additional programs are planned at other Jesuit universities. This effort is particularly significant because it involves a dozen colleges and universities, from all over the country, working in concert to offer initial and ongoing formation to lay ecclesial ministers—an effort called for by the bishops in *Co-Workers*.

A second example of national collaboration comes from St. John's University in Collegeville, Minnesota, and more than twenty national organizations. In 2007 the university's School of Theology and Seminary convened representative leaders from those groups in a first-ever national symposium on lay ecclesial ministry. The goals of the symposium were:

1. To amplify the national will to advance lay ecclesial ministry in the United States;
2. To foster theological and pastoral insight into certifying, forming, authorizing, and sustaining lay ecclesial ministry;
3. To create national recommendations for formation, authorization, pathways, and workplace issues that seek to foster excellence in lay ecclesial ministry;
4. To generate organizational and personal commitments for implementing the symposium recommendations.

In the course of the three-day program the various national groups made commitments to study and integrate *Co-Workers* into the life of their organization; to address inclusion issues and cross-cultural ministry competence; to advance the thinking on national lay ecclesial ministry standards and a certification process; and to deepen theological inquiry into the meaning and practice of authorization for lay ecclesial ministry.

The collective effort represented in all these commitments is significant because it is being carried out by groups whose members are lay ecclesial ministers serving in virtually all the typical parish and diocesan roles. It is national and comprehensive. It is also ongoing. St. John's is planning a second symposium in 2011 at which the organizations can report on progress and chart future courses of action.

CONCLUSION

Co-Workers in the Vineyard of the Lord is not a perfect statement. Some would claim that it breaks no new ground but only reinforces and systematizes what was already the common thinking and practice. Others would focus on its innovative aspects, as did Richard Gaillardetz when he said: "I believe that *Co-Workers* is the most mature and coherent ecclesiastical document ever produced on a theology of ministry. One of the real strengths of this document is the way in which it successfully integrates lay ecclesial ministry within a broader theology of church and ministry."[19]

Both these views of *Co-Workers* are accurate to some extent. In the end, however, its pastoral reception depends less on what we think about the document and more on how we think about ourselves in light of the document. This means that the various tasks that I have identified with a process of reception should be undertaken with larger purposes in mind than simply to advance lay ecclesial ministry. To the extent that its pastoral and theological reception continues in the life of the church, *Co-Workers in the Vineyard of the Lord* should be a resource for situating lay ecclesial ministry more firmly within the broader community of lay and ordained ministers as a single body of persons called to serve the people of God in distinct ways. This is an important accomplishment, to be sure, but it is simply a step toward a larger goal that the bishops set before us when they write: "*Co-Workers in the Vineyard of the Lord* expresses our strong desire for the fruitful collaboration of ordained and lay ministers who, in distinct but complementary ways, continue in the Church the saving mission of Christ for the world, his vineyard."[20]

NOTES

1. U.S. Conference of Catholic Bishops, *Co-Workers in the Vineyard of the Lord: A Resource for Guiding the Development of Lay Ecclesial Ministry* (Washington, DC: USCCB, 2005), 6.

2. National Conference of Catholic Bishops, *Called and Gifted: The American Catholic Laity* (Washington, DC: U.S. Catholic Conference, November 13, 1980).

3. National Conference of Catholic Bishops, *Called and Gifted: The American Catholic Laity.*

4. National Conference of Catholic Bishops, *Called and Gifted for the Third Millennium* (Washington, DC: U.S. Catholic Conference, 1995), 18.

5. Subcommittee on Lay Ministry, *Lay Ecclesial Ministry: The State of the Questions* (Washington, DC: United States Catholic Conference, 1999).

6. See USCCB, *Co-Workers*, 10–12.

7. USCCB, *Co-Workers*, 11.

8. Cardinal Avery Dulles, "Can Laity Properly Be Called 'Ministers'?" *Origins* 35, no. 44 (April 20, 2006): 729.

9. Mary Gautier, ed., *Catholic Ministry Formation Directory 2009* (Washington, DC: Center for Applied Research in the Apostolate, Georgetown University, 2009). The same entry can be found in the 2007 directory.

10. See, for example, several essays in Carole Ganim, ed., *Shaping Catholic Parishes: Pastoral Leaders in the 21st Century* (Chicago: Loyola Press, 2008).

11. Archbishop John Vlazny, "Co-Workers in the Vineyard," *Catholic Sentinel*, June 10, 2009.

12. Bishop Matthew H. Clark, *Forward in Hope: Saying Amen to Lay Ecclesial Ministry* (Notre Dame, IN: Ave Maria Press, 2009).

13. National Federation for Catholic Youth Ministry, National Association for Lay Ministry, and the National Conference for Catechetical Leadership, *National Certification Standards for Lay Ecclesial Ministers Serving as Parish Catechetical Leaders, Youth Ministry Leaders, Pastoral Associates, Parish Life Coordinators* (Washington, DC, 2003).

14. *Catholic Ministry Formation Directory*, 226–27.

15. *Catholic Ministry Formation Directory*, 231.

16. Archdiocese of Chicago, *Formation for Lay Ecclesial Ministry in the Archdiocese of Chicago* (Chicago: University of St. Mary of the Lake, 2005), 8.

17. Howard Hubbard, "Growing Leaders: Ministry Opportunities in the Roman Catholic Diocese of Albany" (no publication information given).

18. David A. Zubik, "The Church Alive: Pastoral Letter to the Church of Pittsburgh," June 29, 2008, n. 32.

19. Richard Gaillardetz, "The Theology Underlying Lay Ecclesial Ministry," *Origins* 36, no. 9 (July 20, 2006), 139.

20. USCCB, *Co-Workers*, 6.

2

The Theological Reception of *Co-Workers in the Vineyard of the Lord*

Richard R. Gaillardetz

Since the publication of the U.S. Conference of Catholic Bishops (USCCB) document *Co-Workers in the Vineyard of the Lord : A Resource for Guilding the Development Lay Ecclesial Ministry*, questions have been raised regarding the authoritative status of this document. Critics (including some bishops) have pointed out that the document was not promulgated as an instrument for teaching doctrine but merely as a resource guide. Consequently, it is held, the document should not be considered doctrinally binding. This statement is true, as far as it goes, but it misses the larger question, namely, is the theological vision of ministry contained in this document likely to be received in the life of the church? It is often thought, quite mistakenly, that the only way that a theological development becomes part of the church's living tradition is through a formal doctrinal pronouncement. Such a view ignores some of the most important insights emerging today around a theology of ecclesial reception.

In the first section of this chapter I will outline some of the central features of a theology of ecclesial reception, concluding with some observations regarding the pertinence of a theology of reception for a consideration of *Co-Workers*. In the second section I will outline some key developments in the document that need to be highlighted with an eye toward assessing their ongoing ecclesial reception.

A THEOLOGY OF RECEPTION

Scholars have used the French term *ressourcement* to refer to the process by which the Second Vatican Council sought to renew the church by recovering often-neglected insights from our ancient tradition. One of the most important of these retrievals was the council's recovery of pneumatology. For much of the history of Western ecclesiology, the role of the Holy Spirit had been eclipsed by a tendency to think of the church almost exclusively in its relation to Christ. The Holy Spirit received very little attention. At Vatican II, however, we find a renewed appreciation that if, in some sense, Christ laid the foundations for the church, it is the Spirit who continues to animate the church, guiding it along its pilgrim journey. Although undoubtedly the Spirit guides the church through its apostolic office, the council also recognized that all the Christian faithful are gifted by the Holy Spirit in the discernment of God's Word. The whole body of the faithful who have received an anointing, which comes from the Holy One, cannot be mistaken in belief. The church shows this characteristic through the entire people's supernatural sense of the faith, when, "from the bishops to the last of the faithful," it manifests a universal consensus in matters of faith and morals. By this sense of the faith, aroused and sustained by the Spirit of truth, the people of God, guided by the sacred magisterium it faithfully obeys, receives not the word of human beings, but truly the word of God, "the faith once for all delivered to the saints." The people unfailingly adhere to this faith, penetrate it more deeply through right judgment, and apply it more fully in their daily lives.[1]

This affirmation of the *sensus fidei*, the spiritual instinct for recognizing the word of God, has further implications for a theology of tradition. For centuries Catholic theology had treated tradition reductively, virtually identifying it with the ecclesiastical organ by which tradition was thought to be handed on, namely, the magisterium. Yet the council recovered a more ancient vision of tradition as growing and developing through the contributions of all the Christian faithful: "This [the growth in tradition] comes about through the contemplation and study of believers who ponder these things in their hearts. . . . It comes from the intimate sense of spiritual realities which they experience. And it comes from the preaching of those who, on succeeding to the office of bishop, have received the sure charism of truth."[2]

Catholic doctrine teaches that the bishops alone possess supreme authority in the church and, by virtue of their apostolic office, are the authoritative guardians of the faith. But the council's teaching reminded us that the bishops, including the bishop of Rome, do not teach new revelation, but only what has been passed on. And how do they receive what has been passed on to them? There is no one answer. Surely they receive it through the celebration of the liturgy, through the study of scripture and the writings of the fathers and mothers of the church, and the contributions of contemporary scholarship. In the nineteenth century, Cardinal John Henry Newman, who may be thought of as a kind of grandfather to the ecclesial vision of the council, reminded us that the bishops also receive what has been passed on through the testimony of the faithful. Newman held a vision of the church in which tradition grew and developed through the *conspiratio fidelium et pastorum*, the "breathing together of the faithful and the pastors."

Newman developed this notion in his essay *On Consulting the Faithful in Matters of Doctrine.*[3] In our age it is all too common to set bishops and faithful in a relationship of opposition and subordination. Yet Newman avoided any harsh separation between a teaching (*ecclesia docens*) and a learning church (*ecclesia discens*). Newman believed that the one apostolic faith given to the whole church was manifested in different forms in the life of the church. To discover this faith one must look to "the mind of the church."[4] Consequently, in some sense the whole church could be seen as both teacher and learner.

The council's theology of tradition gave unprecedented attention to the contributions of the insight of the Christian faithful. Since the council, further developments in a theology of tradition have emerged, most significantly concerning the closely related process of ecclesial "reception." If the term "tradition" draws our attention to the necessary processes by which the Christian faith is "handed on," ecclesial "reception" focuses on how the faith that has been handed on is *received* as the Christian community makes that faith its own.

Although theological reflection on the concept may be relatively recent, the reality of ecclesial reception has always been operative in the church. It is evident, for example, in the way in which local churches received (or at times did not receive) the authoritative pronouncements of synods and councils. For example, it took decades for all the churches to fully "receive" and accept into their life and worship the creeds of the Councils of Nicaea and Constantinople. The formation of the biblical canon was itself the result of a centuries-long process of reception as local churches discerned whether or not to embrace a particular text as divinely inspired. Ecclesial reception often occurred with respect to the liturgy, as when the churches of the West "received" the Eastern liturgical tradition of the *epiklesis* into their liturgy.

Central to a contemporary theology of reception is the insight that the act of ecclesial reception is not a passive one. When a community receives a theological insight, a particular ecclesial or liturgical practice, or even a formal articulation of the faith, in that process of reception what is received is always in some sense reshaped, changed by the receiving party. It is this active element in the process of reception that inserts genuine creativity into the "traditioning" process. This active reception, according to Ormond Rush, occurs across numerous ecclesial axes:

(1) reception between God and humanity; (2) reception between God and the whole community of believers; (3) reception between God and the Roman

Catholic Church as a communion of churches; (4) reception between the episcopal magisterium and the *sensus fidelium* of the whole body of the faithful; (5) reception between a local church and its particular context in the world; (6) reception between local churches in *communio*; (7) reception between local churches and the church of Rome in *communio*; (8) reception between theologians and their local church in its context; (9) reception within and between diverse theologies; (10) reception between the episcopal magisterium and theology; (11) reception between separated churches and ecclesial communities; (12) reception between Christian churches and other religions.[5]

As Rush points out, this process of reception cannot be limited to a single ecclesial relationship. For example, reception is active when a practice, theological insight, or belief emerging in one local church is handed on to other local churches who discern whether to make that practice, insight, or belief their own. It occurs between theologians and bishops and theologians and ordinary believers.

This emerging theology of ecclesial reception provides a helpful framework for considering the contributions of *Co-Workers in the Vineyard of the Lord*. First, it helps us to recall that *Co-Workers* itself represents a moment in the process of ecclesial reception. An important ecclesial development has been occurring in the U.S. church and elsewhere, called lay ecclesial ministry. This document is concerned with that prior ecclesial development. The document is not simply articulating what *ought to* happen as regards lay ecclesial ministry; it is also giving testimony to what has already been happening. Consequently, *Co-Workers* can be understood as a provisional act of episcopal reception of a ministerial structure and a set of ministerial practices that already existed. Since reception is more an ongoing ecclesial process than a discrete act, *Co-Workers* serves as a moment in the process of reception even if it did not represent a formal *doctrinal* approbation.

Second, this framework helps us see *Co-Workers* as an ecclesiastical document that must itself be subject to the ongoing reception of the church. The bishops were not only receiving a set of structures and pastoral practices regarding lay ecclesial ministry that were already operative; they were offering a constructive theological rationale for those practices. That theology will, in turn, have to be received in the ongoing pastoral and theological reflection of the church. It is far too early to know whether this document will ultimately be received as an authentic and fruitful expression of a legitimate future for ministry in the church. However, a theology of ecclesial reception demands that we remain attentive to the document's ongoing theological impact on subsequent theologies and practices of ministry both within the U.S. church and worldwide. In another chapter in this volume Rick McCord outlines the first indications of the document's pastoral reception. In the second part of this chapter, I would like to highlight some of the document's most significant theological contributions. My hope is that this brief exercise will help identify elements in the document that, if fully received, will doubtless reshape the church's ministerial self-understanding.

THEOLOGICAL CONTRIBUTIONS OF *CO-WORKERS* THAT ARE SUBJECT TO ECCLESIAL RECEPTION

A solid case can be made that *Co-Workers* is the most mature and coherent ecclesiastical document ever produced on a theology of ministry. One of the real strengths of this document is the way in which it successfully integrates lay ecclesial ministry within a broader theology of church and ministry. Pope John Paul II offered a helpful theology of the laity in *Christifideles laici*, a positive theology of the priesthood in *Pastores dabo vobis*, and a mature theology of the episcopate in *Pastores gregis*. However, in no ecclesiastical document, papal or episcopal, has there been a truly successful theological integration of the various forms of ministry in the church. *Co-Workers* provides a coherent theology of ministry built on a number of basic theological concepts and pastoral applications.

The Priority of the Baptismal Call of the *Christifideles*

One of the most important initiatives of the Second Vatican Council was its attempt to find new foundations for its consideration of the church. The preparatory draft document on the church given to the bishops at the opening of the council was little more than a synthesis of the ecclesiology that had been operative throughout much of the first half of the twentieth century. It presupposed that the church was, as Pope Pius X put it, an "unequal society" comprised of two ranks, the clergy and the laity.[6] With the fundamental rejection of the ecclesiology reflected in that document, the council set upon a new course. The Dogmatic Constitution on the Church, *Lumen gentium*, offered a new framework for situating any and all distinctions in the church. That new framework was made evident in the well-known decision to place the chapter on the church as people of God prior to the chapter on the hierarchy in the *De Ecclesia* schema. In that chapter the council members "were focusing on the common matrix, the fundamental equality and dignity of each and every follower of Jesus."[7] This matrix is further reinforced by the council's frequent use of the term *Christifideles* to refer to all the baptized and by its appeal to the priesthood of all believers. Before there are ordained and non-ordained, clergy and lay, all church members are the Christian faithful, the baptized, called to a common discipleship in Christ. Indeed, while the council did not itself make use of this metaphor, its theological affirmation of the equal dignity of all the baptized readily suggests a view of the church as the "community of disciples."[8] In baptism we are initiated into Christ's body, the church, and in a sense, discover ourselves fully, our truest identity, in the life of the church. At the same time, by baptism into Christ's body, the church, we are drawn by the power of the Holy Spirit into participation in the triune life of God.

All Christians, by baptism, are called in discipleship to follow the way of Jesus of Nazareth, to grow in holiness, and to help further the reign of God. This commitment, far from being one among many human commitments that one might undertake, is in itself more than a religion. As the early Christians understood it, this commitment brought one into a new form of existence, a new understanding of the human vocation.

The Second Vatican Council augmented its rich treatment of the common matrix of Christian baptism and discipleship with an uneven yet still significant use of the biblical notion of charism. It is a development that was strongly advocated by Cardinal Leon-Joseph Suenens, who gave a very influential speech on the subject on October 22, 1963.[9] This more pneumatological line of thought is evident in the first chapter of *Lumen gentium*, which considered the place of charisms in the context of the whole people of God's participation in the life of the church.[10]

> The Spirit dwells in the church and in the hearts of the faithful, as in a temple, prays and bears witness in them that they are his adopted children. He guides the church in the way of all truth and, uniting it in fellowship and ministry, bestows upon it different hierarchic and charismatic gifts, and in this way directs it and adorns it with his fruits.[11]

The theme is picked up again in the second chapter.

> Moreover, it is not only through the sacraments and the ministries that the holy Spirit makes the people holy, leads them and enriches them with his virtues. Allotting his gifts "at will to each individual," he also distributes special graces among the faithful of every rank. By these gifts, he makes them fit and ready to undertake various tasks and offices for the renewal and building up of the church.[12]

While the terminology employed is not altogether consistent, nevertheless there is a fundamental assertion that charisms are given to all the faithful "for the renewal and building up of the church." There are clear Pauline resonances here as charisms are presented not as private gifts or talents but as gifts of the Holy Spirit offered *to and for* the church *through* the individual believer (compare 1 Cor. 12). *Co-Workers* is to be credited with taking these various strands of a theology of baptism found throughout the conciliar documents and weaving them together to construct a firm baptismal foundation for lay ecclesial ministry.

Ministry Is More than Discipleship

A second foundational contribution of this document is its attempt to clarify what is meant, precisely, by the term "ministry."[13] According to *Co-Workers*, ministry is not the same as discipleship. Not all Christians are called to ministry. All are called to be followers of Jesus, that is, disciples. We have gone from a situation fifty years ago when the term "ministry" was associated with Protestantism, and if used, was used solely in reference to the clergy, to a contemporary situation in which virtually anything from gardening to golf is referred to as "my ministry." One of the distinguishing features of ministry pertains to its public character. A ministry is something to which I am formally called by the community over and beyond my baptismal call. Let us consider the matter concretely. When John Osman and his son go to Cherry St. Mission on a Saturday morning to feed the homeless, they are not doing ministry. Rather, they are responding to their baptismal call as disciples of Jesus to feed the hungry. However, when John's parish leadership calls him forth to be the coordinator of a parish soup kitchen, then he is being called to ministry. Why? Because he is being called forth by the community to serve in some formal and public way in a ministry for which he will be held accountable.

Ministry generally begins with the manifestation of some charism for the building up of the church in mission. Of course every Christian possesses charisms to be exercised in their daily lives. These charisms may appear quite ordinary (making them no less vital), as with the charism of parenting[14] or that of imbuing the atmosphere of one's workplace with the values of the gospel. At other times these charisms may take on a more dramatic and even public character, as in the evangelical witness of Dorothy Day. The exercise of these charisms, however dramatic, does not call for undertaking any new ecclesial relationship for the sake of the church and its mission beyond that constituted by baptismal initiation. However, there are other charisms, the manifestation of which *does* suggest the suitability of entering into a new, public, ecclesial relationship within the church.

What distinguishes these many ordered ministries from the more basic activity of all the baptized in fulfillment of their baptismal call? For a Christian activity to qualify as a formal ministry, that ministry must create for the one who undertakes it some new, formal, and public relationship within the community. The public character of this ministry is evident in the way in which we tend to hold such ministers to a higher moral standard. We recognize the possibility that their moral failings, because of their public character, might be a cause of scandal. Consider the case of the person who in sharing her faith with family and friends manifests great passion and insight. Members of her local community recognize this charism for sharing the faith, a charism already being exercised in her life, and so call her to exercise this charism in a public ministry of the church as catechist. In some cases individuals may sense the presence of this charism as a personal call to service and offer themselves to the church. At other times it is the community itself, in its processes of ecclesial discernment, that will first recognize the presence of a given charism and call that person into ministry. In any case ministry begins with the recognition by the individual and/or the community of an already existing charism. The failure to recognize that evidence of a charism must *precede* one's entrance into church ministry has done great harm to the life of the church. Particularly as regards the ordained, the church has too frequently suffered from the inadequate ministrations of well-meaning priests and deacons called to ministry because of their personal holiness or eagerness to serve but without evidence of a recognizable charism for the ministry they have undertaken.

This insight that ministry is to be distinguished from Christian discipleship is one of the most important contributions of this document as it serves to distinguish lay ecclesial ministry from volunteer service. One does not simply volunteer for ministry without the participation of the community in the discernment of whether a person is in fact called to a particular ministry.

Ministry within an Ecclesiology of Communion

A third contribution of *Co-Workers* was its incorporation of an important concept explored, if only tentatively, at Vatican II, *koinonia-communio*. Two decades ago Pope John Paul II famously referred to *communio* as the central theological concept of the council,[15] and it has played a decisive role in contemporary ecumenical dialogue.[16] *Co-Workers* employs an ecclesiology of communion as an essential foundation for a theology of ministry. It gives particular attention to the Trinitarian dimension of ecclesial communion.

The Trinitarian character of ecclesial communion is vital because Trinitarian doctrine asserts the "fundamentally relational" being of God.[17] The Trinitarian missions of the word and the Spirit draw humankind and indeed all of creation into the divine life of communion. From this Trinitarian foundation, *Co-Workers* then develops the relational nature of the church, attending to the ways in which the sacraments of initiation establish our primary mode of relating within the life of the church, that of discipleship.

The document also draws on an influential trend in contemporary theologies of ministry, one that views the church as an "organic and ordered communion" and sees ministry "as diverse and at the same time profoundly relational."[18] The document consistently avoids a more problematic approach to ministry that defines ministry in terms of the conferral of sacramental power and consequently sees ordained ministry as the only true form of ecclesial ministry. In a relational theology of ministry, both the ordained and those called to exercise the gifts given to them at baptism play vital and complementary roles in the life of the church. *Co-Workers* teaches that "lay ecclesial ministers take on a new relationship to the mission of the church and the other ministers who work to accomplish it."[19] Indeed, the document also asserts that lay ecclesial ministers are given "special graces" for the performance of these ministries.

To its credit, *Co-Workers* applies this relational view of ministry to ordained ministry as well. The ministerial priesthood is placed at the service of the priesthood of all the baptized. The ministry of the bishop is described as a ministry responsible for the ordering of all ministerial relationships within his diocese, and the deacon's ministry is placed at the service of the bishop. What distinctive contributions does this relational approach offer the church?

A theology of ministry based primarily on sacramental powers—the bishop defined by his power to ordain and confirm, the priest by his power to celebrate the Eucharist and administer the sacraments of penance and anointing, the deacon by his status as an ordinary minister of the Eucharist and his authorization to preach during the Eucharist—inevitably puts various ministers in a competitive relationship with one another. Each is defined by what one group can do that others cannot. It encourages a view of hierarchy conceived as a top-down command structure, what we might call a "spiritual trickle down" theory.

Yet from a theological point of view, power is not something that one possesses but a reality that one participates in to the extent that individuals are open to the work of the Spirit. Power is not hoarded; it flows through authentic ecclesial relationships. Vatican II had already taught that the hierarchy does not compete with the rest of the faithful. The Spirit bequeaths to the church gifts both "hierarchic and charismatic."[20] As one assesses *Co-Workers* as a provisional act of episcopal reception, its incorporation of this relational theology of ministry may be its most significant contribution.

Collaboration, Not Competition

Co-Workers affirms the complementary relations of both ordained and lay ecclesial ministries. It insists upon the hierarchical nature of the church, but presents hierarchy not as a vertical command structure but as a right ordering of the church under the bishop's ministry of *episkopē* or "oversight."[21] The relational framework presupposed here constitutes a firm rejection of any theology that would grant to lay ecclesial ministry a mere auxiliary ministerial status. Lay ecclesial ministry, according to *Co-Workers*, has its own ministerial integrity as something more than an auxiliary to the ordained. This establishes the basis for a more collaborative relationship between the ordained and lay ecclesial ministers. It also provides the indispensable foundation for the second part of the document, which impressively affirms the rights of lay ecclesial ministers to such things as just work conditions, due process, adequate ministerial formation, and so forth.

The theology of charism, mentioned earlier, must be considered again here because the appropriation of a theology of charism plays a vital role in the document's noncompetitive conception of ministry. Too often ministry in the church has been conceived as a zero-sum game in which affirmation of lay ecclesial ministry was thought to lessen the importance of ordained ministry, and vice versa. The document's theology of charism helps break that impasse by conceiving the ministry of the ordained, particularly that of the bishop and priest-pastor, as that of discerning, ordering, and empowering the charisms of the baptized.

Ministry within a Theology of Mission

A further insight evident in the document's theology of ministry is its emphasis on mission and discipleship. *Co-Workers* highlights the primary identity of all the baptized as disciples of the Lord. The document asserts that "discipleship is the fundamental vocation in which the church's mission and ministry find full meaning."[22]

It will be important not to overlook one subtle, but very important, development in the document's treatment of mission. Early in the first section *Co-Workers* affirms the teaching of both the council and Pope John Paul II on the "secular character" of the lay vocation. It is a claim that has dominated the theology of the laity, at least in magisterial documents, since the time of the council. This long-standing emphasis is unfortunate since, as numerous commentators have pointed out, the council was hardly offering an *ontological* definition of the laity but merely a *typological* one, that is, a practical definition that captures the "typical" situation of the vast majority of the laity.[23] Yet since the council, the secular character of the laity has been given a quasi-ontological status. Now it is doubtless true that the majority of lay Catholics are immersed in "the ordinary circumstances of social and family life which, as it were, form the context of their existence."[24] However, if pushed too far, this view of the secular character of the laity creates more problems than it solves, a point Edward Hahnenberg has made.[25] There is a risk of turning the distinction between the sacred and the secular into a separation, by presenting the laity as the church's "foot soldiers" sent out into the world by the clergy, who remain safely ensconced in the privileged realm of the sacred.[26]

Co-Workers deftly avoids this danger in a single sentence that is lifted almost verbatim from an earlier document of the subcommittee on lay ecclesial ministry, *Lay Ecclesial Ministry: The State of the Questions.* In that 1999 document we find the following statement:

> All of the *laity* are called to work toward the transformation of the secular world. *Some* do this by working in the secular realm; others do this by working in the Church and focusing on the building of ecclesial communion, which has as *its ultimate purpose* the transformation of the world.[27]

This passage was inserted almost entirely into *Co-Workers* as follows:

> All of the *baptized* are called to work toward the transformation of the world. *Most* do this by working in the secular realm; some do this by working in the church and focusing on the building of ecclesial communion, which has *among its purposes* the transformation of the world.[28]

A single word change suggests a major theological development. *Co-Workers* asserts that not just the laity, as the previous text had it, but "*all of the baptized* are called to work toward the transformation of the world." This reflects the insight of the council's most mature document, *Gaudium et spes*, which attributed the image of leaven not to the laity alone as other conciliar passages had, but to the church itself, which "is to be a leaven and, as it were, the soul of human society in its renewal by Christ and transformation into the family of God."[29]

One of the difficulties that some bishops and conservative commentators like Russell Shaw have had with a theology of lay ecclesial ministry has been the concern that it might distract from the laity's primary orientation toward the world.[30] This concern is both legitimate and misconceived. It is legitimate in the sense that one of the perennial temptations for the church has been to ignore its orientation in mission toward the world. This was the concern of Cardinal Suenens and Archbishop Dom Helder Camara at Vatican II when they insisted that the document on the nature of the church be augmented by a document on the church oriented toward the world. In fact, today ecclesiologists tend to reject the common view that Jesus first instituted a church and then gave it a mission. It is biblically and theologically more accurate to say that Jesus established a mission in the world and then called forth a community of disciples for the fulfillment of that mission. Thus, although the concern about a kind of ecclesial "navel-gazing" is legitimate, this concern is misconceived to the extent that it sees this avoidance of mission as a problem that applies to the laity only. It is the *whole* church that must embrace the demands of mission to the world. This is why the editorial change in the text of *Co-Workers* is so significant; it recognizes that no baptized Christian is exempted from the obligations of church mission and the responsibility toward the transformation of the world.

Vocational Discernment

Yet another contribution of *Co-Workers* lies in its recognition that lay ecclesial ministry is a genuine vocation. This represents a marked departure from the long-standing reluctance of many to conceive of it in vocational terms. The bishops write:

> These lay ecclesial ministers often express a sense of being called. This sense motivates what they are doing, guiding and shaping a major life choice and commitment to church ministry. At the same time, they know that a self-discerned call by the individual is not sufficient. Their call must also become one that is discerned within the church and authenticated by the bishop, or his delegate, who alone is able to authorize someone to serve in ecclesial ministry. (p. 28)

This is no minor point. Once it is admitted that one might have a vocation to lay ecclesial ministry, it becomes necessary to provide institutional processes for vocational discernment analogous to those that have long been established for discerning a vocation to ordained ministry or consecrated life.

Co-Workers not only recognizes the vocational dimension of lay ecclesial ministry; it also attends to the need for a communal context for this vocational discernment. Many lay ecclesial ministry formation programs suffer from the same failings as those of presbyteral and diaconal formation programs. That is, they fall into the trap of discerning impediments to ministry rather than discerning charisms for ministry.

Moreover, the bishops' document highlights the need in this discernment process for someone such as a mentor or spiritual director who can help assess the individual's "human, spiritual, intellectual and pastoral readiness." Of particular note is the emphasis on the human dimension. Elsewhere in the document the bishops refer to this as "mature emotional balance." We have a long tradition, paved by our treatment of vocations to religious life and the ministerial priesthood, of focusing on spiritual holiness. Too often, however, a reductive approach to ministerial holiness has meant a neglect of such basic issues as human wholeness and a sense of emotional balance. Recall the Thomistic maxim, grace builds on nature. Authentic Christian ministry requires a certain basic *health.*

CONCLUSION

None of the theological contributions outlined above are particularly original. All can be found in important theological works written prior to *Co-Workers.* The significance of *Co-Workers* lies not in its theological originality but in its status as a tentative but genuine episcopal reception of a theology of ministry already operative in the life of the U.S. church. This document gives that theology a greater visibility and authority. More importantly, it offers an integrated and coherent theology of ministry as a gift of the U.S. church to the universal church. If it is received by the church universal, *Co-Workers* may prove to be a far more influential document than its provisional doctrinal status might initially have indicated.

NOTES

1. *Lumen gentium,* 12. U.S. Conference of Catholic Bishops, *Co-Workers in the Vineyard of the Lord: A Resource for Guiding the Development of Lay Ecclesial Ministry* (Washington, DC: USCCB, 2005).

2. Dei Verbum, 8, 754.Vatican Council II: The Conciliar and Post-Conciliar Documents, Austin Flannery, O.P., general editor (Northport, NY: Costello Publishing Company, 1984), 363–64.

3. John Henry Newman, *On Consulting the Faithful in Matters of Doctrine* (1859; reprint, New York: Sheed & Ward, 1961).

4. Newman, *On Consulting the Faithful,* 163.

5. Ormond Rush, *The Reception of Doctrine: An Appropriation of Hans Robert Jauss' Reception Aesthetics and Literary Hermeneutics* (Rome: Gregorian, 1997), 206–7.

6. *Vehementer nos,* in *The Papal Encyclicals,* edited by Claudia Carlen (New York: McGrath, 1981), 3:47–48.

7. Kenan B. Osborne, *Ministry: Lay Ministry in the Roman Catholic Church* (New York: Paulist, 1993), 530ff.

8. Years later, in a revised edition of his classic work, *Models of the Church,* Avery Dulles would propose this model (Church as Community of Disciples) as a "bridge model" that drew together the fundamental features of the five models of church (Herald, Servant, Institution, Sacrament, and Mystical Communion) that he had addressed in the earlier edition of his book. Cf. Avery Dulles, *Models of the Church* (expanded edition, New York: Doubleday, 1987).

9. *Acta Synodalia* II/3, 175–78.

10. For a careful analysis of the council's treatment of charisms, see Albert Vanhoye, "The Biblical Question of 'Charisms' After Vatican II," in *Vatican II: Assessment and Perspectives*, vol. 1, edited by R. Latourelle (New York: Paulist, 1988), 439–68.

11. *Lumen gentium*, 4, 351–52.

12. *Lumen gentium*, 12, 363–64.

13. The reader will profit from Bishop Wcela's insightful chapter on this topic.

14. See Wendy Wright, "The Charism of Parenting," in *Retrieving Charisms for the Twenty-First Century* (Collegeville, MN: Liturgical Press, 1999), 85–101.

15. *Christifideles Laici, Origins* 18 (February 9, 1989): 570.

16. As but one example, consider the role the concept of *koinonia* played in the fifth World Council of Churches (WCC) Faith and Order Commission's world conference, which was convened in 1993 in Santiago de Compostela, Spain. *On the Way to Fuller Koinonia*, Thomas F. Best and Günther Gassmann, eds. [Faith and Order Paper No. 166] (Geneva: WCC Publications, 1994).

17. U.S. Conference of Catholic Bishops, *Co-Workers in the Vineyard of the Lord: A Resource for Guiding the Development of Lay Ecclesial Ministry* (Washington, DC: USCCB, 2005).

18. USCCB, *Co-Workers*, 21. For examples of this relational theology of ministry see Susan K. Wood, ed., *Ordering the Baptismal Priesthood* (Collegeville, MN: Liturgical Press, 2003), and Edward Hahnenberg, *Ministries: A Relational Approach* (New York: Crossroad, 2003).

19. USCCB, *Co-Workers*, 25.

20. *Lumen gentium*, 4, 351–52.

21. For different conceptions of "hierarchy" see Terence Nichols, *That All May Be One: Hierarchy and Participation in the Church* (Collegeville, MN: Liturgical Press, 1997).

22. USCCB, *Co-Workers*, 19. See also Kathleen A. Cahalan, "Toward a Fundamental Theology of Ministry," *Worship* 80 (March 2006): 102–20.

23. This distinction was famously made by Cardinal John Wright in his *relatio* presenting the draft of this text to the council bishops. *Acta Synodalia* III/1, 282. This also appeared in the *relatio* introducing chapter 4 of the *De Ecclesia* schema, see *Acta Synodalia* III/3, 62.

24. *Lumen gentium*, 31, 388–89.

25. Edward Hahnenberg, "Ordained and Lay Ministry: Restarting the Conversation," *Origins* 35 (June 23, 2005): 94–99, at 96.

26. Richard R. Gaillardetz, "Shifting Meanings in the Lay-Clergy Distinction," *Irish Theological Quarterly* 64 (1999): 115–39.

27. U.S. Conference of Catholic Bishops Subcommittee on Lay Ministry, *Lay Ecclesial Ministry: The State of the Questions* (Washington, DC: USCCB, 1999), 15, emphasis added.

28. USCCB, *Co-Workers*, 8, emphasis added.

29. *Gaudium et spes*, 40, 939–40.

30. Russell Shaw, *Ministry or Apostolate: What Should the Catholic Laity Be Doing?* (Huntington: Our Sunday Visitor, 2002).

Part II

MINING OUR THEOLOGICAL TRADITION

3

Ministry in the New Testament

Emil A. Wcela

DEFINING MINISTRY

Co-Workers in the Vineyard of the Lord was developed by the Committee on the Laity of the U.S. Conference of Catholic Bishops as "a resource for guiding the development of lay ecclesial ministry." It states: "Today in parishes, schools, Church institutions, and diocesan agencies, laity serve in various 'ministries, offices and roles' that do not require sacramental ordination but rather 'find their foundation in the Sacraments of Baptism and Confirmation, indeed for a good many of them, in the Sacrament of Matrimony.'"[1]

The document expresses the reality of parish and diocesan life throughout the United States. Although in no way slighting the value of the service to the church provided by thousands of laity, is it legitimate, at least according to New Testament usage, to call their contributions "ministry"?

In our times, the word ministry has been used in at least three different ways.[2]

The Classic Definition

The traditional Roman Catholic, Orthodox, and, to a great extent, Protestant position was that ministry is the work of passing on the word and of celebrating the sacraments. Ministry is equated with office, and the Spirit or God or Christ confers office by the church's act of installation or ordination.

33

The More-Inclusive Definition

"Christian ministry is the public activity of a baptized follower of Jesus Christ flowing from the Spirit's charism and an individual personality on behalf of a Christian community to witness to, serve and realize the kingdom of God. . . . [According to Yves Congar] The Church is not built up merely by the acts of the official ministers of the presbytery but by many kinds of services, more or less stable or occasional, more or less spontaneous or recognized, some even consecrated by sacramental ordination."[3]

Pope Paul VI employs this broader sense when he speaks of reader and acolyte as ministries. Using "ministry" and "office" interchangeably, he suggests that conferences of bishops might establish other offices that might be useful in their region (e.g., "porter, exorcist, and catechist, as well as other offices to be conferred upon those who are dedicated to works of charity").[4] Pope John Paul II wrote in similar terms: "Together with the ordained ministry, other ministries, whether formally instituted or simply recognized, can flourish for the good of the whole community, sustaining it in all its many needs: from catechesis to liturgy, from the education of the young to the widest array of charitable works."[5]

The All-Inclusive Definition

According to this usage, the great sacrament of our common calling is baptism. Both clergy and laity have ministries. As one Anglican statement puts it, "there are our churchly ministries . . . of both clergy and laity" (these extending to those who cook, type, and clean) or "our ministries with family, friends and neighbors," "our Monday morning ministries . . . within the structures of the secular world—political, industrial," "our 'Saturday night' ministries in leisure and hospitality and sports and holidays."[6] The scope of ministry has been broadened from word and sacrament to include practically everything in which some kind of Christian witness is possible.

All the definitions agree that ministry is some service to the life and growth of the church. The issue is how widely the term should be applied. To any and all such activities, even those that have no immediate connection to spreading the gospel? To such activities whether public or private? Only to those activities officially sponsored by the church in some way? Can all believers be involved in "ministry" without all being called "ministers"?

To provide a starting point in speaking to these questions, this chapter will consider briefly:

1. Ministry as it can be extrapolated from the public life of Jesus described in the Gospels;

2. Ministry as it emerges in the Pauline letters;
3. The significance of the family of words from the Greek root *diakon-* for understanding ministry;
4. Ministry as reflected in the life of the church in the Gospels and Acts and the more structured ministries in the Pastoral Epistles;
5. Some conclusions about what guidance this might provide for the church today.

MAKING A BEGINNING: WHAT DID JESUS DO?

The Gospels present portraits of the life, teaching, and activity of Jesus colored by thirty to sixty years of reflection on his death and Resurrection and the experience of the first Christian communities. However, it is possible from the Gospel traditions to arrive at some sense of what Jesus did and how he appeared to those who knew him.[7]

Jesus could be described as a prophet according to the model of the Old Testament prophets, Elijah and Elisha. Jesus claimed that his coming marked a crucial point in human history, the final times, no matter how long they would last. God's kingdom, God's will for peace, justice, and good, was at work in a definitive way. The dynamic reality of the kingdom could be experienced in the preaching of Jesus, in his invitation to all people without exception into fellowship with him, and especially in his miracles, where the will of God for healing and life became very real. Yet, in the face of its obvious incompleteness, God's kingdom was still something for the future.

Jesus was also a teacher who not only presented the usual ethical instructions but also gave instructions on how and whether to observe the Mosaic law. People listened to Jesus. Some came out of curiosity. Some were attracted to his message and personality. If Jesus uniquely brought God's reign, to accept this as true would obviously mean some response in belief and in deed from all who heard the message.

Jesus made more demanding claims on some. These individuals had accepted his teaching and Jesus invited them to go further, to share his mission of proclaiming the presence of God's kingdom and even working miracles to demonstrate the power of that kingdom among us. These people were the apostles. The Gospel traditions indicate that three characteristics marked the apostles:

1. *They were called by Jesus.* They did not choose Jesus for their teacher after considering many others. Jesus issued a summons to them to follow him and they responded willingly.

2. *They followed Jesus in the most decisive way.* To be an apostle of Jesus involved more than studying and accepting his teachings. It meant leaving family and employment to accompany him on his preaching journeys.

3. *By following Jesus, they risked danger and hostility.* Jesus told them that in going with him they were making choices about saving or losing their lives. Accepting him and his claims meant denying themselves and taking up their cross. It meant facing opposition, even in their own families.

This group of twelve were among the group of disciples (followers). As exemplars of discipleship and representing the twelve tribes of the reconstituted Israel, they had a very significant role in the ministry of Jesus. Characterized by stability and perseverance, and despite their failings, they embodied what Jesus meant by discipleship. The role of the twelve apostles lasts into the early days of the church, but then rapidly disappears.

THE COMMUNITY GROWS: PAUL REFLECTS

After the death of Jesus, the early disciples and others had formed communities of believers in various places. When Paul,[8] the convert and missionary, writes to a community, he addresses it as an *ekklesia*, a word that has come to be translated as "church" but that more literally means "assembly." Since the people of Israel are often referred to in the Old Testament as the "assembly of Yahweh," it is likely that Paul intends to suggest that the communities of believers are the present extension of that assembly. Each assembly, meeting in a private home, a house church, was the continuity of Israel in that place. Each such gathering, and all of them together, manifested the ongoing reality of God's relationship with believers.

However, another notion overlapped and gave the image of the community of believers as the assembly of God a fuller dimension. It was the church as the body of Christ. What made the gathering of believers different was that it included people of all nationalities and social levels. Through baptism and a common faith, they were formed into a living organism, which was the presence of Christ in the world. They were dependent on one another to form a united whole through which Christ would continue to touch human lives.

The community as a whole, and the individual members within it, were gifted with charisms, "concrete materialization[s] of God's grace."[9] Charisms of speech built up, strengthened, encouraged, guided, and taught the community. Charisms of action made the touch of God's grace concrete through service, assistance to those in need, healing, and other deeds.

DIAKONIA AGAINST ITS BACKGROUND

Words from the root *diakon-* appear regularly in the Pauline letters in passages having to do with service to the assembly.[10] John Collins observes that much of the broadening of the concept of ministry noted in the modern descriptions above depends on the article on *diakon-* words in the standard reference work, *Theological Dictionary of the New Testament.*[11] According to this source, ministry is activity that, under the guidance of the Spirit, contributes to building up the community, the body of Christ. What justifies the widely inclusive understanding of ministry is interpreting *diakonia* as service, especially service at table. This service, seen as something radically new in Jesus, is without institutional hierarchy or any resort to force. It is the humble service of charity—healing, sharing, reconciling. Anyone who fulfills these roles is ministering and is a minister.

Diakon- words are very rare in the Septuagint, the Greek version of the Old Testament, so the basic meaning has to be determined from use in ancient Christian and especially secular sources. From his study of this material, Collins challenges the understanding of *diakonia* as rooted in table service. His conclusion is that the fundamental meaning of this word as a verb is "to serve as a go-between." The *diakonos* or minister is one who is an authorized representative. If the context is religious, the minister has received a sacred commission to carry out some divine purpose. There are thus three basic elements in the notion of ministry as expressed by *diakonia:*

1. It is an action done in the name of another. One acts as the representative or emissary of another, whether divine or human, master or friend.
2. The action performed is given as a command or mandate by the one represented.
3. The actions performed become a personal obligation for the minister or *diakonos.*

WHAT DID PAUL THINK HE WAS DOING?

Although Paul does not use any *diakon-* vocabulary in Galatians, he gives a clear sense of what he thought his ministry was about: "[God] . . . from my mother's womb had set me apart and called me through his grace . . . to reveal his Son to me, so that I might proclaim him to the Gentiles" (Gal. 1:15–16).[12] His ministry was to be an apostle.

Paul regularly uses words with the root *diakon-* to refer to aspects of his mission from and for God and the Gospel. Second Corinthians 3 is filled with references to Paul's ministry. (In the quotes that follow, words from the *diakon-* root will be italic.) The community is "a letter of Christ, *administered* by us, written not in ink but by the spirit of the living God" (v. 3). God "has indeed qualified us as *ministers* of a new covenant" (v. 6). "For if the *ministry* of condemnation was glorious, the *ministry* of righteousness will abound much more in glory" (v. 9).

In the appeal for the collection for the church in Jerusalem (2 Cor. 8–9), Paul refers to that project in *diakon-* terms. The churches in Macedonia "begged us insistently for the favor of taking part in the *service* of the holy ones" (8:4). Titus is Paul's traveling companion "in this gracious work *administered* by us" (8:19). Paul speaks of the "lavish gift *administered* by us" (8:20).

Paul writes: "In everything we commend ourselves as *ministers* of God" (2 Cor. 6:4). "Are they *ministers* of Christ? . . . I am still more" (2 Cor. 11:23). In both these passages, Paul justifies the title for himself with a list of the sufferings and hardships he has undergone for the task entrusted to him of preaching the gospel.

Paul's use of *diakon-* words in writing of his ministry reveals that he considers himself as one entrusted with a special mission, coming from God himself and carrying with it responsibilities of faithful execution.

PAUL'S USE OF *DIAKONIA* IN REFERRING TO THE MINISTRY OF OTHERS

Paul's ministry as apostle was unique to him and some others. They had seen the risen Lord and been commissioned by him as witnesses to God's work through Jesus Christ. This included founding local assemblies of believers. The apostle also had to help the local churches develop whatever kinds of service would foster their inward and outward growth. Individuals would receive the needed spiritual gifts (*charismata*), the forms of service (*diakoniai*), and the workings (*energemata*) (1 Cor. 12:4–6). First on the list of these gifts, services, and workings were "apostles, prophets, teachers" (1 Cor. 12:27–31).

If the apostle had seen the risen Lord and been commissioned by him to preach the gospel, the "prophet" spoke words of inspiration and encouragement under the guidance of the Spirit. From what Paul says, prophecy is not exuberant exclamation but careful reflection on the life of the community. The "teachers" had another responsibility, to know and pass on those foundations on which the communities were based, the traditions about Jesus, and the sacred writings. Some of the other gifts are more or less clear from their names (e.g., "healing"). Some are indefinite enough to cover many situations: "assistance," "administration." The "varieties of tongues" are probably unintelligible sounds of praise that need to be translated into comprehensible language by those with the gift to "interpret."

All these ministries come from God and are entrusted to members of the community "for some benefit." They are not a demonstration of individual prowess. They are also subject to regulation by Paul and the assembly. So everything should be done in an orderly way and for building up the assembly. Only two or three should speak in tongues, and none at all if there is no one to interpret. Two or three prophets should speak, but others in the community are to discern the prophetic speech. What Paul directs is a "commandment of the Lord" (1 Cor. 14:20–40).

In Romans 13:1–7, Paul uses the *diakon-* root even for the role of the state. The authority of the state exercised by rulers is "a *servant* of God for your good" (v. 4). As in other situations, the state has received a commission from God to foster the good and must carry out that responsibility.

Leadership emerges in the local churches (1 Cor. 16:15–18 and 1 Thes. 5:12–13, where Paul advises that the de facto leaders be recognized). These leaders seem to have their positions not through appointment from the community, but from their own proven commitment and concern. Their service is one of the gifts given by God for the benefit of the community.

In Romans 16:1, Phoebe is referred to as a *minister* of the church at Cenchrea who deserves welcome and help because she has been a "benefactor" to Paul and many others. Philippians (v. 1:1) is addressed to, among others, "the *ministers*." In both of these cases, it is hard to know exactly what the title implies, beyond designating those who are playing some important role in church life.

COLOSSIANS AND EPHESIANS

The letters to the Ephesians and Colossians continue the sense of *diakon-* words as a mission entrusted by God, carrying with it responsibility on the part of the recipient of the mission. In Ephesians, Paul is *minister* of the mystery of Christ, a grace granted him by God's power (3:7). Christ gave apostles, prophets, evangelists, pastors, and teachers "to equip the holy ones for the work of *ministry,* for building up the body of Christ" (4:12). Tychicus is a "trustworthy *minister* of the Lord" whom Paul is sending to the community to tell them about Paul and encourage them. In Colossians, Epaphras is a "trustworthy *minister* of Christ on your behalf" (1:7). Paul is a *minister* of the gospel God has entrusted to him (1:23–25). Archippus is to be told, "'See that you fulfill the *ministry* that you received in the Lord'" (4:17).

From the way the root *diakon-* is used in the undisputed Pauline letters and in Ephesians and Colossians, it becomes clearer that *ministry* is not about humble table service but rather closer to its meaning in secular literature. It is an important commission entrusted to a person by God or the community or Paul. What is expected is fidelity to that commission. The purpose of granting the commission is to foster the faith life and charitable practice of that community.

DIAKON- WORDS IN THE GOSPELS AND ACTS

The Gospels themselves, because of their particular focus, do not tell us much about ministry. *Diakon-* words are rare in the Gospels and refer to the commonplace activities of household servants, sometimes interchangeably with *doulos*, which can mean either "slave" or "servant" (e.g., Lk. 12:35–40; Matt. 22:1–14). *Diakon-* words can have different meanings in different contexts.

Two very important *diakon-* passages are Mark 10:45, "For the Son of Man did not come *to be served* but *to serve* and to give his life as a ransom for many," and Luke 22:27, "For who is greater: the one seated at table or *the one who serves?* Is it not the one seated at table? I am among you as *the one who serves.*" Collins comments on the meaning of ministry as expressed in these two passages. Luke took his meaning from the use of the *diakon-* words in his Hellenistic environment. Waiting on table, especially in a religious context, was a service often performed by free men and by masters for their own slaves. For Jesus to be *one who serves* means that, as someone with dignity and authority, he chooses to exercise his important role without pomp or coercion. And Mark clearly understands the "service" of Jesus to be his mission, to carry out the task entrusted to him by his Father, the "ransom for many."[13]

In Acts, which reflects more fully the life of the early church, we get a better sense of what "ministry" was then coming to mean. In the gathering of disciples to choose a successor to Judas, Peter speaks of Judas who "was allotted a share in this *ministry*," which is to be witnesses of the risen Lord. The prayer of the assembled group is for guidance in choosing the one who will take Judas's place "in this apostolic *ministry*" (1:17, 25). In Acts 6, where men were chosen to care for the needs of the poor widows, *diakon-* appears as the "daily *distribution*" (v. 1) as well as "the *ministry* of the word," to which the twelve apostles wish to devote themselves (v. 4). In the face of a famine foretold by Agabus, a prophet who has come to Antioch, the disciples determine to "send *relief* to the brothers who lived in Judea" (11:29). Paul and Barnabas, having "completed their *relief mission*," that is, the delivery of the collection, return to Jerusalem (12:25). In 19:22, Paul sends Timothy and Erastus, "two of his *assistants*," to Macedonia. In addressing the elders of the church in Miletus, Paul says, "I consider my life of no importance to me, if only I may finish my course and the *ministry* that I received from the Lord Jesus, to bear witness to the gospel of God's grace" (20:24). When Paul arrives again in Jerusalem, he "proceeded to tell them in detail what God had accomplished among the Gentiles through his *ministry*" (21:19).

Diakon- takes on the meaning in Acts that it does in Paul's life (i.e., ministry is an important task entrusted to a person or persons with the expectation that he/she/they will carry out the mission responsibly). It might be the commission to preach the gospel entrusted by Jesus, or the commission to assist the hungry by carrying a collection from one Christian assembly to another, or the commission to represent Paul in one community as he remained in another. In Acts, the community plays a very important role in the choice and commissioning of those who are to act as ministers. The community chooses the two possible successors to Judas and then designates Matthias by lot (1:20–26). The community and the twelve apostles appoint seven to care for the needs of the poor (6:1–6). The disciples determine to send assistance from Antioch for famine relief in Judea through Barnabas and Paul (11:27–30, 12:25). Paul has received his ministry from the Lord Jesus (20:24) and then he sends Timothy and Erastus to Macedonia (19:21–22).

FURTHER DEVELOPMENT: THE PASTORAL LETTERS

It will be useful to give special attention to three Pastoral Epistles—1 and 2 Timothy and Titus—because in them we find clear signs of emerging structures, and hence ministries, in the Christian communities. It will be important to note the circumstances that called for the development of these ministries and the societal structures that provided a model from which to build and adapt.

Authorship and Date

One of the reasons for questioning whether these letters were written by Paul and belong to the time of his apostolate is precisely that more advanced church structures are in place. They seem to some to be too developed for the circumstances of Paul's life and ministry. Raymond Brown sums up: "About 80 to 90 percent of modern scholars would agree that the Pastorals were written after Paul's lifetime, and of those the majority would accept the period between 80 and 100 as the most plausible context for their composition."[14] Other notable scholars disagree with this consensus. Jerome Murphy-O'Connor believes that 2 Timothy was written by Paul, and that 1 Timothy and Titus receive recognition because they were connected to 2 Timothy.[15]

Luke Timothy Johnson accepts the authenticity of all three letters,[16] as does Ben Witherington, who emphasizes the long recognized similarities in language and style to Luke and Acts and postulates Luke as the actual writer of the letters whose content came from Paul. "The voice is the voice of Paul but the hand is the hand of a Gentile Christian named Luke."[17] If the letters were written by Paul, they were probably written in the mid-60s. It is unlikely that the authorship and date of the Pastoral Epistles will ever be settled definitively. Whether the letters were written by Paul or not, they still are the inspired word of God. For our purposes, it is not essential to determine date and authorship. It is sufficient to note the development they reflect.

The Cultural Context

Since the Pastoral Epistles witness to a development in structured ministry, it will be helpful to note some characteristics of the world that created a felt need for these structures.

Christians were very much a minority in a culture in which there was little separation between religious practice and civic life. Although residents might privately attend to their personal religious beliefs, failure to honor the local gods of the city and the state, including at times the Roman emperor, was considered disloyal and seditious. Obviously, this caused problems for Christians. The Christian profession, "There is one Lord" (Eph. 4:5), could be considered subversive and dangerous in societies that recognized many "lords" for their well-being. The issue of eating food offered to idols that Paul deals with in 1 Corinthians 8:1–11:1 is an example of the kind of intertwining of religious/political/cultural elements that Christians had to deal with.

Honor was of the utmost importance. Honor can be defined as: "the positive value of a person in his or her own eyes plus the positive appreciation of that person in the eyes of his or her social group. . . . For example, (for a man) as father of a family, his honor is defined in terms of gender (male, father) and position (head of the household). When he commands his children and they obey him, his power is obvious. In this situation of command and obedience, his claim to honor as father and head of the household is acknowledged and onlookers acknowledge that he is an honorable father."[18]

Were the children not to obey him, the father would be dishonored because neither his own children nor onlookers would be acknowledging his position. Christian teachings about the equality of men and women and slaves and free persons, if actually carried into practice, would have caused great stress for an honor ethic in which respect for social position was crucial. These teachings would have jeopardized the traditional position of men in relation to women and masters in relation to slaves.

Christians had to show that they were not a threat to institutions and values that the broader society considered basic to its existence. Cities and states were very wary of movements and religions that appeared to threaten the status quo and took vigorous action against the individuals involved.

Apparently there were also issues within the church community. Some self-appointed leaders were presenting false teachings. It is difficult to describe exactly what these false teachings were, but they seemed to focus, at least in part, on a spiritualized idea of the resurrection as an event that had already taken place for Christians. This called for a life of asceticism, abstaining from marriage and certain kinds of food. Mixed in as well was material from Jewish mythology.

The community also seems to have needed tighter leadership and direction. There was troubling and perhaps attention-attracting agitation about the status of women and slaves. And apparently some leaders in the church had been accused of improper behavior of one type or another. What was required was strong leadership and discipline to restore order and orthodoxy.

HOW THE CHURCH OF THE PASTORAL LETTERS SAW ITSELF: THE HOUSEHOLD OF GOD

The model for the Christian assemblies as reflected in the Pastoral Epistles flowed from its lived experience.[19] According to Acts, the communities grew by the addition of households, for example, that of Cornelius in Caesarea (10:24, 47) and Lydia in Philippi (16:14–15). According to the Pauline letters, the communities met in homes, of Nympha at Laodicea (Col. 4:15), of Prisca and Aquila at Rome (Rom. 16:4–5), of Archippus (Phlm. 2), probably at Colossae.

The household was the basic unit of society. The welfare of the whole social body depended on the health of the household. Household was broader than family, defined not so much by kinship as by relationships of dependence and subordination. Extensive writings from contemporary social commentators spell out lists of responsibilities in a household. There were duties to country, to parents, to children, to spouses, to slaves, to other kin. There were mutual duties between the head of the household and those to whom he was not necessarily related but to whom he offered patronage and protection.

The head of the household, the paterfamilias, was responsible for the well-being of the household and expected obedience and recognition of his position from its members. Each household had its own integrity and identity, which marked its participation in the larger civic unity. The honorable household was a credit to itself and its members and a worthy participant in broader community life.

What defined an honorable household was order and tranquillity (1 Tim. 2:2). A household was one of honor when each member recognized his or her place and acknowledged his or her duties to another. When all the members of every household lived in proper relationship with one another, there would be harmony in society. For the Christians of the Pastoral Epistles, the good ordering of the household was part of the divine plan. There was no radical discontinuity between the structures of the church and society. Here was the "domestic church" in full flower.

A key Greek word in this context is *upotassein* in its various forms. It has a range of meanings revolving around the basic concept of being subject, being obedient. In some of its forms, it has the sense of voluntary subordination. For the household to function well, to be honorable, the members have to renounce their own will for the sake of others. They must accept the place society allots to them. It was according to this pattern that the members of the Christian communities were expected to live out their relationships with one another and with the rest of society.

However, there was a basic difference in the Christian household from others. In the Christian household, the members would submit "in the Lord," would govern or lead "in the Lord." Unlike the situation in the secular world, the master might sometimes behave as a servant. The slave might, by his or her conduct, become a trusted member of the community.

Honorable Behavior in the Household of God

In the household of the Christian assembly, it is, of course, God who is the head of the household, the paterfamilias.[20] The human head of the household serves as the steward, the manager. What determined honorable behavior in the household of God was, in a general way, determined by what was expected in any household in the surrounding society.

Women are to be under the authority of the paterfamilias. They are to live quietly and with dignity in their public roles. Secular writers condemned and satirized women who debated or spoke in public. In the Christian household, women may take roles appropriate to their position but some roles are not for them. They are to wear modest clothes, and good deeds are to be their finery. These requirements are standard in the lists of Greco-Roman and Jewish moralists and have added meaning for Christians since excess in style would be disruptive of worship.

The household of honor requires that slaves keep good order and tranquillity by being satisfied in their station. Slavery was taken for granted in the ancient world. Any disruption of slavery was seen as dangerous to economic and social stability. The pre– and post–Civil War history of our own country reveals how slavery impacts socioeconomic conditions.

From the Pauline letters, it is reasonable to deduce that it was especially among women and slaves that the Christian ideal of equality was becoming very popular. The admonition to slaves not to take advantage of masters who were believers because they were brothers, but to work harder for them (1 Tim. 6:2), most likely reflects a reaction to claims that were being made by slaves on their owners by virtue of their Christian faith.

The letter to the Ephesians notes the difference in the subordination in the Christian household. "Be subordinate to one another out of reverence for Christ" (Eph. 5:21). Christians are to observe the proprieties of the household and society, but the motivation is new. Since Christians saw the natural order of their experience as a reflection of the divine order, they were to observe its requirements as a religious call. There was an additional factor. As the expectation for the Second Coming dimmed with the passing of time, there grew the realization that Christians would have to continue living in the world and within its structures.

THE MODEL FOR MINISTRIES AND THE QUALITIES OF MINISTERS IN THE HOUSEHOLD OF GOD

The Christian communities, in different ways and according to their own circumstances, came to realize that they needed leaders and others to fill special roles if they were to survive divisions and tensions within and a suspicious world without.[21] In a most natural way, they absorbed and adapted structures that were part of the contemporary secular and religious society.

The title of one minister, the *episkopos*, is often translated "bishop." This can be misleading because the bishop with whom we are familiar (i.e., one man in charge of a regional church and assisted by priests and deacons) did not clearly emerge until the time of Ignatius of Antioch (110–115). A better translation at this stage in history is "overseer." In the Old Testament, the overseer is entrusted with specific tasks, military or otherwise.[22] In the Hellenistic synagogue, the overseer was in charge of financial administration and was called upon to settle disputes. At Qumran, the overseer examined candidates and was responsible for the formation of new members. In Greek society, the overseer was selected for some defined civic project (e.g., the building of a road or the repair of a building).

The duties of the *episkopos* or overseer in the Christian communities are not listed. The overseers (*episkopoi*) and ministers (*diakonoi*), in the plural, are simply named among the addressees of the letter to the Philippians. However, the word *episkopos* is used only in the singular in Pastoral Epistles. What the *episkopos* did has to be deduced from the qualities that are required for the ministry and the examples of the function of the overseer in contemporary society.

> Therefore, a bishop must be irreproachable, married only once, temperate, self-controlled, decent, hospitable, able to teach. He must manage his own household well, keeping his children under control with perfect dignity; for if a man does not know how to manage his own household, how can he take care of the church of God? (1 Tim. 3:2–5)

> For a bishop, as God's steward, must be someone who is blameless, married; he must not be arrogant or quick-tempered or addicted to wine or violent or greedy for gain; but he must be hospitable, a lover of goodness, prudent, upright, devout and self controlled. He must have a firm grasp of the word that is trustworthy in accordance with the teaching, so that he may be able both to preach with sound doctrine and to refute those who contradict it. (Ti. 1:7–9)

The qualities required are those that will guarantee that the overseer will be a leader but will not use his authority in a harsh or arbitrary way. He will be faithful, exercise balanced judgment, put community interests above his own, preserve true doctrine within the community, and have a good reputation with outsiders. In other words, the overseer should be a good head of his own household to qualify as the head of the assembly, which is the household of God.

Another ministry or office is that of the *presbyteroi*, transliterated as "presbyters," a word we now use to refer to priests but which in the context of the Pastoral Epistles is more properly "elders." The institution of elders was also familiar from Jewish and secular society. To be an elder, one had to be wise, and wisdom was usually, though not always, a blessing of old age. In the Old Testament, the elders exercise authority and render judgment in various situations (e.g., assisting Moses).[23] Hellenistic synagogues and some other religious associations had a college of elders. They constituted a board that had an administrative role, including raising and distributing money.

Elders appear in the Gospels as members of the religious elite of the Jews.[24] They also appear in Acts referring to religious leadership, whether of the Jews[25] or in a similar position in the Christian community. Paul and Barnabas "appointed presbyters for them in every church" (14:23). The presbyters or elders play a central role in the so-called Council of Jerusalem (Acts 15), which decided the question of the need for Jewish religious practice by non-Jewish converts who had become followers of Jesus. "The apostles and the presbyters" are mentioned together as welcoming Paul and Barnabas (15:4), as meeting "together to see about this matter" (15:6), as sending Paul, Barnabas, and other representatives to carry the letter with their decision to the community in Antioch (15:22).

Again in the Pastoral Epistles, there is no clear description of duties, only a list of qualities. "I left you behind in Crete . . . so that . . . you should appoint elders in every town, as I directed you, someone who is blameless, married only once, whose children are believers, not accused of debauchery and not rebellious" (Ti. 1:5–6). "Let the elders who rule well be considered worthy of double honor, especially those who labor in preaching and teaching" (1 Tim. 5:17).

There were also *diakonoi*, which we should probably render as "helpers" so as not to imagine them exactly as the deacons of today. In synagogues, such men assisted in collecting and distributing community charity. In the communities of the Pastoral Epistles, "deacons must be dignified, not deceitful, not addicted to drink, not greedy for sordid gain, holding fast to the mystery of the faith with a clear conscience. Moreover, they should be tested first; then if there is nothing against them, let them serve as deacons. . . . Deacons must be married only once and must manage their children and their households well" (1 Tim. 3:8–12).

Among the requirements for the helpers, we read, "Women, similarly, should be dignified, not slanderers, but temperate and faithful in everything" (1 Tim. 3:11). There has been ongoing discussion as to whether these women are the wives of the male helpers or are themselves *diakonoi* (the masculine form of the Greek word is used for Phoebe in Romans 16). There are good reasons to opt for the position that they are also "helpers." Their role becomes clearer in time. They especially deal with church situations involving women: preparing women catechumens, assisting women during the ceremonies of baptism and anointing, and so forth. Once again we should not be too hasty in using the language of the Pastoral Epistles to decide current issues such as women as ordained deacons in the modern sense.

A final group about which there is not universal agreement is the widows. In a society without what we call a poverty safety net, widows were vulnerable. If not helped by family, they could be reduced to terrible need. First Timothy 5:3–16 counsels how to care for widows. They should be supported by their own families first, and only if there is no such support available should the household of faith step in to help. Within those instructions, however, the letter seems to envision a special group of elderly widows who have a distinct ministry in the community. Again, the role of this group, if such it was, is not defined. Presumably they would be concerned with ministry to women.

It is important to note that the qualities for ministry in the church have essentially to do with character. The qualities are those expected of other holders of high office in contemporary society, or to put it on a more immediate level, they are the virtues of a good head of household, the virtues of one who can maintain honor and tranquillity in his own household and do the same in the household of the church. It is presumed that the church officials know belief and practice it. What is stressed is the importance of their example and prudent leadership.

SUMMARY AND LINES OF DEVELOPMENT

1. Jesus very soon enlisted others to help him preach the presence of the kingdom of God. Their mission was to spread the kingdom by word and work.
2. As acceptance of Jesus spread after his death and Resurrection, groups of believers gathered into local assemblies.
3. In these local assemblies, there emerged some de facto leaders (e.g., the heads of the households in which the believers came together).
4. As reflected in Paul, each member of each assembly was also expected to contribute to the forming of the group into the body of Christ, witnessing to his presence in the world. There were different needs in the community that had to be attended to if the community was to be healthy and grow. Members had different gifts and ministries from the Holy Spirit to respond to these needs.
5. Some of the ministries might be transient (e.g., prophecy or speaking in tongues), while some, by their nature, lasted longer (e.g., teaching). Teaching required special qualifications (i.e., knowing the traditions about Jesus and the scriptures).
6. None of these ministries was something that the believer took upon himself or herself, nor were they for any personal aggrandizement. They existed for the benefit of all.
7. Even those ministries that seemed to flow immediately from the Spirit (e.g., prophecy and tongues) were subject to control by the community. Paul gives rules so that these gifts might help the community in an orderly way.
8. Ministries reflect the content of the *diakon-* family of words in the secular world. They are a commission from God, Jesus Christ, the Holy Spirit, entrusted to a person to be carried out with fidelity.

9. The community plays a role in this commissioning process. Paul and others could be entrusted with specific tasks in the name of the community. Individuals such as Paul could also commission ministers to act for them.

10. As the community develops, whether chronologically or structurally or both, this commissioning becomes more formal as overseers, elders, and helpers are appointed, at times with a specific act. "Do not neglect the gift you have which was conferred on you through the prophetic word with the imposition of hands of the presbyterate" (1 Tim. 4:14). "Stir into flame the gift of God that you have through the imposition of my hands" (2 Tim. 1:6). "I left you in Crete so that you might set right what remains to be done and appoint presbyters in every town, as I directed you" (Ti. 1:5). "Do not lay hands too readily on anyone" (1 Tim. 5:22).

11. This development within the community took place in the cultural context of contemporary society and in the ecclesial context of the local assembly of believers. As the communities grew, there was a need to provide instruction for converts, material care for the poor, support in the face of a sometimes hostile environment, and so forth.

12. The ministries that developed under the pressure of local circumstances were usually not created ex nihilo but were adapted from secular institutions that seemed appropriate models to serve the needs of the church.

13. There was evidently a fluidity in both the development of ministries and in terminology. Titus 1:5–9, to the church in Crete, seems to equate elder (presbyter) and overseer (bishop). First Timothy, to the assembly in Ephesus, speaks of the overseer (bishop) and helpers (deacons) without mentioning elders, but Acts 20:17–38 tells of Paul calling the elders of Ephesus for a farewell meeting in Miletus.

14. The requirements for ministries as the communities developed were less "charismatic," less spontaneous, and looked more to the personal qualities of the minister to be able to minister effectively within the community and to witness to the outside world.

15. These ministers needed some kind of recognition, some kind of commission from the community. And there was also the power to judge a minister if accusations were brought against him. "Do not accept an accusation against a presbyter unless it is supported by two or three witnesses. Reprimand publicly those who do sin, so that the rest will be afraid" (1 Tim. 5:19–20).

16. There is as yet no indication of ordination in our sense of the word, as the designation of persons exclusively for the celebration of word and sacrament.
17. Women have a place in these ministries, but as circumstances seem to require, these ministries are limited to those roles that were acceptable for women in the culture of the time.

CONCLUSIONS FOR MINISTRY TODAY

If we were to sum up the history of the development of ministries in the church, three guiding principles emerge:

1. All members of the church are called to contribute in some way to the building up of the community into the body of Christ.
2. Within this general call, there is another, to serve in ministry, in some special service to the community recognized and commissioned by the community, usually through its representatives or leaders. The person so recognized and commissioned must have the personal qualities and the competency required to fulfill the ministry.
3. As circumstances in the life of the Christian communities change, the qualifications and competencies required for established ministries might change. There could also arise new ministries appropriate to those circumstances. The forms of those new ministries are regularly affected by structures dealing with similar circumstances in the secular society and call for new ministers, competent and commissioned.

Co-Workers in the Vineyard of the Lord gives the title "lay ecclesial ministers" to "those men and women whose ecclesial service is characterized by:

- *Authorization* of the hierarchy to serve publicly in the local church
- *Leadership* in a particular area of ministry
- *Close mutual collaboration* with the pastoral ministry of bishops, priests and deacons
- *Preparation and formation* appropriate to the level of responsibilities that are assigned to them."[26]

Authorization, pastoral collaboration, and appropriate preparation flow from the New Testament development and apply to all ministries. Leadership in a particular area of ministry may or may not be a characteristic of ministry generally, but it would seem to be one of the distinctive qualities of what is being called "lay ecclesial ministry."

NOTES

1. For a survey of the development of the understanding of ministry, see John N. Collins, *Diakonia: Reinterpreting the Ancient Sources* (New York: Oxford University Press, 1990), 3–44; and *Are All Christians Ministers?* (Collegeville, MN: Liturgical Press, 1992).

2. U.S. Conference of Catholic Bishops, *Co-Workers in the Vineyard of the Lord* (Washington, DC: USCCB, 2005), 9, quoting *Christifideles Laici*, 23.

3. Joseph A. Komonchak et al., eds., *The New Dictionary of Theology* (Wilmington, DE: Michael Glazier, 1987), 660.

4. Apostolic Letter *Ministeria Quaedam.* August 15, 1972. In International Commission on English in the Liturgy, *Documents on the Liturgy: 1963–1975* (Collegeville, MN: Liturgical Press, 1982), 908–11.

5. *Novo millennio ineunte*, (2001), n. 46.

6. Collins, *Diakonia*, 258.

7. The proposals presented here are indebted to the magisterial studies of John P. Meier, *A Marginal Jew: Rethinking the Historical Jesus*, vol. 2, *Mentor, Message and Miracles,* and vol. 3, *Companions and Competitors* (New York: Doubleday, 1994 and 2001).

8. For a fuller treatment, see James D. G. Dunn, *The Theology of Paul the Apostle* (Grand Rapids, MI: Eerdmans, 1998), 533–64.

9. Dunn, *The Theology of Paul*, 553.

10. For the understanding of the meaning of *diakonia,* see Collins, *Diakonia* and *Are All Christians Ministers?*

11. Gerhard Kittel, ed., *Theological Dictionary of the New Testament* (Grand Rapids, MI: Eerdmans, 1964), 2:81–92.

12. All scripture quotations are taken from the New American Bible: Revised New Testament, 1986.

13. Collins, *Are All Christians Ministers?* 145–51.

14. Raymond Brown, *An Introduction to the New Testament* (New York: Doubleday, 1996), 668.

15. Jerome Murphy-O'Connor, *Paul: A Critical Life* (Oxford: Clarendon, 1996), 335–39.

16. Luke Timothy Johnson, *The First and Second Letters to Timothy*, Anchor Bible (New York: Doubleday, 2001), 55–88.

17. Ben Witherington, III, *Letters and Homilies for Hellenized Christians* (Downers Grove, IL: IVP Academic, 2006), 176.

18. Jerome H. Neyrey, ed., *The Social World of Luke–Acts: Models for Interpretation* (Peabody, MA: Hendrickson, 1991), 25–26.

19. For this section, see 1 Tim. 3:1–5, 14–15; 2 Tim. 2:20–21.

20. See Ti. 3:1–2; 1 Tim. 2:1–3, 9–15, 6:1–2.

21. See 1 Tim. 3:1–11; Ti. 2:6–9.

22. See Judg. 9:28; Neh. 11:9, 14–22; 2 Kgs. 11:15, etc. *Paqid* in Hebrew becomes *episkopos* in Greek.

23. For example, Lev. 4:15; Judg. 21:16; 1 Sam. 4:3, 8:4, etc. *Zaqen* in Hebrew becomes *presbyteros* in Greek.

24. For example, Mt. 16:21, 27:1, 3, 12; Mk. 8:31, 11:27; Lk. 7:3, 9:22.

25. For example, Acts 4:5, 6:16.

26. USCCB, *Co-Workers*, 10.

4

Being a Ministering Church: Insights from History

Thomas F. O'Meara, O.P.

Vatican II was an event with unforeseen ramifications. Yves Congar wrote: "It is astonishing how the post-conciliar period has so little to do with the Council. The post-conciliar questions are new and radical. *'Aggiornamento'* [now] means changes and adaptations to a new situation."[1] One of the remarkable developments during the years after Vatican II has been the expansion of ministry in the parish and diocese. For over a millennium there had been effectively only one ecclesiastical office: the priesthood. The priest at the altar had absorbed most of the ministries into his role of celebrating Mass and the sacraments, rapidly, in an alien language. Other ministries, even preaching, were neglected. In the theologies of those centuries the bishop was a special priest, and what was distinctive about laity and religious was that they were not priests. The plurality of the ministries in the Pauline or patristic churches ceased to exist or existed temporarily in monasteries.

In the years that followed the council, ministry and ministries emerged rapidly and variously. The number of people at work in parishes and dioceses increased dramatically. The very model of the parish changed, from one of priests in the sanctuary and sisters in the school to a staff of full-time ministers in a parish community led by the pastor.[2] This newness in ministry was in fact something old: The renewal of various services was a restoration of aspects of the community to which the letters of Paul witness. The New Testament describes charism and ministry in specific services whose names are taken from actions, for instance, preaching, teaching, evangelizing, and counseling. Names and actions differ according to place, culture, and time. As Jesus founded the church in a global way, so ministry as a totality full of implicit forms and powers has a variety and potentiality flowing from the fullness of the body of Christ. Spirit, charism, and ministry offer a primal reality, an original fullness for future times.

THE REEMERGENCE OF THE SPIRIT'S MINISTRIES

The event of the rediscovery and expansion of ministry in the local church (today still in its early stages) is marked by the reappearance at the end of the 1960s of ministries beyond the liturgical ministry of the priest and the apostolates of religious men and women in schools, social service agencies, and hospitals. This event seems to have come from the Holy Spirit, for it was not prescribed by papacy and hierarchy, theologians, or pastoral plans, but appeared suddenly in local churches. The baptized undertook "direct ministries" in and for the church. Certainly themes in the documents of Vatican II stimulated this unfolding: the people of God, broader than the hierarchy; grace as empowerment rather than insurance policy; liturgy as nourishment for social ministry; and a restored theology of baptism. There should not be tension between baptism and authority, for all authority and office presumes and comes from one baptism.[3] The reality of primal Christianity was needed to serve large parishes filled with educated and active people.

Henri Denis speaks of ways in which the church office of priesthood changed at and after Vatican II. The mission of the church was more than the priest's celebration of the Eucharist; Jesus instituted ministries throughout his life and not just at the Last Supper. Every ministry, including those of priest and bishop, is essentially ministerial and not just cultic, active and not just sacral; the priest's ministry is to further the activities of people in the parish and not only through the Eucharistic prayer.[4] The expansion of the ministry, far from eclipsing the pastor and bishop, drew the priest into more ecclesial activity and leadership.[5] An expanded ministerial staff (joined at the diocesan and parish level to the bishop and pastor) mirrors the early church. An expanded ministry did not come into existence because of the decline in vocations to the diocesan priesthood, and it would not disappear if there were a great number of ordinations in dioceses. It is a question not of numbers but of ministerial variety.

We should see the recent multiplication of volunteer groups as part of the expansion of lay ecclesial ministry. A recent survey estimates that there are 25,000 associates of religious orders at work in the Catholic Church. Researchers wonder if "the Spirit is working overtime with the People of God at the dawn of this new millennium. The reality of committed associates collaborating with vowed religious to further the Reign of God has been operative in some congregations of vowed religious for over a third of a century, while in others it is a recent development."[6] Their *diakonia* ranges from teaching to comforting the dying. The activist spirit of young Americans, nourished by retreats and days of prayer, is attracted to the spirituality of the sponsoring institute.

Associates live as part of an intentional church community where liturgy sustains a wider variety of ministries in education and social service. Are they the third orders and confraternities of today? Studies show too that not a few intend to remain involved with church ministry. One can see the associates as a future form of religious life, just as some have seen lay ecclesial ministers as the new form of the minor orders.[7]

This chapter selects *time* as a dynamic form influencing ministry. Christianity narrates and realizes a salvation history. It does not flee God, but expects in cultural ages a special moment of the Spirit's presence in history, a *kairos*. Vatican II accepted a new history in the life of the church. Congar observed that everything is historical, from the person of Jesus Christ to the figure of Pope Paul VI. "The council . . . is basically a historical reality and the vision of the Council—that of *Lumen Gentium*—has been resolutely that of history of salvation, given a destiny by eschatology."[8]

This chapter follows the three dimensions of time. It meditates upon the past (precursors of the expansion of ministry), the present (a new model of circles of ministry), and the future (the situation of baptismal ministry now and in the immediate future). History assists us in understanding the universality, normalcy, and fullness of a baptismal ministry that has become lay ecclesial ministries.

HISTORY, OUR HELPER

Thomas Aquinas observed that time can be our assistant and enabler: "Time is, so to say, a discoverer and a kind of co-operator."[9] History tells of the primal gift of ministry from the Spirit evident in the Pauline letters, and history tells of its metamorphoses in the churches of the first five centuries. Karl Rahner finds the primal gift of ministry not hidden away in eternity but living in historically manifest forms: "Within the time of the New Testament itself there is a history and a becoming of the constitution of the church."[10] The church, far from hoping for the maintenance of a few timeless forms, is itself the place of the presentations and realizations of grace. History tells why the variety and extent of the ministry of all Christians declined in feudal times, and how the new religious orders and spiritualities of the Baroque, up to the nineteenth century, attempted to draw the baptized into the potentially rich life of the church, not only in mystical prayer, but in evangelization and the care of the poor. The following pages ponder first various movements that were precursors of today's lay ecclesial ministry. Then the chapter turns to dynamic lines of the Spirit active in cultures, "trajectories" past and present. Next it looks at the contemporary theological model of circles of ministry. Finally, it turns to the force field of encouraging and opposing forces around ministry now and in the immediate future.

Past Precursors in Ministry

The reappearance of a variety of ministries around 1970 was not without precedents and prior impetuses. As was mentioned, the local life of the church fashioned anew what had been the format of the church in its primal years of the first centuries, and in the following centuries. A history of the Spirit struggling to lead the baptized into ministry has earlier forms, precursors. The ministry declined in variety and in inclusiveness from the eighth to the twentieth centuries, and yet in the feudal and Baroque periods there were always movements struggling to let those who were not priests have some activity for God, to organize an ecclesial service. The Holy Spirit would not leave the entirety of the church to passivity and monoformity; it would not isolate a single group, a small caste, a sacral priesthood to exercise all public roles in the church. Several examples from the period suggest that Christians should not remain in silence and shadows in the church but follow the promptings of the Spirit to work and organize others to work for the kingdom of God.

A prime example was the "third orders" of religious founded in the Middle Ages. At the beginning of the thirteenth century, Dominic and Francis wanted men and women to be involved in preaching inside and outside of church buildings, ordinary people involved in a new vision of spirituality and ministry. They presumed that Christians who were not priests, including women, could be part of this enterprise. Frightened by lay freedom, church authority made the friars' religious orders clerical and led female associates back into the cloister. Consequently, the friars fashioned a third group for the baptized who could associate themselves with Dominicans and Franciscans in ministry. Active women like Catherine of Siena and spiritual nobility like King Louis IX of France belonged to third orders.

The religious orders and congregations founded at the time of the Counter-Reformation—in many ways modeled on the new format of the Society of Jesus—also developed lay groups.[11] The followers of Philip Neri and Ignatius Loyola pursued a new way of living a spiritual life, even as they organized the study of the Bible and founded confraternities of the baptized to help the poor and the sick. These groups were prominent in the seventeenth and eighteenth centuries. For instance, in Munich the brotherhood of Saint Michael was founded by the elector-prince in 1693, and by 1732 had 100,000 members in Bavaria.[12] The sodalities of the nineteenth and early twentieth centuries continued this movement of ministry. The members were, however, not active participants in the liturgy, in adult teaching, or in church administration. Their activity was largely limited to works of charity and remained outside church and liturgy—people seeking ministry, and again ending up in private spirituality, and works of charity.

Building on the confraternities and sodalities were later organizations involved with the poor like the Saint Vincent de Paul Society founded by the French layman Frederic Ozanam, in 1833, and Catholic Charities, drawn from the work of Constantin Noppel in Berlin, after World War I. There were also social movements like the Knights of Columbus, which offered working Catholics recreation and financial services. The Kolping movement, in Germany, and later the Jocists, around the world, helped young people working in large cities, while the Catholic Worker movement emphasized community and an appreciation of agricultural life.[13] Later in America the Catholic Youth Organization, the Catholic Family movement, and Catholic forms of community organization developed. All of this was part of what was called "Catholic Action," which flourished in a variety of organizations worldwide from 1920 to 1960. Countless figures organized groups subsumed under that general term. The popes used the term "Catholic Action" in their writings as a general affirmation of a variety of lay movements. The general dynamic was an attempt to get beyond the location of revelation and grace solely in the interior life.

Finally, there was a further kind of religious order that sought to be modern and anonymous, private and individual, a "secular institute" wherein a person took private vows and met with a spiritual director even as he or she retained a secular profession and work. Their private and anonymous life might sometimes be a form of evangelism of others, albeit slow and indirect. The pontificate of John Paul II encouraged "new movements," organizations of seminarians and priests resembling congregations founded between 1830 and 1930. They were favored because they represented movements prior to the involvement of the baptized after Vatican II.

A historical overview from the third orders to secular institutes shows that these movements had two basic weaknesses. The first was that they resembled past forms of vowed life. They were not focused on baptismal charisms in service for the church. Second, some of the groups found it difficult to find a ministry, one that was distinctive and lasting. A few were born from concrete problems, like those of young workers in European cities or Catholics in rural areas, but most did not know how to find a ministry suited to the twentieth century; the church hierarchy wanted lay activity to remain in the area of helping poor people. The action in "Catholic Action" was vague and limited.

Particularly in English-speaking countries, religious orders—of women as well as of men—were numerous and influential in education. After 1880, their many schools (including colleges and universities) inspired in ordinary Catholic students the idea that they too had a calling to a public life in the church, and that entry into the priesthood or religious life was not the only way to serve the church, or to bring the gospel into society. Those many schools in existence for over a century and a half had an enormous impact on U.S. Catholicism, planting the ideas that any Catholic might have a ministerial work and that women educators were and could be leaders in the church.

Clearly it is a mistake to think that the widespread ministry of the baptized begun in the late 1960s came from nowhere. Centuries of Catholics worked to broaden ministry in church and society. Furthermore, the past eight centuries hold a paradox. On the one hand, there is a dominance of one official ministry only: the priesthood, with the introspective spiritualities of the ages of the Baroque (Pierre Bérulle); Vatican I (Curé of Ars); and the early twentieth century (Columba Marmion).[14] That brings more and more clericalism, more and more definition of ministry as a sacral liturgy or a sacral life, more and more lay passivity. If after 1630 and 1830 that movement to clericalism becomes intense and monopolistic, on the other hand, there are countless prophetic founders and foundresses working to offer the baptized ministry. Even as the emphasis on the priesthood became more and more intense, the Holy Spirit drew prophetic men and women to lead hundreds of thousands of baptized into ministries. One can estimate that 60 percent of the ministry in the past century and a half in the U.S. Catholic Church was accomplished by the baptized, and largely by women. Yet, church authority worked to curtail this; religious and their sodalities were kept apart from the clerical monopoly.

Trajectories to the Present Moment

The present moment of expanding ministries is a time of change. Ministry in the entirety of the body of Christ is important, and it releases important theological energies. Composing a proximate background to the dynamics of today's ecclesial ministry are the ways selected by Dolores Leckey, through which she observes that the baptized are "stirring the church." They are seeking and cultivating a spirituality; they see the presence of grace as God's co-creating presence in family and society; they represent new roles for women; they expect and work for the vitality of their parish; and, finally, she notes "their entrance into ministry and their willingness to share responsibility for the mission of the church."[15]

A further way of looking at the present moment in Catholic Church life is to see that not one but four different important movements have reappeared, clamoring for understanding and realization: (1) the Pauline theology of the body of Christ with its various activities; (2) the public and social inadequacy of the historically conditioned distinction between clergy and laity; (3) public roles of ministry for women;[16] (4) an ecclesiology of full-time and part-time ministers around the community leader as the complement of the priest.[17] These trajectories have led into a new millennium, drawing forward the living drama of history, composed by culture and time.

Today's Model: Circles of Ministry

The Spirit seems to be intent upon retaining the primal Pentecostal ecclesiology where all the baptized are called to ministry. Historical lines lead to a new model for the local church with its ministries. The new image coming from ecclesiologies old and new is one of circles. A presence of grace coming from the Spirit vitalizes church life and structure so that a new pattern of ministry displays circles of ministries around the leader of the community. Karl Rahner spoke of the "ministerial basis"[18] of the entire church, which is grounded in a transcendental modality of the sharing Spirit. This new model recognizes a variety of ministries and permits degrees of ministries. The communal leader does not stand above or in competition with other ministries. Other ministries are not all the same but they are all truly ministry: the ordained and those who work full time in a church along with various kinds of part-time ministers, volunteers, and assistants in the parish. The model of circles sustains both a basic ecclesial similarity in ministry and differences and distinctions among degrees of ministry. Yves Congar observed:

> The Church of God is not built up solely by the actions of the official presbyteral ministry but by a multitude of diverse modes of service, stable or occasional, spontaneous or recognized, and (when the occasion arises) consecrated, if not by sacramental ordination. These modes of service already exist. . . . They exist now; but up to now were not called by their true name, *ministries*, nor were their place and status in ecclesiology recognized.[19]

Reflections on ministry today bring up an interesting parallel. The expansion of ministry occurred along with an expansion of theological education for the baptized through an array of graduate programs. Schools and universities initiated multiple programs to educate the baptized who wished to work in ministry. When theology was joined to priesthood, only the seminarian could study theology; this lasted from medieval times to the middle of the twentieth century. After the foundation of the Tridentine Seminary and the labor to establish seminaries throughout the world in the seventeenth century, theology became little by little almost exclusively located in the seminary. University theology became less significant in the church and, with the Enlightenment's interest in reason, science, and secularity, marginalized. In short, during the millennium prior to Vatican II, only priests and future priests could study theology. Around 1955, German universities began to admit women to doctoral programs. In the United States, the study of theology was possible for nonseminarians only through studying patristic theologians in a faculty of Greek and Latin literature, until Sister Mary Madeleva, in the mid-1950s, established at St. Mary's College in Indiana the first graduate program in theology for those who were not seminarians. The first students were women religious; the idea of a layperson studying theology lay ten years ahead. In the 1960s, the theology schools of the religious orders (partly seminaries) and universities offered graduate programs ranging from biblical studies to the new field of pastoral theology. Schools were ready to educate tens of thousands of Catholics who wanted to work in ministry.

Christian Ministry Today: Forces and Counterforces

Precursors of ministry led to the present expansion. Today there is the ongoing development of education and formation for the lay ecclesial minister; there is the development of the structure of a staff of ministries with leadership; there is the relationship of ministers to Sunday liturgy and to Christian life; there is the need for a just salary, perceptive hiring practices, and continuing education. Nonordained ministers in the church are not failed aspirants to the one sacerdotal ministry and not outsiders to a superior ordained state.

What lines of force are furthering and countering lay ecclesial ministry? We need not dwell on the "laity" since they, the baptized, are realizing their diaconal charisms on a considerable scale. Second, the religious orders and congregations have not seen wider ministry as a competitor: indeed, they have provided in North America most of the schools and educational programs for lay ministry. Similarly, Catholic colleges and universities—often sponsored by religious orders—have for over forty years educated tens of thousands in various masters programs in ministry. Finally, most pastors and some bishops have welcomed lay ministers.

Although ministry is the normal realization of the Spirit's gifts of the baptized, not infrequently it is not assisted by church leadership. Preparation for ecclesial ministry has become the task of the baptized themselves and of the schools generously educating them. Documents addressing lay ministry from the Vatican contain the old theology of a laity that must be passive lest it assume the activities of the real ministry of the priest.[20] John Paul II, in

1994, grudgingly allowed the biblical word "ministry" to be applied to the "lay faithful." Strangely, he says that ministry refers originally to the church's members continuing the "mission and ministry" of Christ, but its "full, univocal meaning" lies with ordained ministry.[21] Vatican documents offer not an ecclesiology of a ministering church but a pastiche of thoughts about the secular ministry of the baptized linked to a priestly ministry of devotions and Eucharistic sacrifice. They show a preference to move the baptized into the secular realm and to exalt the sacral status of the priest as set apart, hoping that spotlighting theatrical clothes and rituals will encourage vocations. What should be an enthusiastic and whole-hearted support for the staff of ministries in parishes and dioceses is a cool disinterest or even an active hostility, and the local church less and less contributes to the education of the baptized.

One reason for the lack of support is the fear that lay ecclesial ministry might further the absence of vocations to the celibate diocesan priesthood. Therefore, there is the commitment to maintain ecclesiastical and theological models that have room only for the celibate priesthood. However, if the model of a single, sharply drawn distinction between clergy and laity once gave a small set of officeholders all ministry and power, it has lost its public social reality and does not correspond to the reality of ministry in parishes, dioceses, and universities. That division between Christians came from the abstract order of Roman law and was sustained by the neo-scholastic description of the world as ordered abstract beings.[22] It cannot do justice to any sort of variety, either in charism or ministry.

Furthermore, related to this is the influence on the spirituality of the priest from the French school of spirituality, in the seventeenth century, which defined ministry largely as a metaphysical continuance of the Incarnation in a baroque theater, with few aspects of serving a church community. The theology of the priest serving solely as another Christ for a few minutes at the altar is inadequate.

In addition, the neo-Platonic model of descending hierarchy exercises ongoing influence. There is certainly authority in the church, but that authority is not arranged by divine authority into a hierarchy of higher and lower levels, where the baptized are passive, a model not conducive to dialogue and cooperative ministry. A hierarchical model not only holds back any power from lower levels but states that there can be no illumination, no teaching, from lower to higher groups. In this model the church is a pyramid with the inactive laity at the bottom. Yves Congar states of this ecclesiastical pyramid: "If authority is exercised well, then order will be assured. This order is unitary and ultimately hierocratic. The people are at the base of the pyramid."[23] Also coming from this neo-Platonic perspective is the view that the bishop shares particles of his ministry with others, in other words, that baptismal ministry does not come directly from the Spirit, but from a priest's needs for assistance in his ministry.[24]

A further model present today that has its limitations is that of the three *munera*, three offices for all the baptized that offer some framework for involvement in ministry or office. The theological terminology of the baptized as prophet, priest, and king is from Calvin, but was used in the twentieth century by Catholic theologians to offer some justification for baptismal ministry and then was employed at Vatican II. While priest, prophet, and king can inspire service and spirituality, each is a metaphor. A baptized person is not really a priest or a king. An approach through metaphors distracts from the reality of ministerial activity. Real ministers with specific activities and goals are vaguely described by words that leave baptism, charism, and ministry in the community in a cloud of metaphor.

The expansion of ministry is not only a new possibility; it is a clear necessity. But it is left unanalyzed and unsupported by many church policies. There is a lack of planning for which ministries parishes in the United States will need in the future. Too often, a diocese wonders about future pastors without referring to the need for deacons, youth ministers, or Rite of Catholic Initiation of Adults (RCIA) directors. The situation created by the continued decline of vocations to the diocesan priesthood, the retirement or death of a large number of active priests, and acceptance of candidates for the ministry of presbyter who are psychologically incapable of sustained work among normal adults is not discussed. The reality of laity and religious leading parishes, the high percentage of women among those interested in lay ministries, and the continuing interest among young adults in ministry are not pursued.

The parallel between involvement in ministry and the expansion of theological education was mentioned earlier. Today, as part of reaction against and restoration after Vatican II, there is a stance against lay ministry—and a paradox in theological education. Ministers and the baptized can receive a mature, professional, and open theological education drawing on the best sources and teachers. Seminarians, the priests of a diocese, and U.S. bishops, on the other hand, may experience a limitation in their theological education. They may read and hear only theologians who are shallow, introspective, neo-scholastic, even Protestant evangelical. The hierarchy's exposure to theology is limited to a small number of acceptable books and lectures by people who were not involved in Vatican II and who avoid post-conciliar developments in the church.

If we look ahead we see new ministries and new forms of basic ministries. For instance, there will be more Christians working in the area of abuse, in a spirituality and liturgy for the handicapped of all ages, in the ever-expanding campuses of higher education, and in health care. Ministries clearly on behalf of the church, but with new programs with and within social and political groups, will emerge, and they will require new forms of education in ministry. If the number of Catholics in North America and around the world is a factor, so too is their increasing level of education and interest in Christian life and in service. There will be more regionalization, as the differences between the Catholic Church in Boston and Minneapolis, Miami, and Seattle will unfold in a regional constellation of ministries for the dioceses and parishes. Corresponding to this will be a pastoral theology suited to this or that area in the United States, with greater sensitivity to the diverse cultures present throughout the country. At the same time, there will be a recognition of the vitality and diversity of churches in the many nations around the globe, and initiatives in the pastoral theology of ministry born in the United States will play an international role.[25]

The ministries of bishop, presbyter, and deacon are in the midst of further changes in their style of leadership, in the demands of being a theological educator, and in the options of the ordained being married or being a woman. Ministry is at a new beginning. Catholics have for over a millennium been forgetting ministry, living in a state of amnesia. Now the regimentation of the Pneuma does not accept attempts to control its presence.

CONCLUSION

In the renewed ministry of the baptized directed by the Spirit we have not a radical alteration but a rediscovery of the self-understanding of the churches after Pentecost. Paul's theology of charismatic ministries corresponds to the modern emphasis on persons and activities: Ministry comes from a personal experience of grace and from an existential hearing of the word and a deeper understanding of the sacraments.[26] The expansion of the ministry continues because the number of Catholics increases and because society and church life recognize the need for more services. In the local church, there needs to be more, not fewer, opportunities for young and middle-aged Catholics vivified by baptism to study and learn the gospel, so that they might serve the kingdom of God.

NOTES

1. Letter from Yves Congar to Thomas O'Meara (December 9, 1970).
2. Yves Congar wrote of the documents of Vatican II: "These ecclesiological values [hierarchy, authority, papacy] are not denied, not even forgotten, but they are not presented as the places of entry into the reality of the 'church' or as dominant values." ("Situation ecclésiologique au moment de 'Ecclesiam suam' et passage à une Église

dans l'itinéraire des hommes," in *Le Concile de Vatican II. Son Église. Peuple de Dieu et corps du Christ*, edited by R. Rémond [Paris: Beauchesne, 1984], 16).

3. Aidan Kavanaugh wrote of developments over centuries that "occluded" baptism, blocked baptism, as the moon can eclipse the sun. Religious life and the priesthood were "baptismal surrogates," ways of a first-class church life over against a proletariat that were controlled. *The Shape of Baptism. The Rite of Christian Initiation* (New York: Pueblo Publishing, 1978), 158f.

4. H. Denis, "La Théologie du presbyterat de Trente à Vatican II," in *Les Prêtres* (Paris: Cerf, 1968), 198–201.

5. See O'Meara, "The Ministry of Presbyters and the Many Ministries in the Church," in *The Theology of Priesthood*, edited by Donald Goergen and Ann Garrido (Collegeville, MN: Liturgical Press, 2000), 67–85; "The Ministry of the Priesthood and Its Relationship to the Wider Ministry in the Church," *Seminaries in Dialogue* 11 (1985): 1–8.

6. Mary E. Bendyna, "Foreword," in *Partners in Mission: A Profile of Associates and Religious in the United States* (Washington, DC: Georgetown University, CARA, 2000):i; Ellen Rose O'Connell, "Lay Associates: Called, Gifted and Formed for Associate-Religious Life," *Listening* 40 (2005): 59–65.

7. Winfried Haunerland, "The Heirs of the Clergy?: The New Pastoral Ministries and the Reform of the Minor Orders," *Worship* 75 (2001): 305–20.

8. Congar, "Situation ecclésiologique," 27; *Jean Puyo interroge le Pere Congar: une vie pour la vérité* (Paris: Le Centurion, 1975), 43. "All the work of the Council is a half-way station" (*Jean Puyo*, 149).

9. Aquinas, *Commentary on the* Ethics *of Aristotle*, 2:4.

10. Karl Rahner, *Das Amt in der Kirche* (Freiburg: Herder, 1966), 11; see Rahner, "On the Theology of Revolution," *Theological Investigations* 14 (New York: Seabury Press, 1976), 324–27.

11. Interestingly Thomas de Vio, Cardinal Cajetan could write in the early sixteenth century: "Each faithful believes he is a member of the church, and as a member of the church believes, hopes, administers the sacraments, receives, teaches, learns, etc. and does them on behalf of the church as a part of the whole to whom they [the activities] all belong" (*Commentaria Cardinalis Caietani* on Thomas Aquinas, *Summa theologiae* II-II, q. 39, a. 1; Sancti Thomas Aquinatis, *Opera Omnia* [Rome: Typographia Polyglotta, 1895], 307).

12. Peter Steiner, *St. Michael Berg am Laim* (Munich: Schnell & Steiner, 1983), 3.

13. Priest-workers was not a movement toward lay ministry but one of priests and sisters joining laity in their workplace; see Jacques Loew, *Mission to the Poorest* (New York: Sheed & Ward, 1950).

14. See O'Meara, "What Can We Learn from the Tridentine and Baroque Church?" in *The Catholic Church in the Twenty-First Century. Finding Hope for Its Future in the Wisdom of the Past*, edited by Michael Himes (Liguouri, MO: Liguouri Press, 2004), 56–64.

15. Dolores Leckey, "From Baptismal Font to Ministry. The Surprising Story of Laity Stirring the Church," in *Catholic Identity and the Laity*, edited by T. Muldoon (Maryknoll, NY: Orbis, 2009), 27–29.

16. "More and more women either are in the ministry (but unrecognized by the church) or want to enter ministry (with public recognition). If they are Christians professionally trained and involved in a full-time effort to serve the presence of the Spirit in the world, are they not ministers? . . . Recently they have begun to participate in the ministry of leadership in parishes. Why is ordination as public commission withheld? Why is ministry not officially diversified?" (O'Meara, "Clerical Culture and Feminine Ministry," *Commonweal* 98 [1973]: 524).

17. See O'Meara, "Ministry in the Catholic Church Today: The Gift of Some Historical Trajectories," in *Together in God's Service: Towards a Theology of Ecclesial Lay Ministry* (Washington, DC: USCCB, 1998), 70–83.

18. Karl Rahner, "The Role of the Layman in the Church," *Theological Investigations* 8 (New York: Herder and Herder, 1971), 57, 72.

19. Yves Congar, "My Path-Findings in the Theology of Laity and Ministries," *The Jurist* 32 (1972): 181.

20. Edward Schillebeeckx, criticizing John Paul II's *Christifideles laici*, writes: "The clergy become the apolitical men for the church; the laity are the less ecclesially committed politically involved 'men of the world.' In this view, the ontological status of the 'new humanity' reborn with the baptism of the Spirit was not recognized in his or her own individual worth but only from the standpoint of the clergy." *The Church with a Human Face* (New York: Crossroad, 1985), 157.

21. John Paul II in an address of 1994 quoted in "Some Questions Regarding Collaboration of Nonordained Faithful in Priests' Sacred Ministry," *Origins* 27 (November 27, 1997): 403. Two theological presuppositions influence what that document says. A theology of the laity stresses the secular character of lay vocation and activity, and the ministries of the baptized are placed in the context of the almost unique possession of sacred power by the ordained (see Richard Gaillardetz, "Shifting Meanings in the Lay-Clergy Distinction," *Irish Theological Quarterly* 64 [1999]: 115–39).

22. Yves Congar wrote: "In the scholastic period . . . the Latin tradition gives the theology of the Holy Spirit particularly a conceptual clarity—the mystery of the Holy Spirit increasingly becomes a conceptualized theological treatise—as it passes from considering the economy of salvation to presenting an ontology." "Pneumatologie ou 'christomonisme" dans la tradition latine?" *Ecclesia a Spiritu Sancto edocta* (Gembloux: J. Duculot, 1970), 62.

23. Yves Congar, *L'Église de Saint Augustin à l'époque moderne* (Paris: Cerf, 1970), 427.

24. "Charism does not owe its ecclesial character to hierarchical blessing." Karl Rahner, *Theology of Pastoral Action* (New York: Herder and Herder, 1968), 60.

25. An example of this is Andreas Henkelmann, ed., *"All Are Welcome!" Gelebte Gemeinde im Erzbistum Chicago* (Munster: Aschendorff, 2009).

26. See Rémi Parent, *A Church of the Baptized: Overcoming Tension between the Clergy and the Laity* (Mahwah, NJ: Paulist Press, 1989), 49–53.

5

Theology of Lay Ecclesial Ministry: Future Trajectories

Edward P. Hahnenberg

.

What is the future for the theology of lay ecclesial ministry? How will we understand this phenomenon in ten or twenty or one hundred twenty years? Where will faithful reflection on this ministerial reality lead?

These are impossible questions to answer. But they are questions well worth asking. They are worth asking because, by inviting us to look into the future, they challenge us to pay attention to the present. By asking us to imagine tomorrow, they call us to investigate today—to examine what is already going on, to note what is significant or particularly problematic, and to suggest what will last or what needs to begin. Where are we? Who are we? And what are we about as the church and as ministers of the church? Thus this chapter does not pretend to predict the future. Instead it tries to learn from the present. It does not so much look ahead as it looks around: What is the present *experience* of lay ecclesial ministers? And what might this suggest about future trajectories for theological reflection?

This chapter takes the lived experience of lay ecclesial ministry as the starting point for identifying theological questions in need of further exploration. I begin with a brief reflection on the importance of attending to ministerial reality. Then I survey the rise of lay ecclesial ministry as a new form of ministry in the church so that, finally, I might suggest three aspects of the lay ecclesial minister's experience and identity that call for future theological reflection.

ATTENDING TO REALITY

We often get caught up in our ideas and, in the process, miss what is going on around us. This is a particular danger for theologians, whose training takes us into the world of books and beliefs, dogmas and definitions. Ecclesiology (the study of the nature and mission of the church) is all about ideas. But these ideas are ultimately rooted in reality—the church itself. And this church is a concrete community, a historical reality, a human institution. Theologians and ordinary believers alike draw on categories from the Bible and the tradition to help interpret what is going on in the actual life of the community. When certain categories "catch on," when certain ecclesiological models become broadly accepted, it is because they account not only for doctrinal claims, but also for human experience. They are successful because they offer an accessible way to address important issues facing real people.[1]

Therefore, we can say that theology follows reality—a recognition that calls us to pay attention to the concrete realities of Christian experience and church life. This is particularly true when we start to theologize about ministry. On this point, the Jesuit historian John O'Malley makes an important observation. O'Malley points out that when Catholics write about the history of priesthood or ministry, they tend to focus on the evolution of *ideas* about priesthood or ministry, but not on what is actually *happening*. He sees this tendency in the amount of attention given to official church documents and the lack of attention given to other sources, such as letters, diaries, and reports from the field.[2] The result is an incomplete picture. To take just one example, in the sixteenth and seventeenth centuries, Catholic ministry underwent one of its most innovative and exciting transformations in history. But reading the official decrees of the Council of Trent, you would never know it. During this period, the mendicant orders saw tremendous growth in both size and influence; and new apostolic orders, like the Jesuits, burst onto the scene, experimenting with everything from directing retreats, spiritual counseling, and social ministries to using schools, artists, and the press as instruments of ministry. The catechetical and missionary outreach were intense, immense, and unprecedented—a thrust seen nowhere more dramatically than in the massive efforts directed toward evangelizing the newly "discovered" worlds of the Americas and Asia. But, as O'Malley ironically observes, just as this global missionary movement was at its peak in the mid-sixteenth century, the bishops gathered at Trent bypassed it "without a word."[3]

This observation does not deny the tremendous achievement of Trent in confirming doctrine and initiating real reform within the church. But it suggests the limitations of relying too heavily on official documents to describe the ministerial reality of an era. To bring the point closer to home, it would be like a scholar a hundred years from now turning to Vatican II's statements about the laity as the only source for information about the reality of ministry in our own era. These passages from the Constitution on the Church or the Decree on the Lay Apostolate would give a glimpse into the various lay movements and theologies leading up to the council. But they would give little indication of the scope and the scale of the ministerial transformation about to occur. The council's few passing references to professional forms of lay ministry (what we are now calling lay ecclesial ministry) might easily be overlooked; and one might miss the way in which the broader ecclesiological vision of the council—the church as the People of God; the dignity of the baptized; the universal call to holiness; the participation of all the Christian faithful in the priestly, prophetic, and kingly work of Christ—served to inspire genuinely new forms of ministry within and on behalf of the church.

Fortunately, in recent years Catholic theologians have turned their attention more explicitly and intentionally to what happens "on the ground"—not only in ecclesiology, but in all areas of theology. Our incarnational and sacramental sensibility recommends such a turn. And the twentieth-century recovery of experience as a source for theology equips us to carry it out. Indeed, even with their historical blind spots, the most important theologies of ministry to appear over the past twenty or thirty years all emerged as a response to the concrete reality of ministerial transformation that came in the wake of the council. These theologies were not dreamt up or imposed from above. They were instead attempts to reflect on what was happening in the life of the church. In many ways, the U.S. Conference of Catholic Bishops' document *Co-Workers in the Vineyard of the Lord* falls within this broader trajectory of theological response to pastoral reality. For even though *Co-Workers* is an official document full of ideas about ministry, it is at root a response to reality—the emergence and expansion of a new form of ministry.

A NEW MINISTERIAL REALITY

The opening section of *Co-Workers in the Vineyard of the Lord* is titled "Describing and Responding to New Realities." The new reality that is the focus of the document is what the bishops have come to call lay ecclesial ministry. The roots of this reality can be traced back forty years to a new position that started to appear in Catholic parishes: the "coordinator" or director of religious education (DRE). The many lay ecclesial ministers now working in the United States are the pastoral legacy of those first few parish volunteers and women religious who, in the mid-1960s, were hired by their pastors to bring some order to parish Confraternity of Christian Doctrine (CCD) programs.[4] As religious education programs grew, parishes themselves were changing. Liturgical reforms needed explanation and implementation; adult parishioners sought out opportunities for faith sharing, study, and direct service; newly emerging questions about civil rights, war, and poverty were recognized as concerns that parishes needed to address. The DRE soon served as a model for other roles on the parish staff. General assistants, called pastoral ministers or pastoral associates, appeared, as did youth ministers, liturgical coordinators, and directors of social concerns. The work of organists and other liturgical musicians was recognized as ministry. At the same time, colleges and universities began to offer graduate courses and programs in theology for laypeople. Laymen and laywomen filled summer sessions and received degrees in religious education and theology. National organizations for lay ministers emerged and expanded, promoting professionalization, competency standards, and networking beyond the parish.

When the U.S. Conference of Catholic Bishops began to study parish lay ministries, they found a fairly well-defined group of professionally prepared and committed ministers. The first time this new group of ministers was recognized in a document of the U.S. bishops, they were described simply as "lay persons who have prepared for professional ministry in the church."[5] The studies of parish lay ministers conducted by the National Pastoral Life Center in 1992 and 1999 put numbers to the experiences of many Catholic parishioners, drawing attention to the large and growing corps of laypeople working on parish staffs. The latest study, published in 2005, indicates that over thirty-thousand lay ecclesial ministers are currently serving in Catholic parishes across the United States.[6]

What this brief history reminds us of is the fact that *Co-Workers in the Vineyard of the Lord* came as a *response* to a reality already there. The rise of lay ecclesial ministry in this country has been very much a grassroots movement—the work of the Spirit lifting up new ministries and new ministers in the community. There was no Vatican directive mandating these ministries, no national pastoral plan encouraging them. Instead, as Zeni Fox put it, the rise of lay ecclesial ministry was a lot like Topsy; it "just grew."[7] And as it grew, lay ecclesial ministry took a shape never quite seen before, never quite on this scale. In other words, what has come into existence are not just new positions in ministry, but new ways of ministering, new ways of being a minister, new configurations of the church's ministerial structures, and new arrangements of its pastoral life. *Co-Workers* affirms unequivocally that it is in continuity with the church's theological tradition and doctrinal history. But that is only half the story. For, while the theology in this document is not an innovation, the very reality that this theology attempts to explain is itself genuinely new.

To their credit, the bishops acknowledge as much, pointing to the real shift that has taken place. They write: "Lay ecclesial ministry has emerged and taken shape in our country through the working of the Holy Spirit. In response to these new opportunities and situations, lay men and women have responded generously to renewed awareness of the implications of their Baptism and to the needs of their Church communities."[8]

What, then, is the appropriate context for comprehending this new ministerial reality? What exactly has been going on? I believe that we are living in one of the most significant periods of ministerial transformation in the history of the church.[9] I make this claim well aware of the fact that we always tend to overstate the importance of our own era. We human beings always see the present moment as the pivotal moment. Still, when we look around at what has been going on in the Catholic Church over the past forty years, it is hard to escape this conclusion. The emergence of lay ecclesial ministry since the council stands out as one of the top four or five ministerial shifts of the past two thousand years. It ought to be compared to the changes in the church brought on by the rise of communal forms of monasticism in the fifth century, the birth of mendicant orders in the thirteenth century, the creative constitution of apostolic orders in the fifteenth century, or the explosion of women's religious communities in the seventeenth century.

This comparison is not meant to suggest that lay ecclesial ministry is a new type of religious order. But it is a new way of ministering—just as those new forms of religious life were in their day. We often fail to recognize the innovation that has always come with the founding of new religious orders. We fail to see it because we tend to read the history of religious life through the lens of the evangelical counsels (the vows of poverty, chastity, and obedience). When we do so, we tend to emphasize the continuity across time and across different religious communities. Under the lens of the vows, all religious communities seem simply to be variations on the monastic life; they are all basically alike. However, when we look at religious life not through the lens of the evangelical councils, but through the lens of ministry, then we see not so much continuity as we see change. In other words, when we look at the kinds of active service that these communities actually provided, then what we start to recognize is the diversity, the freshness, and the originality that each major wave of religious life has brought.[10]

With this originality, with the novelty in ministry that new orders embodied, the church again and again faced a challenge. Each new form or new family of religious life brought a challenge to the ministerial order of the time. More often than not, these new forms did not fit. And whether it was the mendicant friars of the Middle Ages or the active sisters of the early modern period, it took time for the institutional church to adjust. But for all the slowness and setbacks involved in incorporating these orders into the ministerial life of the church, the new ministries enriched the life of the church of their era and so advanced the mission of Christ. They stretched our church in a positive way.

Lay ecclesial ministry is stretching our church again. In significant ways, the reality of lay ecclesial ministry does not fit into the boxes we have traditionally used to order our ministries. True, this is not the first time in history that laypeople have been actively involved in church ministry. Nor are lay ecclesial ministers the total sum of lay ministry today. Alongside the thirty thousand lay ecclesial ministers employed in parishes are many more thousands of U.S. Catholics who serve in important ways through volunteer or occasional services and ministries. Particularly within poorer parishes or among minority communities, these part-time volunteers are indispensable to the church's life. (And this is not even to consider the many millions of Catholics who advance the reign of God not through direct church ministry but through lives of active discipleship.) Still, what our brief overview highlights is the fact that, over the past forty years, many laywomen and laymen have chosen to make a significant life commitment to ministry in the church. They seek out education, join parish staffs, collaborate closely with the pastor, and often work full time coordinating an area of ministry on behalf of the community. The generic title "lay ecclesial ministry" has come to highlight the distinctive dimensions of these individuals' service. Together, these characteristics describe a ministerial form that has never existed in quite this way and on quite this scale. And our theology is still struggling to make sense of this reality.

So while "the experience" of lay ecclesial ministers cannot be captured in any one essay—for it is as diverse as the number of different roles filled by these ministers; indeed, it is as diverse as the number of individual ministers who fill these roles—still, lay ecclesial ministers share a certain ministerial identity within the church. In attending to "the experience" of lay ecclesial ministers, there are all kinds of particular experiences that deserve further study. Since I am interested in lay ecclesial ministry as an ecclesiological reality, and since I want to comment on avenues for future theological development, let me discuss in turn how lay ecclesial ministers experience their relationship to God, their ministerial context, and the church as an institution. These are the realities of call, community, and recognition.

THE REALITY OF CALL

The first aspect of the lay ecclesial minister's experience that invites further theological exploration is the experience of being called by God to this way of ministering. In preparing *Co-Workers in the Vineyard of the Lord*, the bishops' Subcommittee on Lay Ministry held a number of consultations with different groups around the country, meeting with diocesan leaders, theologians, directors of ministry formation programs, canonists, human resource professionals, and—most importantly—lay ecclesial ministers themselves. Early on in this process, in the course of one of these consultations, several lay ministers rather spontaneously shared their experiences of being called by God. They spoke of their vocation to this ministry. The bishops present were clearly moved by this personal testimony, and they spent some time afterward discussing whether lay ecclesial ministry represented a new vocation in the church. It seems that a new awareness was sinking in. Perhaps the bishops present were used to this kind of witness at clergy retreats or in communities of religious women, but had not heard it articulated so clearly among laypeople engaged in ministry.

Here was a powerful example of lived experience coming up against traditional categories. After all, lay ecclesial ministry does not seem to fit neatly within the traditional definition of vocation. It is not a state of life. It does not entail the same degree of permanence or totality of life that has been associated historically with clerical or religious vocations. And yet lay ecclesial ministers do make a significant commitment to ministry, and they enact that commitment in concrete ways (by pursuing education on their own and at their own expense, by moving a family to take a new position, by planning programs or projects that extend into the future, and so on). The latest study reports that nearly three-fourths (73.1 percent) of lay parish ministers believe that they are pursuing a lifetime of service in the church.[11] Clearly, their response to God's call is a life-orienting decision, one that profoundly impacts their faith, their families, and their future. Moreover, their own personal sense of call is consistent and strong. Those few lay ecclesial ministers who shared their experiences with the subcommittee are not the exception, but the norm. Talk to any lay formation director in charge of the lay ministry programs run out of dioceses or universities around the country, and you will hear what they hear: The language of vocation and call comes naturally for candidates entering these programs. It is how they articulate what they are doing and why they are interested in ministry. DeLambo's study reports that more than half (54.2 percent) of lay ecclesial ministers say that the factor that most influenced them to pursue a lifetime of ministry in the church is a "call" from God. Seven in ten (69.3 percent) list "response to God's call" among the top three reasons for doing what they do. "So dominant was the response to God's call as a motivating factor that the next highest factor cited by laypersons totaled only 15.0 percent."[12]

The bishops acknowledged the reality of this experience. In an initial report of the subcommittee, published in 1999, they wrote: "Lay ministers speak often and reverently of their call or vocation to ministry, a call that finds its origin in the call of God and its confirmation in the appointment to a specific ministry within the Church. . . . We conclude that this call or vocation is worthy of respect and sustained attention."[13] Over the course of drafting *Co-Workers*, those involved continued to struggle with this question of vocation. The final document ends with a frank admission: "The preparation of *Co-Workers in the Vineyard of the Lord* has already indicated a need for a more thorough study of our theology of vocation."[14] Here the experience is stretching the categories; the reality is stretching the theology.

These observations suggest that the category of vocation represents an important trajectory for future theological development. One of the things that the experience of lay ecclesial ministers has done is wake us up to the fact that, for half a century now, our theology of vocation has been caught in a coma. Vatican II's unambiguous affirmation of the universal call to holiness challenged the widespread assumption among Catholics that God's call belonged only to a select few. The recognition that *everyone* has a vocation loosened up the category. It freed vocation from a narrow identification with priesthood and religious life and made it possible for lay ministers to appropriate this language in coming to understand and describe their own experience. Still, despite this broadening, many of the older theological assumptions have remained in place. We are left today with two distinct views of vocation: a broad vision of God's call that is practically equivalent to discipleship and a narrow vision that identifies God's call with a state of life. Lay ecclesial ministers are caught in the middle. Their deep sense of call to direct ministry on behalf of the church seems to be something more than the universal call to holiness (even as this ministry—like all ministries—remains always grounded in the baptismal vocation). But lay ecclesial ministry is not a state of life. Their experience "in the middle" is a dilemma for traditional understandings of vocation, but it might also suggest a way forward for future exploration.

To advance the theological discussion, we might begin by rethinking the strong identification between vocation and state of life. This association lies behind any number of bishops' letters, Sunday homilies, popular articles, or high school textbooks that divide vocation into priesthood, religious life, and marriage (with a few awkwardly adding the vocation to single life). Such presentations speak a certain truth about roles in the church and paths people follow, but the static language of "states" comes more out of medieval society than Christian theology. It is foreign to our developmental sense of human life and commitment. Such an observation is not meant to dismiss the importance of permanent commitments or imply that lifelong promises are impossible in today's day and age. Indeed, in a world marked by such profound flux and fragmentation, we ought to be suspicious of any too-easy appeal to process and revision. But that caution is not an excuse to constrain vocation. If anything, it is an invitation to a more rigorous analysis of commitment itself—a category too often overlooked in contemporary theology. Indeed, better attention to commitment may free us for a more honest recognition of the dynamic nature of vocation. As scripture testifies, God's call is often a call *from* and a call *toward*. It involves conversion and change. God wants to move us—but not in the sense of asking us to drop one commitment for another, and then another, and then another, but rather by challenging us to grow and change *in and through* our commitments. We all know that the promise to love that a couple makes on the day of their wedding changes radically as that couple moves together through their married life—the early years of independence, the birth and growth of children, the onset of illness, old age, and the inevitability of death. Commitment and change exist in a dialectical, mutually informing relationship. These are dynamic realities, just like vocation.

The experience of lay ecclesial ministers breaks open an older identification between significant, public ministry and a state of life. Lay ecclesial ministry represents a call to a new way of *doing ministry*, but it also represents a new way of *being a minister*. For here we have a serious, long-term, full-time commitment to a position of ministerial leadership outside of the clerical state and distinct from religious life. But it will not do to imagine lay ecclesial ministry as a new vocation alongside (or overlaid on top of) priesthood, religious life, and married life—if our primary association is that of a state of life. And our theological response will founder if it expects a static status or the kind of permanent commitment from the individual that marks these other venerable vocations. Lay ecclesial ministry is not a state of life, but a living commitment. As a way of embodying a life of Christian service, lay ecclesial ministry has shown a remarkable freedom and fluidity. This reality calls for a theology of vocation articulated in more dynamic, developmental, and relational terms.

THE REALITY OF COMMUNITY

Lay ecclesial ministers experience their call in the context of a changing church. In *Co-Workers in the Vineyard*, the bishops note the variety of settings within which nonordained Catholics take on professional ministerial roles. They serve as chaplains in hospitals and nursing homes; they minister in prisons and seaports; they work in high schools, diocesan offices, and college campuses. Despite this rich diversity of place, however, lay ecclesial ministry has always been primarily a parish phenomenon. The parish is the place where this ministry was born, and for the vast majority of lay ecclesial ministers today, it remains the basic ecclesial context for their service. Thus, to attend to the reality of lay ecclesial ministry is to pay attention to the parish.

Much could be said about the shifting shape of the Catholic parish. I want to focus on one aspect: size. As a whole, the Catholic Church in the United States has seen relatively steady growth in population over the past century. From 1900 to 1950, the number of Catholics increased from just over ten million to just under thirty million. From 1950 to today, the population more than doubled in size again, bringing us to a current total of approximately sixty-five million Catholics. What is interesting is what happened to the parish during this time. In the first half of the twentieth century, new parishes were erected at a rate that kept up with the overall growth in population. Thus the average number of Catholics per parish in 1950 (1,843) was roughly the same as the average number of Catholics per parish in 1900 (1,759).[15] However, in the second half of the century, parish construction did not keep pace with Catholic growth. And since 1995, the total number of parishes has been declining each year, as dioceses close or consolidate parishes in response to changing demographics, financial concerns, and the clergy shortage. The result is that parishes today are significantly larger, on average, than at any other time in the past. The number of Catholics per parish in 2009 (3,567) is almost double what it was in 1950.

It is no news flash that parishes look a lot different today than they did fifty years ago. In their wonderful pastoral letter, "As I Have Done for You," Cardinal Roger Mahony and the priests of the archdiocese of Los Angeles begin by describing a paradigmatic parish, Saint Leo's, and comparing how it looked in 1955 with how it looks in 2005.[16] With the parish having grown from 1,500 to 5,000 families, the letter paints a picture of the creative ways the community has responded to the new scale and scope of parish life. As parishes have become larger and more complex, new programs, ministries, and structures have taken shape. Indeed, the expansion of lay ecclesial ministry itself is directly related to this growth and diversification of parish life. Still, for all the creative ways we have been living into a new ecclesial reality, I am not sure that we have fully thought through theologically the implications of this shift in our experience of community—particularly what this shift means within the context of larger cultural currents reshaping the lives and habits of U.S. Catholics.

Our parish communities exist within an increasingly consumption-driven, digitally mediated culture. Something as harmless, ubiquitous, and, for many of us, strangely mysterious as Facebook signals a profound shift in human interaction already under way. Facebook, smart phones, and the almost infinite number of online social networking tools have increased our ability to connect with one another in amazing ways. When, after all, has it ever been so easy to interact so quickly with so many people in so many places? But this interconnectivity has implications that bear directly on community life. Blogs, online discussion groups, Twitter, news and opinion sites—these become for many people virtual communities. They are a significant form of association, serving a purpose once served by clubs, civic organizations, neighborhoods, and, yes, churches. Since the introduction of television pulled us out of public spaces and into our living rooms, much has been written about the social implications of communication technology.[17] While it is important to acknowledge that this trend is not simply a story of decline and deterioration, it still has had a profound impact on how we relate to one another and to the larger communities of which we are a part. And I do not think we as a church have spent enough time thinking about it.

One dynamic in particular that deserves attention from Catholic theologians is what Vincent Miller calls "deterritorialization."[18] There is a way in which modern means of travel and communication have loosened our connections to geographic territory and to the people who share the physical space we inhabit. People are no longer bound to their surroundings the way people were bound in the past. With the Internet, we are connecting to more and more people (a gain), but not necessarily connecting to people around us (a loss). Our immediate environment is no longer the only (or even the first) place we look to establish relationships. Just a few years ago when I first started teaching, I remember walking into classrooms that were buzzing with student chit-chat and conversation. Now, my more common experience is to step into a classroom that is silent—full of students waiting for class to start, all looking down and tapping away on their phones. When we lose the habit of interacting with those immediately around us, we also lose the ability to deal with friction, to deal with disagreement, or simply to deal with people who are different. It is true that physical location promotes its own form of homogenization, and that the Internet opens up a world of diversity that no neighborhood could ever match. But I wonder if most of us turn to the web to engage truly different perspectives, to meet people who might genuinely challenge us, or simply to find like-minded friends and opinions that confirm our own point of view. When Facebook replaces face-to-face encounter, a theology of incarnation calls for critique. The body of Christ demands more than a virtual community. Miller concludes that here the old notion of the territorial parish becomes surprisingly relevant.[19] While parishes are always in danger of becoming parochial, they still hold the potential to be a form of association that is rooted in a specific place and that draws people into face-to-face, ongoing relationship with one another—an alternative to the disembodied, anonymous echo chamber of the web. Here is the promise of an experience of community that is local, embodied, and truly relational.

And so the closing, consolidation, and increasing size of our parishes comes at just the wrong time. Precisely at the moment when we need to be cultivating concrete communities that operate on a human scale, our parishes are growing larger and more impersonal. I recently came across a diocesan reorganization plan that recommended—largely in response to the clergy shortage—the consolidation of four rural parishes within a twenty-mile radius. The plan was to shutter the four churches and build a new and larger facility, one that would be able to accommodate the combined communities for Sunday liturgy. When we step back from this particular decision (a decision being made by dioceses all across the country), we see where a lack of significant theological reflection on changing community leads. In contemporary church debates, access to the Eucharist is frequently pitted against mandatory celibacy for priests—with progressives often accusing the hierarchy of sacrificing Eucharist on the altar of celibacy. But there is a third element that is too often overlooked in this debate, namely, the community. Plans such as the one above suggest that, while bishops may have given up on any discussion of celibacy, they have not given up on the Eucharist. In fact, they are going to great logistical lengths to provide regular access for as many Catholics as possible. But while they seem intent on saving Eucharist, they appear willing to sacrifice community. Consolidating four small parishes may make sense from a managerial perspective: Demographics are not insignificant and financial concerns are real concerns. But each of these communities has its own history and traditions, each embodies in the present a distinctive way of being church, each continues to pass on the practices of the faith and a lived sense of discipleship to the next generation. They are true communities, the local embodiment of the church of Christ. No one needs to make a case for mourning the closing of a parish. But perhaps greater attention to the larger cultural trend toward weaker and weaker local communities might inspire us to make a stronger case for dedicating as much time and energy to sustaining local parish communities as is being dedicated to ensuring access to the Eucharist.

If the reality of call invites us to further theological reflection on the *minister*, the reality of community invites us to further theological reflection on the *ministry* that lay ecclesial ministers offer. As noted, lay ecclesial ministers serve in a variety of parish positions and ministerial roles. But all of these are *ministry*, that is, all serve in some way to build up the body of Christ for the mission of the church. Given the cultural pressures currently pulling at community, the building up of this body is going to involve a lot of joint work. In other words, ministry today must help strengthen those sinews that hold together the members of Christ's body. Lay ecclesial ministers are called to make connections: finding ways to foster community within large parishes and across ethnic and ideological groups, linking up families, creating space for conversation and debate, developing habits of service and advocacy that draw parishioners beyond the parish into the concrete context of the world where discipleship is really lived. We need a theology of community organizing, a theology of the charism of coordination. By virtue of their leadership roles, lay ecclesial ministers are not just ministers in relationship with others, they are ministers with a special responsibility for fostering ministerial relationships among others. Lay ecclesial ministers are called to get the various members of Christ's body working together so that this community might better serve its mission of fostering the life of discipleship and transforming the world in the light of the gospel. In order to serve this purpose, the future theology of lay ecclesial ministry has to take more seriously how the communion and mission that these ministers serve is embedded and embodied in our current, constantly evolving cultural context.

THE REALITY OF RECOGNITION

A third reality that invites continued theological reflection is that of ministerial recognition. From the perspective of the *minister*, recognition entails acknowledgment, affirmation, and support for the individual in her or his work for the church. From the perspective of the *ministry*, recognition involves the identification, promotion, and structuring—the "ordering"—of these new ministerial roles by the church institution. Recognition on both levels is crucial and is already a part of the current reality (although I can imagine many lay ecclesial ministers would argue that it is not recognition, but the *lack of* recognition that calls for theological investigation). Still, a number of questions remain. In the paragraphs that follow, I will focus on the questions raised by the second perspective: How is lay ecclesial ministry, as a new form of ministry, being incorporated into the formal ministerial structures of the church? And what theological work needs to be done to better understand the ordering and authorization of various ministries today?

Historically, the church has recognized important ministries by incorporating them into the sacrament of holy orders, religious communities, or ecclesiastical offices. Typically, lay ecclesial ministers in the United States are formally incorporated into ministry by being hired. *Co-Workers in the Vineyard* is careful not to define lay ecclesial ministry in terms of employment, and a number of unpaid ministers fit the description laid out in this document—in the bishops' eyes, these volunteers are no less lay ecclesial ministers. Still, for the vast majority of lay ecclesial ministers, the fact of their employment constitutes one of the most significant dimensions of their recognition and authorization by church. In most cases it is the pastor who hires the lay ecclesial minister, sometimes with the help of a parish hiring committee. In the case of chaplains, campus ministers, and other lay ecclesial ministries outside the parish, the specific institution is responsible for hiring. This practice has had the advantage of allowing for a diversity of roles and ministries, each of which responds to the particularities of a local community. However, its disadvantage has been a tendency to reduce the relationship between the official church and the lay ecclesial minister to an employment contract.[20] Occasionally the hiring of a new parish minister is ritualized through a blessing or commissioning, but this still remains the exception rather than the norm.

One of the more difficult implications of this history of parish-based hiring is the ambiguity it has fostered about the relationship of the lay ecclesial minister to the larger church beyond the parish. A concrete example may help illustrate this ambiguity. Over the past thirty years, alongside lay ecclesial ministry has arisen another new form—or newly recovered form—of ministry: the permanent diaconate. Both represent a diversification of church ministry since Vatican II, both have taken a variety of forms, both have been implemented and experienced in different ways in different dioceses around the country. Still there is a notable difference between the way in which the church authorizes deacons and lay ecclesial ministers—in some cases dramatically demonstrating the asymmetry between the reality of ministry and the recognition it receives. Deacons pursue a clearly outlined formation program according to standards set forth by the Vatican and the U.S. Conference of Catholic Bishops. They are incorporated into the ministerial structures of the diocese through sacramental ordination and are guaranteed an official role in the local church—even though their participation in ministry is, in many cases, limited to part-time or occasional assistance. In contrast, lay ecclesial ministers follow any number of pathways into ministry—from volunteering to graduate degree programs. Many devote their lives to full-time ministry, yet they are not ordained and enjoy little in the way of formal job security. The permanent deacon working for a law firm and preaching once every other month at Sunday liturgies began his ministry with sacramental ordination celebrated at the diocesan cathedral, while the full-time lay liturgical coordinator who organizes four services every Sunday and countless parish programs began her ministry with a brief commissioning prayer after the homily at her parish church.

A first phase in the post-conciliar rise of lay ministry occurred during the 1970s and 1980s, a time marked by broad and enthusiastic promotion of new ministries at all levels. A second phase, beginning in the 1990s and continuing into the present, acknowledges the expansion of ministries and reflects more critically on its structural and ecclesial implications. The questions now being asked concern how better to integrate professional lay ministries into the ministerial structures of the church, into the church's *ministerium*.[21] Individual bishops have begun to take concrete steps to formalize their relationship to these new ministers. Many dioceses have developed their own certification standards, procedures for hiring, and guidelines for different lay ministry positions.[22] Grievance procedures for parish ministers are beginning to be instituted. Some dioceses are actively working to recruit and screen potential applicants for positions in parish religious education, liturgy, and social outreach. Sample contracts and diocesan employment policies have been published. Gatherings of diocesan clergy are beginning to include not only permanent deacons but also lay ministers working in parishes. These developments are not simply a professionalization or standardization of employment policies. They are, consciously or not, initial movements toward ordering the ministerial relationships of the community.

   Co-Workers in the Vineyard of the Lord calls for the bishop to take a greater role in integrating lay ecclesial ministry into the total ministerial life of the diocese. Thus it is a moment within this second phase of post-conciliar development. This attention to the broader ecclesial context is, I believe, a positive contribution. But it calls for ongoing theological reflection. In particular, we need to bring our theology of lay ecclesial ministry into dialogue with recent theological developments in our understanding of the local church (the diocese) and the bishop. Two comments need to be made. First, this shift in theological attention from parish to diocese need not contribute to the drift away from the concrete, local, face-to-face level of community discussed in the previous section. Alongside our stress on the parish, we have to recognize at the same time that, for all its importance, the parish has never been for Roman Catholicism the fundamental ecclesiological category. In Catholic tradition, the fundamental unit of church is the local church, the diocese with the bishop at its center. But our theology of the local church can move in one of two directions. It can see the diocese as *replacing* local forms of community or as *serving* them.[23] Obviously, given our concerns about current cultural trends, it is the latter approach that is necessary: How can the diocese incorporate lay ecclesial ministries into larger church structures precisely in order to serve the diverse ways in which the Spirit is at work in these ministers at the local level? A second comment concerns the role of the bishop. To call for a more active role for the bishop in directing new forms of ministry demands an adequate theology of the episcopacy. Such a theology will be one that recognizes the bishop as a catalyst and coordinator of many ministers, rather than the sole creator and judge of all ministerial initiatives.[24] In these concerns about the local church and the bishop, we begin to situate the practical issues surrounding the recognition and authorization of lay ecclesial ministers within a larger, properly theological context.

CONCLUSION

Together, the three realities of call, community, and recognition help to constitute the place of the lay ecclesial minister within the church today. They are at root relational categories, categories that name the relationship of the minister to God, to the ministry that is needed at this present cultural moment, and to the larger church community of which we are all a part. By speaking of God as a loving communion of persons, by calling the church a communion on a mission, by exploring lay ecclesial ministry in relation to the various other ministries serving our church, *Co-Workers in the Vineyard of the Lord* offers the framework for a thoroughly relational approach to ministry—naming the reality today and laying out a challenging theological agenda for the future.

NOTES

1. For a fuller treatment, see Edward P. Hahnenberg, "The Mystical Body of Christ and Communion Ecclesiology: Historical Parallels," *Irish Theological Quarterly* 70 (2005): 3–30.

2. John W. O'Malley, "Priesthood, Ministry, and Religious Life: Some Historical and Historiographical Considerations," *Theological Studies* 49 (1988): 223–57, at 225–26.

3. John W. O'Malley, "One Priesthood: Two Traditions," in *A Concert of Charisms: Ordained Ministry in Religious Life*, edited by Paul K. Hennessy (New York: Paulist, 1997), 9–24, at 17.

4. See Maria Harris, "DREs in the U.S.: The First Twenty Years," *The Living Light* 17 (1980): 250–59; Debra Campbell, "The Struggle to Serve: From the Lay Apostolate to the Ministry Explosion," in *Transforming Parish Ministry: The Changing Roles of Catholic Clergy, Laity, and Women Religious*, edited by Jay P. Dolan et al. (New York: Crossroad, 1989), 253–78; Maria Harris, *The D.R.E. Book* (New York: Paulist Press, 1976); and the important early book by Joseph C. Neiman, *Co-ordinators: A New Focus in Parish Religious Education* (Winona, MN: St. Mary's College Press, 1971).

5. National Conference of Catholic Bishops, "Called and Gifted: The American Catholic Laity," *Origins* 10 (November 27, 1980): 372.

6. David DeLambo, *Lay Parish Ministers: A Study of Emerging Leadership* (New York: National Pastoral Life Center, 2005), 19.

7. Zeni Fox, *New Ecclesial Ministry: Lay Professionals Serving the Church*, rev. ed. (Chicago: Sheed & Ward, 2002), 4

8. U.S. Conference of Catholic Bishops, *Co-Workers in the Vineyard of the Lord: A Resource for Guiding the Development of Lay Ecclesial Ministry* (Washington, DC: USCCB, 2005), 14.

9. Edward P. Hahnenberg, "The Vocation to Lay Ecclesial Ministry," *Origins* 37 (August 30, 2007): 177–82.

10. O'Malley, "Priesthood, Ministry and Religious Life," 223–57.

11. DeLambo, *Lay Parish Ministers*, 71.

12. DeLambo, *Lay Parish Ministers*, 72.

13. U.S. Conference of Catholic Bishops Subcommittee on Lay Ministry, *Lay Ecclesial Ministry: The State of the Questions* (Washington, DC: USCCB, 1999), 27.

14. USCCB, *Co-Workers in the Vineyard*, 67.

15. Mary Gautier, "Parishes Past, Present and Future: Demographic Realities," in *Multiple Parish Pastoring in the Catholic Church in the United States*, Symposium Report (February 7–9, 2006), 18, available at http://www.emergingmodels.org/article.cfm?id=20 (accessed March 9, 2010).

16. Cardinal Roger Mahony and the Priests of the Archdiocese of Los Angeles, "As I Have Done for You: A Pastoral Letter on Ministry," available at http://www.archdiocese.la/archbishop/letters/ministry/ (accessed March 9, 2010).

17. See, for example, Robert D. Putnam, *Bowling Alone: The Collapse and Revival of American Community* (New York: Simon and Schuster, 2000).

18. Vincent J. Miller, "Where Is the Church? Globalization and Catholicity," *Theological Studies* 69 (2008): 412–32, at 417.

19. Miller, "Where Is the Church?" 429. See Miller, "Body of Christ or Religious Boutique? The Struggles of Being a Parish in a Consumer Culture," *Church* (Summer 2007): 15–19.

20. DeLambo observes that almost six in ten (56.8 percent) lay ministers report working under an employment contract—surprisingly higher than the private sector. DeLambo, *Lay Parish Ministers*, 101.

21. See Matthew Clark, "The Relationship of the Bishop and Lay Ecclesial Minister," *Origins* 30 (April 5, 2001): 678.

22. Noting the gap that still exists between what dioceses are doing and what lay ecclesial ministers expect, DeLambo suggests that a larger role for the diocese in recruiting, screening, training, certifying, and commissioning lay ecclesial ministers would not be unwelcome by these ministers. DeLambo, *Lay Parish Ministers*, 118.

23. This tension is also seen in the larger theological debate surrounding what is known as communion ecclesiology, with some arguing that the notion of communion underscores the church's universality and others arguing that it strengthens our appreciation of local particularity. See the well-publicized debate between Cardinal Walter Kasper and then-Cardinal Joseph Ratzinger, summarized in Kilian McDonnell, "The Ratzinger/Kasper Debate: The Universal Church and Local Churches," *Theological Studies* 63 (2002): 227–50; Hahnenberg, "The Mystical Body of Christ and Communion Ecclesiology," 20–27.

24. See Edward P. Hahnenberg, "Bishop: Source or Center of Ministerial Life?" *Origins* 37 (June 28, 2007): 104–7.

6

Lay Ecclesial Ministry and Ritual

Catherine Vincie, RSHM

Taking a fresh look at *Co-Workers in the Vineyard of the Lord* from the U.S. Conference of Catholic Bishops provides an opportunity to reflect upon lay ecclesial ministry and the role of ritual in the life of the church. Our concerns are both theological and anthropological. From a theological perspective, particular questions regarding lay ecclesial ministry and ritual participation must be addressed. Specifically, we might raise such questions as to the theological propriety of lay ministers presiding at corporate public prayer. To put it another way, is it not only proper but even necessary for lay ministers to do so in order to take their rightful place in the ecclesial body? We might also ask whether there is any theological or pastoral precedent for them to have a ritual role at liturgies when other members of the hierarchy preside. In addition, are blessings and rituals crucial for the authorization of lay ecclesial ministers in the parish setting, and is ritual or liturgy a useful social tool in the development of lay ecclesial ministry?

From an anthropological perspective, general issues of ritual and the social process that immediately come to mind are the role of ritual in social stability, identity formation, and facilitating social change. Other issues regarding status and status change are pertinent here, as well as ritual competency of individual members and the community as a whole. Performance and praxis approaches to ritual activity as well as ritual as a social strategy will also be important to explore. These issues will provide background for understanding the development of lay ecclesial ministry in the church and the ritual implications for the same.

In this chapter I will use the term "ritual" as a generic term including all ritualizing practices of communities, whether they be religious or not. We are fortunate that the social sciences, particularly social and cultural anthropology, have made significant contributions to our understanding of ritual in recent years. The field has developed to such an extent that "ritual studies" has become a distinct discipline of its own. Because religious ritual or liturgy (in our more common ecclesial use) is a subset of human ritual, what the social scientists have learned about society and its ritualizing process will be very informative to our reflections on the emergence and development of lay ecclesial ministry vis-à-vis ritual. Although the church has a long and storied tradition of liturgy, it has much to learn from the social sciences about the relationship between its ritual actions and the society and dynamics of the church itself. My goal here is to bring some new insight into the role of ritual in the development of lay ecclesial ministry and so to come to a deeper understanding of how ritual functions in the development of this recently formed ecclesial reality.

LAY ECCLESIAL MINISTERS AND LITURGICAL PRESIDENCY

Before turning to the social sciences for their insights into ritual, we need to address our present practice regarding liturgical presidency and the theological presuppositions regarding this practice. At the present time our liturgical books take into account that within the hierarchically ordered life of the church certain members are granted permission to preside at certain liturgies. Because we have taken on the ancient Roman *cursus* of promotion in rank, those of higher rank can do all of what lower ranks can do, but the reverse is not true.[1] The question at hand is what determines the suitability of certain members of the ecclesial body for presiding at certain liturgies.

The theological rule of thumb that applies here is that a pastoral charge carries with it a liturgical charge. If one's pastoral task involves oversight of a diocese (i.e., the bishop), then he presides over those liturgical rites pertinent to that ministry. This means that the bishop is the ordinary and sole presider at the rite of dedication of a church and altar, ordinations, blessings of abbots and abbesses, to name a few. He is the ordinary presiding minister of Eucharist in the diocese, although priests, as assistants to the bishop, may also preside at this liturgy. The bishop is the ordinary minister of the sacrament of confirmation; however, priests may be delegated to celebrate this sacrament at times, such as when they initiate adult catechumens and welcome candidates into full communion. A priest, on the other hand, presides at those rites that pertain to his pastoral charge of a parish. Thus he is the ordinary presider of parish Eucharist, the sacrament of reconciliation, anointing of the sick, and the rite of religious profession, among other liturgies. The deacon, in his turn, may preside at the minor exorcisms, blessings, and anointings of catechumens during the period of the catechumenate. As one with a special ministry to the word, he is also the preferred presider at Sunday celebrations in the absence of a priest (SCAP) and may be delegated to witness marriages and to baptize. The understanding is that the bishop may do all that a priest or deacon does as well as his own distinct liturgies; the priest may do whatever the deacon does as well as his own distinct liturgies; and the deacon may do whatever a layperson may do as well as his own distinct liturgies. Members of a "lower" rank cannot do anything ascribed to those of the "higher" orders unless specifically delegated to do so in accordance with canon and liturgical law.

What the church seems to be saying is that if one has a pastoral charge, then one ought to have a liturgical charge that corresponds with that pastoral responsibility.[2] Hervé-Marie Legrand argues historically that "those who preside over the life of the Church preside at the Eucharist."[3] A contemporary indication of this is given in the rite of Christian initiation of adults (RCIA). Paragraph 16 says, "Catechists, who have an important office for the progress of the catechumens and for the growth of the community, should, whenever possible, have an active part in the rites." It likewise says in the rite of confirmation (RC 46a) that priests may assist the bishop with confirmation when they have a diocesan role such as diocesan vicar or dean. In other words, there is a theological and pastoral appropriateness to connect liturgical presidency, or at least a liturgical role, with pastoral service. Thus it would appear to be an anomaly in our tradition to have a pastoral charge with no liturgical expression, or a liturgical role without a pastoral charge.

This obviously brings us to the question of whether there are liturgies of the church at which the *lay ecclesial minister* may or ought to preside or assist. At the present time our liturgical books do not address this specific question except in the case of the catechist mentioned above. What they do address is whether *laypersons* in general may preside at certain liturgies. Indeed they may, and a significant list of liturgies is included. Among them are: presiding at the liturgy of the hours, SCAP, the vigil and committal rite of the order of Christian funerals, the minor exorcisms and blessings during the catechumenate, many of the blessings in the Book of Blessings, and so forth. What is obvious is that liturgical practice has not caught up with the emergence of lay ecclesial ministry. Liturgical books were revised prior to or simultaneously with the emergence of lay ecclesial ministry and did not take this reality into account.

The question remains then whether in the future a lay ecclesial minister may or ought to preside at certain of the church's official and unofficial liturgies. I would suggest that a positive reply to this question is the next step in the development of the roles of lay ecclesial ministers. It is becoming a generally recognized practice that those working on the pastoral staff of a parish may and often do preside at certain liturgies in the absence of a priest or deacon. This is particularly true of parish life coordinators (or those serving the pastoral needs of a parish by whatever name) where an ordained minister is not assigned full time. Thus it is not unusual to find parish staff persons presiding at funeral vigil services and committals as well as SCAPs, among other liturgies. This practice would be in line with the present theologically grounded rationale that for ordained members of the hierarchy, a pastoral charge is accompanied by a liturgical role. What lay ministers are wondering is whether they ought to have some liturgical role that would match the pastoral role they already have. This would apply in the presence or absence of ordained members of the hierarchy.

The absence of any liturgical role for the lay ecclesial minister when a priest or deacon is at hand is particularly painful when an ordained minister comes to a parish monthly to celebrate Eucharist. The parish life coordinator who has been caring for the community throughout the month has no liturgical role at all and becomes invisible to the community. One might suggest that they at least have a place in the sanctuary to acknowledge their ongoing pastoral role in the parish. The directory on SCAPs makes a point of the importance of leaving the presider's chair vacant to indicate the ordained's pastoral role even in his absence. One might wonder if having another chair occupied by a lay ecclesial minister at a monthly Eucharist is not equally as important a symbol. In the absence of the deacon, one might also wonder whether lay ecclesial ministers are not the most suitable persons to proclaim the prayers of the faithful. In addition, other actions or roles might be added to the Eucharist if we took seriously the theological and pastoral tradition of always associating a liturgical role with a pastoral charge.

Co-Workers in the Vineyard does not provide any commentary on this point, and it would be helpful if the next edition of this document or some future document would take up this issue. It does address the question of liturgical rites and authorization, but I will cover that below under another topic.

As in the case of lay preaching at non-Eucharistic services, provisions would have to be made for suitable training in liturgical leadership, but such training is already taking place in many schools of ministry, and many dioceses have implemented training programs for those delegated to preside at SCAP. There is no reason to presume that training in a particular ecclesial ministry necessarily equips one with ritual competence, but training in liturgical leadership can be easily provided.

RITUAL AND SOCIETY

In the early stages of social and cultural anthropology (the last half of the nineteenth century and early twentieth century), anthropologists were interested in the role of ritual in social life. Émile Durkheim (1858–1917), for instance, explored the role of religion in society and argued that religion was a way of socially organizing groups of individuals. According to ritual theorist Catherine Bell, Durkheim concluded that "religion is a set of ideas and practices by which people sacralize the social structure and bonds of the community. In this way, religion functions to ensure the unconscious priority of communal identification."[4] It is through rites and rituals that religion accomplishes this social task. They help individuals bond together and recognize themselves as part of a bigger reality while lending support to the social structures of the community.

Although Durkheim developed a somewhat ahistorical approach to religion and society, his insights into the social function of religion and its rituals are nonetheless important. Others, such as Alfred Reginald Radcliffe-Brown (1881–1955), extended Durkheim's theories to take greater account of the role of ritual in securing and maintaining the unity of a group. Still others, such as Bronislaw Malinowski (1884–1942), put more stress on emotional states and suggested that religious ritual functioned to alleviate stress and anxiety, fear and doubt.

Radcliffe-Brown argued instead that religious ritual could just as easily create anxiety as relieve it. In either case, ritual does not only express mental states; it can also create them.[5] Among social functionalists, as these anthropologists became called, society was generally seen as being in a static state; religious ritual had a functional role and was a means to regulate and stabilize the life of this system. While later theorists would challenge this static view of society, these theorists accounted for at least some dimensions of the social function of ritual, and their insights remain valuable.

What may one conclude from this approach to ritual and its implications for lay ecclesial ministry? I would like to stress here that religious ritual, at least sometimes, has the function of supporting social structures. In other words, ritual can express and reinforce the current structures of a society. Regarding lay ecclesial ministry, we have been witnessing over the past forty years the development of a new structure in the Roman Catholic Church. While I will refrain from discussing whether lay ecclesial ministry constitutes a new "order" in the church, I can at least say that it is an important and growing social reality in the church. According to the anthropological theory summarized above, it would be reasonable to assume that the ritual practice of the community would express the actual composition of the church and support it. In other words, if the insights of our anthropologists are to be trusted, the existence of lay ecclesial ministry would naturally be reflected in the ritual practice of the community and the practice would reinforce its position in the church.

The ritual practice of acknowledging and exercising liturgical roles of lay ecclesial ministers would give added status and stability to this emerging reality. Just as the practice of having distinct roles for bishops, presbyters, and deacons is ritually expressed in the liturgies of the church and as such reinforces those roles, so too the ritual expression of the distinct roles of lay ecclesial ministers has the potential for solidifying their role in the life of the church. In addition, as Durkheim and Malinowski suggest, we can expect that such ritual performance would express and perhaps create mental states. Thus it would not be surprising that changes in ritual practice would have an emotional effect on the community. Depending on one's ideological stance toward the development of lay ecclesial ministry, the emotional impact can vary. What is certain is that the liturgical expression of lay ecclesial ministry would raise the visibility of this reality in our community and present it for our reflection. I will return to this concept of reflection below, but for now it is enough to stress that ritual visibility of lay ecclesial ministry would assist in stabilizing its place in the life of our community.

Other insights from the social sciences are also useful in helping us to understand what is going on in the development of lay ecclesial ministry and in its ritual expression. I am thinking here of the insights of Arnold van Gennep and Victor Turner on "rites of passage." Van Gennep was writing at the turn of the twentieth century, and Turner extended his thought on rites of passage in the second half of the twentieth century. In brief, rites of passage, life-crisis or lifecycle rites, mark a person's transition from one state of being to another. Some examples are those rites surrounding birth, puberty, marriage, and death. While these rites are often related to biological changes, they are often a society's effort to order the biological into the social. In other words, while the onset of menses and the appearance of facial hair may indicate physiological changes in youth, only cultural actions such as lifecycle rites of initiation actually "make women" and "make men." In the thought of Claude Levi-Strauss there is a deep human need "to take the raw changes of the natural world and 'cook' them . . . thereby transforming physical inevitabilities into cultural regularities."[6]

According to Van Gennep and Turner, rites of passage have a threefold pattern. There is a movement of separation (when one is separated from one's former status), a period of liminality (an in-between time when one is neither one thing nor another, the old nor yet the new), and a movement of reincorporation (when one takes one's place in a new status). The result of this process is that one moves from one status or situation into another. In puberty rites, one changes from the status of girl to that of woman, from a boy to a man. For those early theorists who favored a static view of society, these rites helped to order chaotic social change in a controlled and sanctioned way. For those theorists like Turner who favored a "processual" or process notion of society and culture, these rites provided a time for individuals to reflect upon the values, beliefs, and traditions of the community and possibly reconfigure them in a new way. In other words, rites of passage can be as much about social stability as they can be about social change.

Once again we ask how these insights about ritual and society can help us to understand the phenomenon of the emergence of lay ecclesial ministry. At this point we need to address the suitability of blessings and rituals in the authorization process of lay ecclesial ministers. Here *Co-Workers in the Vineyard* weighs in with extensive comments. It makes very clear that the authorization of laywomen and laymen for ecclesial ministry is given by competent authority—particularly the bishop, who according to canon law is granted oversight of the pastoral care carried out in his diocese. While acknowledging the unique role of the bishop in the authorization process, the document gives consideration to the pastor in selecting candidates for these ecclesial positions.[7] Great care is given in the document to the certification process, allowing for diversity in preparation, but insisting on the necessity of appropriate theological, pastoral, spiritual, and human formation. Appointments should be made in writing with particular attention paid to special delegation to perform functions proper to the ordained (e.g., baptizing outside of emergencies and witnessing the exchange of matrimonial consent).[8] *Co-Workers* is clear about the use of terms to designate different kinds of authorization, such as "entrust" (a diocese is entrusted to a bishop, a parish to a pastor). This language is usually confined to those holding an ecclesiastical "office" in the church, which has stability as part of its essential makeup. The document goes further, suggesting that not every ministry in the church is an "office," and that care should be taken "before establishing lay ecclesial ministries in this manner."[9]

While I will leave to other authors consideration of these limitations, I would particularly like to address the document's comments on blessing and ritual in the authorization process. The section begins by stating that "public prayer and ritual can be significant for the lay ecclesial minister and for the community, highlighting the new relationships that the person is beginning in the life of the community."[10] The point of the ritual, according to *Co-Workers*, is to emphasize the relationship of the lay minister to the diocesan bishop and the community. The document states that care should be taken so that such lay ministers would not be seen as a substitute for the priest and, curiously, that the rite itself would *not* be seen as conferring the appointment. On one hand, *Co-Workers* makes it clear that the authorization comes from the bishop, but it is not as clear whether ritual also gives its own particular kind of authorization.

We need to consider other kinds of authorization given in the church. The first rituals that come to mind are those of ordination to the episcopacy, the presbyterate, and the deaconate. It is clear in our tradition that these sacramental rituals give the grace they signify. In other words, through the actions and words of the rite a man is consecrated and becomes a bishop, priest, or deacon. Theologically we call them sacramental actions, but we also call them performative actions—meaning that the action/saying does something here and now.

We also see this in other sacramental and nonsacramental rituals in the church. I am thinking of marriage, in one case, or the making of a catechumen in another. We can also look at such rituals as the installation of a bishop in his diocese and the installation of a pastor in his parish. Although it is clear that authorization for such "offices" is given by hierarchical authority, it is also true that the ritual itself gives a certain authorization for the new relationship established in the community vis-à-vis the bishop or the pastor.

Giving attention to the actual dynamics of ritual in the life of a community, it is inadequate to simply say that the ritual does not confer the appointment. The actual experience of a community ritually praying over someone for the grace to exercise a ministry in the church does, in fact, convey a certain authority. As *Co-Workers* indicates, this ritual practice is extremely helpful to both the lay ecclesial minister and the community, but it does more. Looking at the insights from anthropology, the blessing rituals can function as rites of passage. They actually change the relationship of the lay ecclesial minister within the community. The community is acknowledging that the lay minister has the blessing of the church on their pastoral care in the parish or other pastoral setting. In a way, the ritual "orders" the lay ministers into a new configuration in the life of the community. As I argued earlier, it gives approbation to the existence of such a reality and facilitates the acceptance of lay ecclesial ministry in the community. In certain cases the ritual can create a mental state of acceptance of this new reality. That this is helpful to the candidate and the community is beyond question.

Ritual is not the only phenomenon in the life of a community, but it is a significant action especially in the Roman Catholic church, which has placed such an emphasis on the mediation of grace through sacramental and nonsacramental rites. Although we might not consider a ritual blessing of a lay ecclesial minister to have the same importance or stature as our ordination rites, it nonetheless places a person in a new status in the community. By doing so it can establish that person in a new position within a community structure that already exists, thus maintaining the status quo; or it can reconfigure the community itself by establishing lay ecclesial ministry as a new reality in the life of the church. In 1972 Pope Paul VI established the ministries of reader and acolyte in his *motu proprio Ministeria Quaedam* and declared that the ministries would be conferred through the liturgical rites *De institutione lectoris* and *De institutione acolythi*. It would appear quite possible, then, to decide to confer lay ecclesial ministries similarly through the celebration of a suitable rite.

RITUAL AS SOCIAL PRACTICE

We must also address some more contemporary insights regarding ritual and the social process from the social sciences and ritual studies. Recently ritual theorists have turned from a more communicative approach to ritual (i.e., that ritual communicates a community's values, meanings, beliefs, etc.) and to an interest in how rituals do what they do. Since the 1970s interest has shifted to the study of "cultural performances" such as rituals, carnivals, festivals, and theater, and scholars have drawn insights from these dynamic events. Pursuant to our interest in rituals, theorists used performance metaphors to help focus "on what ritual actually *does*, rather than on what it is supposed to mean."[11] A performance approach suggests a very active role for ritual participants who are able to reinterpret symbols as they use them. In other words, the focus on performance led theorists to ask "how symbolic activities like ritual enable people to appropriate, modify, or reshape cultural values and ideals."[12] Accepting the presupposition that rituals do communicate the values and ideals of a culture, those interested in performance approaches suggest that "ritual actors" actually use the ritual experience to either appropriate or reconfigure the values communicated in the ritual. Ritual actors can be creative and purposeful in their ritual participation. Previously it was thought that rituals had the power to shape individuals and communities; more recently it has been appreciated that "ritual does not mold people; people fashion rituals that mold their world."[13] This obviously suggests that societies are not static, but dynamic entities that are changed through the participation of their members in cultural performances.

Not unrelated to performance approaches are what we call *praxis* approaches to ritual activity. Praxis as it has been understood recently is the result of an upward spiral of practice, reflection, and theory, and further practice, reflection, and theory, and so on. In the context of this chapter, a praxis approach implies that communities use rituals as a way "to continually reproduce and reshape their social and cultural environments."[14] In other words, rituals, among other practices, are creative strategies used by societies to think and rethink their values and attitudes, their structures, and their symbol systems. This implies a thoughtful and reflective approach to the shape of one's culture and society.

It is important to note that the reflection is not done in the abstract, but through the ritual practice. Rituals are embodied practices that have the capacity to affirm or to reconfigure the status quo. Ritual participants can shape and reshape their world. Theorists such as Marshall Sahlins argue that practice brings together "structure and history, system and event, continuity and change. In other words, ritual enables enduring patterns of social organization and cultural symbolic systems to be brought to bear on real events; in the course of this process, real situations are assessed and negotiated in ways that can transform these traditional patterns or structures in turn."[15]

Sahlins also thought that ritual could create a meaningful event out of a new and potentially threatening situation. It allows the community to dynamically interact with its changing environment, be that internal or external. Pierre Bourdieu extends Sahlins's thought on this issue by suggesting that rituals are "strategic practices for transgressing and reshuffling cultural categories in order to meet the needs of real situations."[16] Ritual can also be a tool for cultural jockeying; it can be a medium for the negotiation of power in relationships.[17]

Finally, I would like to include the thought of Catherine Bell on this topic of ritual as a social practice. She argues that the goal of ritualization is circular. Ritual creates ritualized agents or actors "with a form of ritual mastery, who embod[y] flexible sets of cultural schemes and can deploy them effectively in multiple situations so as to restructure those situations in practical ways."[18] In summarizing the advantages of the performance approach to ritual, she suggests that ritual is not so much a vehicle for the *expression* of authority as much as it is a vehicle for the *construction* of relationships of authority.[19]

The implications of these theories for the development of lay ecclesial ministry are most provocative. They suggest that ritual exercises can be understood as occasions where the participants not only are formed by the ritual, but can use the ritual to form the community, its values and its meanings, its structures and its symbols. In the case of lay ecclesial ministry, blessing rituals of authorization need to be invented. Yes, not only is ritual inherited, but at times it is invented by specific individuals for specific purposes. In this case, the blessing rituals are or can be a form of reflection, critique, and reconfiguration of the status quo. Specifically, they are ways of rethinking the place of theologically trained and spiritually formed individuals in the life of the church.

In a sense, it is understandable that *Co-Workers* cautions that the rituals are not meant to give the impression that the individual in question is a substitute for the priest or that the ritual itself gives authorization. But its concern does not take seriously enough the power of ritual in social systems, and it does not pursue what such rituals would actually do. Indeed, according to our ritual theorists, the ritual is not only about blessing the lay ecclesial minister; it is also about reconfiguring the way the church has traditionally understood itself and the role of the laity. It is not enough to do this thinking and reconfiguration in theory or in the pages of academic journals or church documents; it must be ritually acted out.

Rituals such as blessings of lay ecclesial ministers are public social praxis, a public social strategy for reframing the structure of the church and the laity's place in it. They place laypeople as the recipients of the community's ministrations, its gestures, its words of prayer and blessing. Through embodied action, they ask the community to rethink what it knows of pastoral leadership. They also raise expectations of what the lay ecclesial minister may do in the life of the church. If the blessing is done in the sanctuary area of the church, the ecclesial ministers might find a permanent place there. Think again of the appropriateness of having the parish life coordinator remain in the sanctuary when the ordained minister comes to celebrate Eucharist on his monthly rounds. That, too, would be a ritual performance where we would think and rethink the church's social organization and leadership roles. According to Bourdieu, such ritual practice would be a way for transgressing and reshuffling cultural values. It is quite possible that such reshuffling would be contested by members of the clergy or the laity, and it may even happen that that contestation would take place during the ritual. It is also likely that the community would use other social strategies in addition to ritual practice to work through these changes in meaning and value, structure and forms. Nonetheless, it seems clear that ritual is a reflective exercise reviewing and perhaps reconfiguring the lay ecclesial minister's place in the life of the church.

A final reference must be made to anthropological studies of ritual in regard to two issues: ritual as a technology of the self, and the revised understanding of power in social relations. Regarding the former, we need to review the work of two scholars, Talal Asad, a British scholar of ritual and Benedictine monasticism, and the French philosopher Michel Foucault.[20] Asad bases his work on Foucault's project of sketching out the different ways (techniques or technologies) that humans develop knowledge about themselves.[21] His fourth category of technologies, and the one that interests us here, is that of "technology of the self." In Foucault's words, technologies of the self "permit individuals to effect by their own means or with the help of others a certain number of operations on their own bodies and souls, thoughts, conduct, and way of being, so as to transform themselves."[22] In his view rituals as practiced by individuals or groups are operations that shape the self. In Benedictine monasticism, as codified in the *Rule of Benedict*, the monk practiced three sets of activities (chanting the Divine Office [*opus Dei*], manual labor, and holy reading [*lectio divina*]) to inculcate certain virtues that are put to the service of God. In other words, all three of these were means by which the monk acquired Christian virtue. They were techniques or technologies that aimed at the creation of a virtuous self. As theologian Nathan Mitchell summarizes, "the virtues of a monastic man or woman were thus formed by cultivating the ability to behave, bodily, in certain ways."[23] He goes on to say that "in [the] *R[ule of] B[enedict]*, ritual is thus perceived as bodily inscription, as embodied practice, rehearsal, routine."[24] Rituals are not necessarily cultural codes that need interpretation (although at times that may be the case), but rather involve *abilities to be acquired*. Ritual teaches the body how to act in certain ways. It is also a competence that is not mental but bodily, and that competence is oriented to the creation of a new self.[25] Mitchell adds that "ritual is not only a way Christians negotiate their access to the Sacred; it is also their way of editing experience, 'rewriting' personal history, and appropriating a new identity."[26]

The second item of interest here is the reconfiguration of power in social relations pursuant to ritual. In the classical consensus on ritual, which operated among ritualists up to the 1980s, ritual was seen as an instrumental agent used in such a way as to impose social control and transmit tradition (meaning and values). However, as Mitchell states, "the power linked to ritual cannot simply be defined, then, as political manipulation or as the violent oppression of the weak by the powerful."[27] Rather, as we have described above, ritual is "a strategic mode of practice" that "produces nuanced relationships of power, relationships characterized by acceptance and resistance, negotiated appropriation, and redemptive reinterpretation of the hegemonic order."[28] Rather than understanding power as that held solely by those in authority, power can be better understood as something distributed throughout the social body. According to Mitchell, *"Power is thus the way ordinary people define and negotiate the reality of their daily lives."*[29] Specific to our concerns, rituals are strategic modes of practice that community members use to define and redefine themselves and their place in the body politic. All have access to this kind of power; all can use ritual strategically to define their individual and corporate "selves." As Mitchell summarizes, "The power of ritual is thus far more local, strategic, messy, imprecise, ordinary, flexible, ambiguous, and indeterminate than the high church liturgist might wish us to believe."[30]

Once again, we shift to inquire into the implications of this work for the phenomenon of lay ecclesial ministry and the rituals that we use to authorize its place in the church. I began with comments about ritual as a technology of the self, an embodied practice that effects transformation on those who practice such rituals. Here the application to lay ecclesial ministry is quite direct. We can suggest that the newly created rituals of blessing and authorization are social schemes whereby, through operations on the body, we inculcate certain virtues and attitudes, beliefs about ourselves and one another. Earlier I mentioned the ministrations of blessing and prayer delegated to the lay ecclesial minister. Here too we suggest that such ritual activity "creates" a new self now empowered to act with authority in the community. The corporate assembly redefines itself in relationship to these individuals through these rituals and in a very public fashion redraws its lines of authority. As an embodied practice, ritualization creates ritual competence that can be used in the service of certain goals—in this case the redefinition of lay ecclesial ministry in the church. As Mitchell stated, ritual is a way of editing experience and appropriating a new identity. This is why I indicated earlier that rituals of blessing are indeed necessary in the negotiation of the new identity and authority of lay ecclesial ministry. They are at least one strategy whereby the body politic rewrites the history of the church and the laity's role in it.

The last concern, that of power, is not unrelated to what I have just explored. As indicated above, we have shifted our understanding of power from that which one dominant person exercises over a less influential one, to an understanding that power is distributed throughout the social body. Thus we can infer, in contrast to the premise of *Co-Workers*, that the negotiation of the place of lay ecclesial ministry is not determined solely by the actions of those in authority. The actual reality is more complex and, as Mitchell indicates, "more messy." If power is more properly understood as distributed throughout the social system, then lay ecclesial ministers are not merely being "acted upon"; they are active agents in the negotiation of their new identity and authority in the community.

SUMMARY

This chapter began by asking theological and pastoral questions about the suitability of lay ecclesial ministers presiding at certain liturgies and about the necessity of rituals of blessings or authorization. It was suggested that it has been the tradition of the church that because a person has a pastoral charge that person necessarily has a liturgical charge within that same community. I pointed out that this tradition applied to those in holy orders, but I suggested that it might be applicable also to lay ecclesial ministers, particularly those exercising significant leadership in pastoral settings. At the moment our liturgical books are not precise in designating such delegation for lay ministers, but as the reality of lay ecclesial ministry grows, a reasonable conclusion is that new versions of the liturgical books will take that into account. I also argued that parish life coordinators ought at least to be seated in a chair in the sanctuary area when the pastor comes to celebrate Eucharist in order to honor the pastoral leadership and ministry the lay person actually exercises.

I also reviewed several theories regarding ritual from the social sciences and ritual studies that have significant implications for lay ecclesial ministry. I explained that there was development in understanding ritual and its place in the social process. Early theorists favored a more static understanding of society and therefore suggested that ritual would support the status quo. Later scholars argued that society was much more dynamic and that ritual participated in that dynamism. I suggested that if these theories were to be taken into account, rituals of blessing and authorization would have an important part to play in the development of lay ecclesial ministry in the life of the church. Rituals would reflect this new reality and therefore solidify it. What remains necessary is to explore further the relationship between authorization by ecclesiastical authority and rituals of blessing or commissioning. The two need to work in concert with each other.

Insights into rites of passage suggest that rituals of blessing can have the effect of facilitating the change of status of lay ecclesial ministers. Rites of passage are ways for a society to deal with the new situations that come into its life not as inevitable but as "digested," so to speak, by the community. I suggested that despite claims to the contrary, rituals do communicate a certain kind of authorization. Although the church has developed a tradition of ordaining deacons, presbyters, and bishops and instituting those in the role of reader and acolyte, it has yet to develop an adequate vocabulary or ritual for bestowing authority on lay ecclesial ministers. This is one of the important agenda items of the future.

I examined performance and praxis approaches to ritual and suggested that they both provide an active understanding of ritual participants and that they recast rituals by focusing on what they do rather than what they mean. Rituals are embodied practices that can reconfigure the status quo; they allow participants to reshape their worlds. The implications for lay ecclesial ministers are many. Blessing rituals and other rituals of authorization can be understood as strategic practices for reflection, critique, and reconfiguration of the status quo. Ritual is a public performance that allows the church and lay ecclesial ministers to rethink their identity and relationships.

Finally, I reviewed work on ritual as a technology of the self and a new understanding of power in the social body. I also suggested that ritual practice is a way for participants to inculcate certain values, virtues, and attitudes. Ritual is an ability to be acquired and used to edit experience and appropriate a new identity. The new understanding of power allows for power to be perceived throughout the whole social body. Ritual is one example of a strategy a community may use to negotiate one's identity and social place.

In sum, the church should be very interested in ritual performances. They have the potential for reshaping identity and reforming ecclesial relationships and are exercises of power within the social body. Lay ecclesial ministry needs ritual if this ministry is to be well integrated into the life of the church.

NOTES

1. See Mary Collins, "The Public Language of Ministry," in *Worship: Renewal to Practice* (Washington DC: Pastoral Press, 1987), 137–73.

2. See the important article on this issue by Hervé-Marie Legrand on "The Presidency of the Eucharist According to the Ancient Tradition," in *Living Bread, Saving Cup*, edited by Kevin Seasoltz (Collegeville, MN: Liturgical Press, 1982), 196–230.

3. Legrand, "Presidency," 211.

4. Catherine Bell, *Ritual: Perspectives and Dimensions* (New York: Oxford University Press, 1997), 24. I rely on Bell's summary of the development in anthropology throughout my text.

5. Bell, *Ritual*, 28.

6. Cited in Bell, *Ritual*, 94.

7. U.S. Conference of Catholic Bishops, *Co-Workers in the Vineyard of the Lord: A Resource for Guiding the Development of Lay Ecclesial Ministry* (Washington, DC: USCCB, 2005), 37–41.

8. USCCB, *Co-Workers*, 40.

9. USCCB, *Co-Workers*, 40.

10. USCCB, *Co-Workers*, 41.

11. Bell, *Ritual*, 73. Theorists included Kenneth Burke on dramatism, Victor Turner on ritual as social drama, Irving Goffman on rituals that structure the performances of social interaction, among others.

12. Bell, *Ritual*, 73.

13. Bell, *Ritual*, 73.

14. Bell, *Ritual*, 76.

15. Cited in Bell, *Ritual*, 77.

16. Cited in Bell, *Ritual*, 78.

17. Bell, *Ritual*, 79.

18. Bell, *Ritual*, 81.

19. Bell, *Ritual*, 82.

20. I am grateful to Nathan Mitchell for his introduction to Asad's and Foucault's work in this area. See his *Liturgy and the Social Sciences* (Collegeville, MN: Liturgical Press, 1999), 64–80.

21. Luther H. Martin, Huck Gutman, and Patrick H. Hutton, eds., *Technologies of the Self: A Seminar with Michel Foucault* (Amherst, MA: University of Massachusetts Press, 1988).

22. Cited in Martin, Gutmann, and Hutton, *Technologies of the Self*, 18, as quoted in Mitchell, *Liturgy*, 65.

23. Mitchell, *Liturgy*, 72.

24. Mitchell, *Liturgy*, 72.

25. Mitchell, *Liturgy*, 73.

26. Mitchell, *Liturgy*, 75. See also Talal Asad, "On Discipline and Humility in Medieval Christian Monasticism," in *Genealogies of Religion* (Baltimore: Johns Hopkins University Press, 1991), 125–67.

27. Mitchell, *Liturgy*, 87.

28. Catherine Bell, *Ritual Theory, Ritual Practice* (New York: Oxford University Press, 1992), 196.

29. Mitchell, *Liturgy*, 88. [Emphasis in the original].

30. Mitchell, *Liturgy*, 89.

7

Lay Ecclesial Ministry and Parish Leadership Options: Canonical Reflections in Light of *Co-Workers in the Vineyard*

Sharon A. Euart, RSM

Co-Workers in the Vineyard of the Lord: A Resource for Guiding the Development of Lay Ecclesial Ministry[1] was approved by the U.S. Conference of Catholic Bishops (USCCB) in 2005 following more than a decade of research and discussion by the USCCB Subcommittee on Lay Ministry.[2] This theological and pastoral reflection provides a common frame of reference for the future development of lay ecclesial ministry based on the experience of the bishops in the United States over some forty years and what they have learned from that experience. The bishops provide an outline of a theology of ministry that serves as a guide for both current and future discussion and development of ministry in this country. They invite adaptation to the goals, strategies, and resources they offer, keeping in mind fidelity to the church's teaching and canonical norms, on the one hand, and application to pastoral needs and diverse situations, on the other.[3] The canonical framework for reflection on lay ecclesial ministry presupposes a theological vision of ministry that is rooted in Catholic tradition, especially in the notions of communion and mission, and from which the canonical articulation flows.[4] It is in response to this invitation to offer reflections and recommendations for the future that I wish to frame my comments on the continued development and adaptation of lay ecclesial ministry within the context of the universal law of the church.[5]

The focus of my reflections will be the experience of lay ecclesial ministry in the life of the parish, highlighting: (1) the impact of canon law on the development and growth of lay ecclesial ministry, (2) the canonical notion of parish and the code's options for parish leadership, and (3) implications for the application of canon law to parish life and leadership in the future. Although the thrust of this chapter is limited to lay ecclesial ministry in the parish setting, it is important to recognize that although the parish is a major venue in the life of the church that has witnessed the most growth of lay ecclesial ministry, it is not the only one. Laymen and laywomen have served with women and men religious for decades in Catholic schools and colleges, health care facilities, social service agencies, diocesan chanceries, and other types of ministry, both as volunteers and as salaried professionals. In these settings, too, they have contributed greatly to the building up of the church.

REVISION OF THE CODE OF CANON LAW

In addressing the three areas identified above, it is important to begin with some reflections on the Code of Canon Law and the principles guiding its application. It was just over fifty years ago that Pope John XXIII set things in motion on January 25, 1959, when he announced the three-part plan for his papacy: (1) a synod for the diocese of Rome, (2) an ecumenical council, and (3) a modernization (*aggiornamento* or updating) of the Code of Canon Law. He created a Commission for the Revision of the Code of Canon Law (actually the *recognitio*, a rethinking of the code) in 1963, shortly before his death. His successor, Pope Paul VI, set the commission to work telling the members that they were to do more than simply update the fifty-year-old document; they were to reorganize the church's discipline and accommodate it to the teachings of the Second Vatican Council and to new and changing circumstances. They were to reform the church's canonical style, give it a "new way of thinking" (a *novus habitus mentis*), responsive to new needs.[6] The renewal and reform of Vatican II and its focus on the pastoral dimensions of the life of the church necessarily led to practical considerations and behavioral consequences that required a reform of law or, specifically, a reform of the Code of Canon Law.

Following completion of the council, the Code Commission began to undertake a reform of law, relying on a set of ten guiding principles of revision that emerged from the Synod of Bishops in 1967. It became clear that the commission's task was no longer a technical revision but an in-depth reform of law in accordance with the pastoral teaching and guidance of Vatican II. The council's purpose was a reform and renewal of the church; therefore, the code had to have the same purpose. This was no small challenge. The code was not only required to be faithful to, interpret properly, and apply the documents of Vatican II, it was also to be adequately flexible to respond to the needs of the times. The first code had been in place for forty-two years before the need to reform it was announced. The current code has already weathered over twenty-five years, a quarter of a century in which there have been major changes in the church and in our society.

Twenty-Five Years Later

In January 2008, Pope Benedict XVI addressed the Congress on Canon Law held in Rome to commemorate the twenty-fifth anniversary of the promulgation of the code. In that address he said that "Church law is, first and foremost, 'lex libertatis': law that makes us free to follow Jesus." He went on to say:

> [It is] necessary to present to the People of God, to the new generations and to all who are called to make canon law respected, its concrete bond with the life of the Church, in order to safeguard the delicate interests of the things of God and to protect the rights of the weakest, and of those who have no other means by which to make their presence felt, and also in defense of the "goods" which every member of the faithful freely received—the gift of faith, of God's grace, first of all—which the Church cannot allow to be deprived of adequate protection on the part of the Law.[7]

Pope Benedict also described canon law as essential for the proper exercise of *munus pastorale* (the pastoral office) of the church. In order that it might fulfill this service, canon law must be well structured, that is, bound to its theological foundation yet flexible enough to "keep up with the changing circumstances of the historical reality of the People of God." Therefore, Benedict went on to say, it is "necessary to abrogate norms that are antiquated; modify those in need of correction; interpret . . . those that are doubtful and . . . fill possible *lacunae legis*."[8] Pope Benedict's invitation to reflect on the current law in light of its mission of service in our changing circumstances provides the occasion for reflection on the code's impact on the life of the church, its effectiveness and reception, as well as identification of those areas of the law that might be in need of future revision—a timely invitation, along with that of the U.S. bishops in *Co-Workers*,[9] to consider the experience and development of lay ecclesial ministry from a canonical perspective.

In the context of the parish, what are some of the developments over the past twenty-five years that might impact the church's law and its application?[10] Some examples include:

- The establishment of instant communications through the Internet and its impact on evangelization, both positive and, in some instances, negative;
- The impact of secularism on religious and spiritual values and the "cafeteria" approach to selecting what one likes and rejecting what is not appealing;
- The increasing number of laypersons working for the church on a full-time basis in parishes and other ministries, especially where there is a shortage of priests;

- The growth in the permanent diaconate—over sixteen thousand or more than twice the number from twenty-five years ago;
- The decline in the number of priests available for parish ministry—a 29 percent reduction in the number of diocesan and religious priests in the United States;
- The impact of the rite of Christian initiation of adults (RCIA) and the increasing sense of what it means to be a parish community;
- The declining number of vowed religious in many parts of the world—a 48 percent decrease in women religious in the United States—and the more than seven hundred new groups in some stage of growth toward becoming religious institutes;[11]
- The increasing number of Hispanic Catholics in the United States and the high percentage of youth and young adults in this ethnic group;[12]
- The increasing number of Catholics who are members of ecclesial movements or associations in the church;
- The accelerated pace of change in our parishes as demographic shifts occur, leading to parish consolidations, mergers, and closings. Over the past twenty-five years, there has been a 5 percent decrease in the number of U.S. parishes and an increase of over 200 percent in the number of parishes without resident pastors.[13]

How has the Code of Canon Law kept pace with these changing circumstances? The experience of Catholics over the past twenty-five years indicates that it has been "workable," not perfect by any means, but it has responded to their changing circumstances fairly well.[14]

Code of Canon Law and Lay Ecclesial Ministry

Several of the principles for revision that were approved by the Synod of Bishops in 1967 as guidelines for the process of revising the entire Code of Canon Law served to enhance the position of the laity in the revised law. Principle 6, for example, identified the "fundamental equality of all members of the Christian faithful" as a common juridic status and urged that "the rights of persons be appropriately defined and safeguarded."[15] The revised code's acknowledgment of a proper role for the laity in the mission and ministry of the church has helped to advance and expand the role of laypersons in the ministry of the church. It has opened up opportunities for lay involvement in the threefold mission entrusted to the church.

The scope of opportunities permitted in the code for lay ecclesial ministry encompasses a variety of works or ministries undertaken by the lay faithful to carry out the church's teaching, sanctifying, and governing mission.

For example, in the *munus docendi* (teaching office), a layperson may offer opinions on ecclesial matters to pastors and other members of the Christian faithful (c. 212§3), assist the pastor in the parish catechetical ministry (c.776), serve as catechist in missionary lands to teach on behalf of the church (c.785), teach the sacred sciences in institutions of higher learning (c. 229§3), and participate in the teaching function through the church's effective use of the instruments of communication (cc. 822§3, 823§1, 830§1).

In the *munus sanctificandi* (sanctifying office), a layman or laywoman may serve as liturgical minister in performing the functions of lector, commentator, and cantor (c. 230§2),[16] special minister of Communion (cc. 230§3, 910§2), and minister of sacramentals (c. 1168). It is interesting to note that many of the liturgical functions that laymen and laywomen may perform are permitted only when a priest or deacon is not available. It would seem that roles associated with the sanctifying function of the church are still thought of primarily in terms of clergy.

Finally, in the *munus regendi* (governing office) laywomen or laymen may hold certain offices identified in the law. They may serve in the tribunal ministries of auditor (c. 1428), assessor (c. 1424), promoter of justice and defender of the bond (c. 1435), and procurator and advocate (c. 1483). Administratively, a layperson may be chancellor and notary for cases not involving clerics (c. 483§2). A layperson may also serve as diocesan financial officer (c. 494§1), member of a parish pastoral team (c. 517§2), and secretary general of the episcopal conference (c. 451).

Also in the area of governance, there are consultative functions open to laymen and laywomen: membership on plenary and provincial councils (c. 443§§3, 5), diocesan synods (c. 463), diocesan pastoral (c. 512) and finance (c. 492) councils, and parish pastoral (c. 536) and finance (c. 537) councils. In addition, the pope can call to an ecumenical council those whom he wishes and determine their degree of participation (c. 339§2). All of these functions are established by universal ecclesiastical law, possess objective stability and a spiritual purpose, and can thus be considered official ministries (c. 145).

Additional offices or ecclesial ministries, constituted by particular ecclesiastical law, that is, the law of a local church, may vary from diocese to diocese. Identifying all the ecclesial ministries open to laypersons is left to the determination of each diocesan bishop for his respective diocese. There is no doubt that the enhanced role given to the participation of the laity in the mission and ministry of the church in the Code of Canon Law has contributed significantly to the development of lay ecclesial ministry and to the tremendous growth in the numbers of lay ecclesial ministers serving in the dioceses of the United States.[17] The influence of the code is particularly evident in the parish where some of the issues and implications for the future of lay ecclesial

ministry are reshaping parish life and leadership. How is this happening and
what are the implications?

PARISH AND PARISH LEADERSHIP

For the majority of Catholics, the parish is the most familiar experience of
church. It is where Catholics are baptized, receive the sacraments of Holy
Communion and confirmation, often marry, and from which they are buried.
It is central to the discovery and ongoing nurturing of the spiritual identity
of most Catholics. In 1997 Pope John Paul II, in addressing the bishops of
France during their *ad limina* visit to Rome, spoke about the basic elements
of parish and parish leadership. He said that "it is essentially the parish which
gives the Church concrete life." This means, he continued, that the church
"must be a home where the members of the Body of Christ gather together,
open to meeting God the Father full of love, and the Savior his Son, incorporated into the Church by the Holy Spirit at the time of their Baptism, and
ready to accept their brothers and sisters with fraternal love, whatever their
condition and origins." The parish must also "be a meeting place for generations," especially young people, giving them "a place to which they are fully
entitled."[18]

To develop this kind of parish Pope John Paul II recognized the key role
of leadership in forging the future of parishes. He said an "essential question
is that of leaders. To guide and enliven pastoral units, the collaboration of
priests and lay persons is increasingly necessary." "All this presupposes," the
pope went on to say, "that priests and lay people clearly coordinate without
confusion, the concerns of the ministerial priesthood and of the universal
priesthood."[19] This is the setting in which Catholics find themselves today,
an appropriate context for reflection on *Co-Workers*, the Code of Canon Law,
and lay ecclesial ministry now and in the years ahead.

Canonical Notion of Parish

The Code of Canon Law defines a diocese as a portion of the people of God, a
description that is of fundamental importance. First and foremost the believing
people are the primary reality, then those who minister to them. The people are
entrusted to a bishop for their pastoral care. In providing that care, the bishop
is assisted by the priests of the diocese. The people of God, gathered with their
bishop and the priests, with the Holy Spirit, the gospel, and Eucharist, constitute an embodiment of the one holy, catholic, and apostolic church (c. 369).
The diocese is not simply an administrative unit of the universal church; rather

it is the people of God who form a particular church. The bishop is the central figure, described in terms of his role as shepherd and pastor.

Similarly, the code is somewhat general in its articulation of the nature of a parish. The 1917 code referred to a parish almost in passing, simply as a territorial part of a diocese, describing it mainly in terms of its pastor. The parish was understood to be an institution to serve the spiritual needs of the faithful. At the same time it was described as a "benefice," that is, a title or office with a source of income to the pastor. The elements of a parish were: a territorial section of the diocese, a church building, an assigned Catholic population, and a pastor who was responsible for the care of souls, the *cura animarum*.[20] The 1983 code altered this approach by defining a parish as "a certain community of the Christian faithful stably constituted in a particular church" and then stating that the pastoral care of that community is entrusted to a pastor under the authority of the diocesan bishop (c. 515§1). It is the believing community of the Christian faithful that is the principal reality. The parish is viewed fundamentally as a community of believers, a description faithful to the theologically and biblically rich title, the people of God. This parish community is established on a stable basis, meaning its members can expect that it will remain in existence for some time, that it is not a temporary arrangement. The canon goes on to say that the "pastoral care of the parish is entrusted to a pastor as its own shepherd under the authority of the diocesan bishop" (c. 515§1). Here, and in several canons that follow, the code defines the office of pastor as teaching, sanctifying, and governing in the community with the diocesan bishop in the name of Christ. Thus, Canon 515 identifies four fundamental elements in its description of the parish: community, stable basis, pastor, diocesan bishop.

The notion of parish in the 1983 code emphasizes that the parish is not primarily an administrative division of the diocese, but rather a community of the faithful established for the pastoral care of persons within the particular church. Pope John Paul II reiterated this perspective in 1997, stating, "Whatever its [the parish] size, it is not merely an association . . . it is a building to be erected, a body to bring to life and develop together, a community where God's gifts are received and where the baptized generously make their response of faith, hope and love to the call of the Gospel."[21]

The code's notion of parish and Pope John Paul II's vision of the parish in ecclesial life call for a clear understanding of the ecclesiology of parish and the ecclesiastical legislation regarding the parish, pastors, others serving the parish community, and its structures. In this regard, one of the more notable changes in the code is the various options for parish leadership, particularly when there is a shortage of priests available for parish ministry and the implications of this legislation for the development of lay ecclesial ministry.[22]

Options for Parish Leadership

The canons describing parish leadership options make up one of the sections of the revised code that has received considerable attention over the past twenty-five years, especially as more and more dioceses in this country and throughout the world experience the decreasing availability of priests for parish ministry. It is also an area of the law that is subject to misunderstanding and misinterpretation.

Canon 515 identifies as one of the fundamental elements of a parish the entrusting of the pastoral care to a pastor (*parochus*) under the authority of the diocesan bishop. The normal arrangement for providing pastoral care in a parish is for each parish to have its own priest-pastor. The revised code, however, permits other options for parish leadership.[23] For example, several neighboring parishes can be entrusted to the same pastor (c. 526§1). One or several parishes may be entrusted to a team of priests (c. 517§1) or, when there is a lack of priests, a participation in the pastoral care of a parish may be entrusted to a deacon, a person who is not a priest (such as a religious sister or brother, or a layman or laywoman), or to a community of persons (c. 517§2). In these latter cases, when the pastoral care is entrusted to persons who are not priests, a priest is appointed with the faculties of a pastor to direct the pastoral care.

What are the differences among these leadership options? Canon 526§1 reflects the general principle that a pastor is to have the pastoral care of only one parish, but the canon allows the exception that because of a lack of priests or other circumstances, the pastoral care of several neighboring parishes may be entrusted to the same pastor. For the first time, specific exceptions to this general principle have been incorporated into the revised code.

Canon 517, a new canon with no precedent in the 1917 code, contains two exceptions that grew out of the experience of the shortage of priests existing in several regions of the world. It is new in church law and reflects notions of team ministry, collaboration, and pastoral service that have roots in the teaching of the Second Vatican Council. Canon 517§1 permits the diocesan bishop, when circumstances call for it, to entrust the pastoral care of one or more parishes to a group of priests jointly (*in solidum*), with one of the priests appointed as moderator of the group. The role of the moderator is to direct the joint action of the priests and answer for it to the bishop. The canon does not indicate what circumstances might call for the implementation of this arrangement, thus permitting the diocesan bishop to determine when he considers it necessary or advisable for one or more parishes in his diocese.

Canon 517§2 contains another exception. It allows the diocesan bishop, when there is a lack of priests, to entrust to a deacon, another person who is not a priest, or a community of persons who are not priests participation in the pastoral care of a parish. If the bishop does so, he must also appoint a priest who has the faculties of a pastor to direct the pastoral care.

Both the provision for a priest to be pastor of more than one parish (c. 526) and the option for a bishop to entrust the participation in the pastoral care of a parish to one who is not a priest (c. 517§2) have been implemented in many U.S. dioceses. As options for parish leadership, they call for an accurate application of the canons and attention to the precise meaning of the terms found in the law. What do these options look like and what are their ramifications for parish life and leadership?

Canon 526: Multiple Parish Pastors

Canon 526§1 is key for addressing multiple parish ministry. The canon states:

> A pastor is to have the pastoral care of only one parish; nevertheless, because of a lack of priests or other circumstances, the care of several neighboring parishes can be entrusted to the same pastor.

The canon expresses both the traditional rule of one priest for each parish and the new exception to the rule. What was once forbidden as an abuse based on avarice in earlier times, namely serving as pastor of more than one parish, is now permitted for pastoral reasons: a shortage of priests or "other circumstances."[24]

The reference to "neighboring" parishes in Canon 526§1 might be understood not to mean necessarily physically contiguous, but close enough as to make it pastorally possible for the priest to minister to both parishes. We know, however, that in some parts of our country this could mean as much as one, two, or more hours' drive between parishes. The code provides various models for pastoring multiple parishes: for example, pastor of several parishes (c. 519), pastor of one or more and administrator of one or more (c. 539), or pastor of one or more and the priest endowed with powers of a pastor (c. 517§2). No one model of multiple parish ministry fits all situations. The appropriate structure or model may evolve over time with cooperation, trust, and collaboration between leadership and the people of the affected parishes.

Since the mid- to late 1990s many bishops have restructured parishes within their dioceses, usually as strategies to address a shortage of priests. These restructuring efforts, whether resulting in closures, mergers, or consolidations, are often precipitated by demographic shifts, declining populations, financial concerns, condition and size of buildings, as well as fewer priests. Today the number one response for addressing the declining numbers of priests available for parish ministry is multiple parish pastoring.[25] It is likely that as fewer priests become available for parish ministry, the number of parishes that share a pastor will continue to grow.

Until recently little has been published addressing the impact of changes in parish structure on the priests who are experiencing them firsthand. Katarina Schuth's 2006 book, *Priestly Ministry in Multiple Parishes*,[26] provides a valuable resource on the implementation of Canon 526 and the experience of those affected by it. In this study, Schuth surveyed more than nine hundred priests who serve multiple parishes in this country; she reports on the extent of this practice and identifies successful models of leadership for maintaining the vitality of the parishes. The study also provides recommendations for the future of multiple parish ministry.

The extent to which appointing priests to serve as pastors of multiple parishes continues to be a viable solution to the availability of fewer priests for parish ministry in the future will depend on the impact of this arrangement on what it means to be a parish community; the ability of pastors to fulfill adequately their pastoral duties in all the parishes entrusted to them; the quality of the relationship between pastor, lay ecclesial ministers, and parish communities; and the effect of the physical, human, and spiritual demands on the priests assigned to these parishes.[27] The preference for this option for parish leadership, which is also the preferred option in the 1997 instruction *Ecclesiae de mysterio* of the Congregation for the Clergy,[28] continues to raise concerns regarding its impact on parish ministry and, to some extent, the structure of the particular church, for many of the reasons mentioned above.[29] Some caution that extensive use of the option of Canon 526, in which the priest focuses on providing sacramental ministry and the lay or religious pastoral associate/coordinator handles the day-to-day responsibilities, could lead to a view of the priest as a "sacramental provider who enters and exits the parish" to administer the sacraments, then moves on to another parish.[30] Careful consideration of these factors in comprehensive planning efforts and the development of diocesan policy will be critical to the future of parish ministry and the role of lay ecclesial ministers whose ministry is of utmost importance in parishes served by pastors of multiple parishes.

Parishes under Canon 517

Canon 517 offers a new solution to the church's growing pastoral needs, a solution that acknowledges the decreasing number of priests available for parish ministry as well as the responsibility to provide for the pastoral care of parishes. Canon 517 faithfully reflects the conciliar teaching on the laity by providing broadened opportunities for the participation of laypersons in the life and ministry of the church.

Canon 517§1 refers to the experience of what is commonly called "team ministry," that is, the entrusting of the pastoral care of a parish to a team of several priests *in solidum* (meaning they act as one) with one of them serving as moderator, directing the team's activity and answering to the bishop. While the notion of team ministry has roots in the gathering of the ancient *presbyterium* around the bishop,[31] its inclusion in the code as an option for parish pastoral leadership is new. In the United States, following the Second Vatican Council, several dioceses allowed experimentation in the area of team ministry. The extent to which it was successful varies from parish to parish and from team to team. Differing understandings of parish/pastoral leadership and shared responsibility as well as the matching and, in some instances, the mismatching of personalities have contributed to a diversity of experience with team ministry. Since Canon 517§1 requires all members of the team to be ordained, the decreasing number of priests in many dioceses makes this option for parish leadership somewhat less attractive.

It is the second section of Canon 517 that presents a new canonical possibility for parish leadership, namely, the possibility that a diocesan bishop is unable to assign a canonical pastor to a parish because of a scarcity of priests. In such instances, the bishop may then entrust participation in the pastoral care of the parish to a deacon, a layperson, or a community of persons with a priest supervising the pastoral care.

Canon 517§2 provides an extraordinary option for parish leadership. It states:

> If the diocesan bishop should decide that due to a dearth of priests a participation in the exercise of the pastoral care of a parish is to be entrusted to a deacon or to some other person who is not a priest or to a community of persons, he is to appoint some priest endowed with the powers and faculties of a pastor (parochus) to supervise the pastoral care.

The canon first appeared in the 1977 *schema* of the proposed code in Book II, "On the People of God." From the discussions that took place in the *coetus* (group) dealing with the topic, it seems that some of the consultors, citing the shortage of priests in many regions of the world, noted that at times it was impossible to assign a pastor for a single parish, and in such cases a single pastor was appointed for two or three parishes or a group of priests was jointly appointed for several parishes. The consultors further noted that in some instances even this was not possible, and that there might be a need to grant some share in the exercise of pastoral care to some persons "not marked with the priestly character" or to some group of such persons. When this occurs, it would be necessary to appoint a priest who enjoys the power of a proper pastor as moderator of the pastoral care.[32]

The legislative history of Canon 517§2 suggests three observations: first, Canon 517§2 provides a canonical response to a pastoral need, namely, the shortage of ordained priests; second, the positive experience of entrusting a share in the pastoral care of parishes to laymen and laywomen already taking place in several parts of the world was affirmed; and third, the role of the priest moderator evolved from that of proper (canonical) pastor who enjoyed the power of a pastor to one endowed with the powers and faculties of a pastor who supervises the pastoral care of the parish.

When implementing this option for parish leadership, certain circumstances must exist and specific conditions are to be met. The most obvious circumstance is the shortage of priests. The canon leaves to the diocesan bishop the determination of whether or not there is a shortage of priests and the responsibility to decide if and at what point the diocese will use the solution of Canon 517§2 to meet its pastoral needs.

An important condition for implementing Canon 517§2 is the requirement of a supervising priest or priest moderator. The supervising priest is not the equivalent of a proper or canonical pastor. The role of the supervising priest evolved from that of a proper pastor to a "priest endowed with the powers and faculties of a pastor." Having the powers of a pastor means he is able to perform all the functions granted by universal law to pastors, such as hearing confessions within the jurisdiction of the parish (c. 968§1), assisting at marriages within the parish (c. 1108§1), and representing the parish in all juridic affairs (c. 532). He does not, however, have a term of office or stability in office, nor is he obliged by all the obligations of a pastor such as the obligation of residency (c. 533§1) or the profession of faith (c. 833, 6°). The evolution in the role of the supervising priest of Canon 517§2 was the result of a desire on the part of the *coetus* not to restrict excessively the role and responsibilities of either the priest or the new figure entrusted with a participation in the pastoral care of the parish.[33] Canon 517§2 provides flexibility and room for adaptation to local situations and leaves many details about the roles and responsibilities of both these new figures to particular law. What does seem clear from the canon is that the legislator's main concern is the assurance that there be a priest who is responsible for each parish, and that the relationship between the bishop, the presbyterate, and the pastoral care of souls is retained.[34]

One model that has evolved in some dioceses is the appointment of two distinct figures to fulfill the "priest" requirement of Canon 517§2, the supervising priest and one who has been called the "sacramental minister," who is available to fulfill those sacramental functions in the parish that require ordination: assist at marriages, confirm adults received into the church, hear confessions, and celebrate the Eucharist.[35] Whether or not the title "sacramental minister" is the most appropriate title for this person remains a question.

If this role is distinct from that of the supervising priest, this priest might be called the presider or celebrant of the sacraments for the Canon 517§2 parish. A recent development is to identify the supervising priest as the "priest director," to emphasize his leadership role as one who directs the pastoral care of the parish.

The appointment of the deacon, layperson, or group of persons entrusted with a participation in the pastoral care of the parish is a third important consideration. How this role is to be carried out is not specified in the code, thereby making it possible for a diocese to respond to particular pastoral situations with some creativity, while always in accord with the provisions of law. This figure, sometimes called pastoral or parish life coordinator, parochial minister, pastoral administrator, pastoral leader, parish director, or resident pastoral minister,[36] is appointed by the diocesan bishop and ministers under his authority. He or she participates in the threefold functions of teaching, sanctifying, and governing in accord with the law of the church and coordinates the day-to-day operation of the parish. Initially, the vast majority of the individuals appointed to this role were women religious, though this trend has shifted from 75 percent in 1990 to 35 percent in 2008.[37]

In recent years there has been an increase in the number of deacons appointed to this position. In a 2008 study conducted by the Center for Applied Research in the Apostolate (CARA) for the Emerging Models Project, the number of parishes in the United States in which participation in pastoral care has been entrusted to a deacon rose steadily from 13 percent of the 268 parishes under Canon 517§2 in 1993 to 30 percent of the 477 parishes in 2008.[38] The same data show that the number of parishes under Canon 517§2 decreased between 2007 and 2008, perhaps due to parish mergers and a preference by some diocesan bishops to utilize the option of assigning pastors to multiple parishes rather than employing the option of Canon 517§2.[39] Future studies could assess what, if any, impact such trends might have on the future development of lay ecclesial ministry in general and on parish life coordinators in particular.

ISSUES AND CHALLENGES FOR THE FUTURE

The dramatic expansion of lay ecclesial ministry continues to develop in response to current pastoral needs and situations. Grounded in a theology of communion that recognizes the diverse gifts and manifestations of the Spirit for the building up of the church, lay ecclesial ministry "can reveal the nature of the Church itself, which is an organic and ordered communion made up of diverse parts."[40] It is in this context and spirit that questions and challenges have evolved from the implementation of new canonical arrangements for parish leadership in many dioceses of the United States over the past twenty-five years. While the various issues that have been raised regarding the implementation of the options for parish leadership and their implications for the future development of lay ecclesial ministers cover a range of perspectives, four arising from a canonical perspective are considered below.

Clarity of Roles

The language used to describe the roles involving lay ecclesial ministers serving in parish leadership is becoming increasingly significant for parish life.[41] Whether real or perceived, the lack of clarity regarding who is responsible for what, canonically and pastorally, and the blurring of roles and responsibilities often result in confusion and misunderstanding on the part of staff and the faithful of the parish. In highlighting the functions of various roles in the church, Pope Benedict XVI explained that the identity of priests and laity must be seen in light of the "essential difference between priestly ministry and the 'common priesthood.'"[42] He went on to caution that it is important to avoid the "secularization of clergy and the 'clericalization' of the laity." The development of job descriptions and the correct assignment of functions in the areas of education, pastoral services, worship, and administration are crucial to maintaining clarity regarding the responsibilities of those in parish leadership. In identifying lines of accountability, position descriptions can preclude or at least minimize the blurring of roles and functions between clergy and laity. With appropriate orientation for the priests and lay ecclesial ministers serving in parish leadership and clear expectations on the part of the bishop, parish leadership, and staff, a great deal of the potential misunderstanding, misuse, and abuse of legitimate parish leadership options can be avoided. Descriptions of roles and responsibilities are also important for the parish communities that are transitioning from a parish with a single pastor to either a parish sharing a pastor (c. 526§1) or a parish under Canon 517§2. Such information can minimize ambiguity yet maximize creativity and contribute to a better understanding of change and a richer experience of what it means to be a parish community.

Temporary versus Permanent Options

The question of the temporary versus permanent nature of Canon 517§2 is an issue that has been raised regarding the long-term use of Canon 517§2, but there is little doubt that lay ecclesial ministry will continue to develop and flourish in the church through the working of the Holy Spirit. The roles laymen and laywomen assume in the life of the church will continue to evolve in response to pastoral needs and changing circumstances. As new situations call for new solutions, laypersons will be called to exercise lay ecclesial ministries within the communion of the church and in service to mission.

Canon 517§2 came into existence as an extraordinary solution for addressing the decreasing number of priests available for parish ministry. The dearth of priests for parish ministry is a necessary condition for implementing the canon, suggesting that the intent of the canon is that once a sufficient number of priests are available, the option will cease to be implemented. The discretion of the diocesan bishop to choose the option of Canon 517§2 also suggests that the solution might be adopted by one bishop but not by his successor, or by a bishop for a particular parish at a particular time and with a different option chosen at a later time. In other words, it might be more useful to consider Canon 517§2 as an exceptional short-term initiative rather than a genuine long-term alternative for parish leadership—that is, once a parish comes under Canon 517§2 it does not necessarily mean that it will always be a Canon 517§2 parish.

This perspective would also apply to parishes served by a pastor of another parish. The code does not envision either solution as a permanent designation for parishes. This understanding was affirmed by Pope Benedict XVI in stating that "the shortage of priests must not come to be considered as a normal or typical state of affairs for the future."[43] He urges bishops to encourage new vocations to the priesthood and to assist other dioceses in need of additional pastors. Likewise, U.S. bishops participating in focus groups on the use of Canon 517§2 supported this notion, identifying the solution of Canon 517§2 as a "temporary" measure until the time when priests can be assigned as pastors.[44]

Titles for Canon 517§2 Roles

Another issue concerns the titles assigned to the various roles in parishes under Canon 517§2. While not of particular importance during the first years following the implementation of the code, job title has increasingly become a topic calling for some resolution. Titles matter; they describe or illustrate the role and functions performed by the person holding the office. The 1997 interdicasterial instruction on collaboration between the nonordained faithful and the sacred ministry of priests sought to provide guidance on the use of appropriate titles by indicating that titles such as pastor, administrator, director, or coordinator are not acceptable.[45] Around that same time, the USCCB Committee on Pastoral Practices attempted to standardize the titles used in this country but was unsuccessful, since many of the bishops wished to retain titles that were already in place in their respective dioceses. The USCCB study identified some twenty-four titles used to describe the person entrusted with participation in the pastoral care of the parish.[46] A decade later, there are more than thirty-six titles used to describe this role.[47] Today, the suitability of terminology remains an unresolved issue. Following the Ministry Summit sponsored by the Emerging Models Project in Orlando, Florida, in April 2008, one of the top recommendations from the discussion regarding the canonical option of Canon 517§2 was a request to the U.S. bishops by the more than 1,200 participants for common titles for the roles involved in Canon 517§2 parishes. While *Co-Workers* suggests that the identification of a common title for this role remains unfinished business,[48] it seems important for the future that an effort be made to identify, if not a common title, two or three titles that might be selected as appropriate designations for this new role.

Canonical Education for Lay Ecclesial Ministers

Formation for lay ecclesial ministers involved in parish leadership is a critical focus for the future. In *Co-Workers* the bishops direct their resources to those "who educate and form prospective lay ecclesial ministers," and identify ongoing formation for lay ecclesial ministers as a "permanent necessity" for enhancing their ministerial skills.[49] The bishops outline the obligation for appropriate formation and urge the development of formation programs for lay ecclesial ministers. *Co-Workers* describes the four-pronged framework for such programs: human, spiritual, intellectual, and pastoral, thereby fostering balance for personal growth and ministerial service.[50]

At the same time, the skills training, education, and competency required for certain leadership positions cannot be overlooked. A 2005 study of lay ecclesial ministers found that canonical education was one of the top educational needs identified by the participants.[51] In fact, canon law was one of the areas in which lay ecclesial ministers felt least prepared for their ministry. The same can be said for pastors who, in a separate study, identified canon law as an area for which neither they nor parish business managers were adequately prepared.[52] Education and training for seminarians as well as for deacons regarding the canonical provisions of Canon 517§2 and the skills needed for collaborative models of parish leadership will enable those who will be assigned to parishes under Canon 517§2 or multiple parish ministry to provide ecclesial leadership that promotes the building up of the parish community as a community of faith. Diocesan training programs for ministry in parishes served by lay ecclesial ministers should include canon law as one of the key components of the program. Adequate education and training for lay ecclesial ministers, including knowledge of the canonical provisions governing parish pastoral leadership and their application, warrant serious consideration by those responsible for the formation and education of lay ecclesial ministers. Similarly, providing canonical education regarding the provisions of Canon 517§2 and its implementation for those parishes under Canon 517§2, as well as for the faithful of dioceses in which this leadership option is implemented, can serve to increase understanding of the option and alleviate confusion and apprehension regarding parish pastoral leadership.

CONCLUSION

Co-Workers in the Vineyard of the Lord provides a valuable service to the church in general and to lay ecclesial ministry in particular. In inviting "local adaptation, application, and implementation to achieve consistency where possible and to encourage diversity where appropriate,"[53] the U.S. bishops have set in place a process for ordering and integrating lay ecclesial ministry into the life of the local church where many of the questions and concerns will be addressed considering the needs, resources, and experience of the faith community. This exploration of the theology and experience of lay ecclesial ministry, as it continues to unfold and develop in the church, and particularly as it impacts parish leadership roles, will necessarily call for further reflection and dialogue from the perspective of canon law. Such reflection will require the collaboration and cooperation of many—theologians, canonists, bishops, lay ecclesial ministers, men and women, clergy and lay—all called to devise creative and reasoned responses to the experience and praxis of lay ecclesial ministry.

NOTES

1. U.S. Conference of Catholic Bishops, *Co-Workers in the Vineyard of the Lord: A Resource for Guiding the Development of Lay Ecclesial Ministry* (Washington, DC: USCCB, 2005).

2. For a historical overview of research by the USCCB, see chapter 1, by Richard McCord, in this volume. In addition, the USCCB commissioned a study of the growth in lay ministry by the late Monsignor Philip J. Murnion and the National Pastoral Life Center. The results were first published in *New Parish Ministers* (New York: National Pastoral Life Center, 1992). Subsequent studies were conducted by Murnion in 1999 and, following Murnion's death, by David DeLambo in 2005.

3. USCCB, *Co-Workers*, 6.

4. See especially, "Understanding the Realities in Light of Theology and Church Teaching," in USCCB, *Co-Workers*, 17–26.

5. This invitation was reaffirmed by Bishop Gerald Kicanas, chairman of the subcommittee, in a 2006 address to the National Association of Lay Ministry in Cleveland in "Why and How Lay Ecclesial Ministers Matter," *Origins* 36, no. 9 (July 20, 2006): 138. For a canonical analysis of *Co-Workers*, see Rose McDermott, *"Co-Workers in the Vineyard of the Lord*: A Canonical Analysis," *The Jurist* 67 (2007): 432–60.

6. Preface to the Latin edition, *Code of Canon Law Latin-English Edition*: New English Translation (Washington, DC: Canon Law Society of America, 1998), xxxvi. All English translations of the canons of the Code of Canon Law are taken from this text.

7. Pope Benedict XVI, "Address to the Study Congress of the Pontifical Council for Legislative Texts," January 25, 2008, printed in the Canon Law Society of Great Britain and Ireland (CLSGB&I) *Newsletter* 154 (June 2008): 21.

8. Pope Benedict XVI, "Address to the Study Congress of the Pontifical Council," 20.

9. USCCB, *Co-Workers*, 6; compare Kicanas, "Lay Ecclesial Ministers," 138.

10. For various listings, see Francis Morrisey, "Twenty-Five Years of the 1983 Code: Reflections on the Past, Thoughts on the Future," *CLSA Proceedings* 70 (2008): 2–5. See also John A. Alesandro, "The Code: 25 Year Reflection on the Past and Looking to the Future," *CLSA Proceedings* 69 (2007): 17.

11. Center for Applied Research in the Apostolate, *Emerging Communities of Consecrated Life in the United States, 2006* (Washington, DC: CARA, 2006).

12. Pew Hispanic Center, "Changing Faiths: Latinos and the Transformation of American Religion," 2007), 2, available at http://pewhispanic.org/reports/report/php?ReportID=75. (accessed April 30, 2007).

13. See CARA, "Frequently Requested Catholic Church Statistics," 2009, available at http://cara.georgetown.edu/bulletin/index.htm (accessed March 12, 2010).

14. Alesandro, "The Code," 18.

15. Preface to the Latin edition, *Code of Canon Law Latin-English Edition*, xxxvii.

16. Canon 230§1 states that only men can be admitted to the ministries of lector and acolyte on a stable basis.

17. See, for example, David DeLambo, *Lay Parish Ministers: A Study of Emerging Leadership* (New York: National Pastoral Life Center, 2005), 19 and 44.

18. Pope John Paul II, "The Vocation of the Parish," January 25, 1997, address to the third group of bishops of France on the *ad limina* visit. Reprinted in *Church* 13, no. 2 (Summer 1997): 43–46.

19. John Paul II, "Vocation of the Parish."

20. James Coriden, *The Parish in Catholic Tradition: History, Theology and Canon Law* (Mahwah, NJ: Paulist Press, 1997), 59. See also John A. Janicki, "Parishes, Pastors, and Parochial Vicars," in *The Code of Canon Law: Text and Commentary*, edited by J. Coriden et al. (Mahweh, NJ: Paulist Press, 1985), 415.

21. John Paul II, "The Vocation of the Parish."

22. Another notable change is the establishment of required and recommended structures of participation at the diocesan and parish levels that reflect the conciliar teaching on communion.

23. For a fuller explanation of alternatives for providing pastoral care in parishes, see James Coriden, "Parish Pastoral Leaders: Structures and Questions," *The Jurist* 67 (2007): 466–67.

24. See Canon 460 of the 1917 Code of Canon Law; see also John Lynch, "Parochial Ministry in the New Code of Canon Law," *The Jurist* 42 (1982): 395.

25. See Mark Mogilka and Kate Wiskus, "The Multiple Parish Pastoring Project," Best Practices of Parish Leadership: National Ministry Summit, April 21, 2008, available at http://www.emergingmodels.org/article.cfm?id=70 (accessed March 12, 2010).

26. Katarina Schuth, *Priestly Ministry in Multiple Parishes* (Collegeville, MN: Liturgical Press, 2006).

27. Walter Kasper, *Leadership in the Church* (New York: Crossroad Publishing, 2003), 68. See also Schuth, *Priestly Ministry in Multiple Parishes*, 166–73.

28. Congregation for the Clergy et al., "On Some Questions Concerning the Cooperation of the Lay Faithful with the Ministry of Priests," *Ecclesiae de mysterio*, (August 15, 1997): art. 4,1,b, *Origins* 27, no. 24 (November 27, 1997): 404.

29. See James Coriden, "Pastoral Ministry in the Parish: A Theological Consensus and Practical Issues," in *Institutiones Iuris Ecclesiae I*, Essays in honor of Sister Rose McDermott, SSJ, edited by Robert J. Kaslyn, SJ (Washington DC: Catholic University of America, 2010), 112.

30. See Cardinal Roger Mahony, "Fostering the Baptismal Priesthood in the Year of Priests," *Origins* 39, no. 17 (October 1, 2009): 279. See also Benedict XVI, "The Role of Priests Is Irreplaceable," address to prelates from the National Conference of Brazil on their *ad limina* visit, Vatican Information Service, September 21, 2009.

31. Janicki, "Parishes, Pastors and Parochial Vicars," 417.

32. *Communicationes* 8 (1976): 24.

33. *Communicationes* 13 (1981): 149.

34. See John A. Renken, "The Canonical Implications of Canon 517§2: Parishes without Resident Pastors?" *CLSA Proceedings* 50 (1988): 256–57. This requirement is reaffirmed in the 2004 *Directory for the Pastoral Ministry of Bishops*, which states that in these situations "it is necessary to establish clearly and concretely, not simply juridically, that it is the priest who is in charge of the parish and it is he who is answerable to the Bishop for its governance while the deacon, religious and laypersons assist him with their collaboration." Congregation for Bishops, *Apostolorum Successorum Directory for the Pastoral Ministry of Bishops* (Rome: Libreria Editrice Vaticana, 2004), 215.

35. For a fuller explanation of this experience, see Alexander Anthony Vadakumthala, *Lay Person as Caretaker of A Parish: A Juridical and Theological Study of Canon 517§2* (Roma: Pontificia Universitas Urbaniana, 1992), 194–99. For the findings from a study conducted in 1987 on the implementation of Canon 517 in the United States, see John A. Renken, "Canonical Issues in the Pastoral Care of Parishes without Priests," *The Jurist* 47 (1987): 512–13.

36. CARA reports that the title most often used for this role is parish life coordinator. See *CARA Report* (Summer 2009): 11.

37. See CARA *Report* (Summer 2009): 11.

38. See Mark Gray, "Deacons Entrusted with the Pastoral Care of a Parish according to Canon 517.2," available at http://www.emergingmodels.org/article.cfm?id=49 (accessed March 12, 2010), and *CARA Report* (Summer 2009): 11.

39. See Mogilka and Wiskus, "The Multiple Parish Pastoring Project." For a discussion of the preference for deacons in parish leadership roles, see Coriden, "Parish Pastoral Leaders," 476–78.

40. Aurelie Hagstrom, "Lay Ecclesial Ministry and Questions of Authorization," *Origins* 37, no. 7 (June 28, 2007): 108.

41. See Coriden, "Pastoral Ministry in the Parish," 14–15.

42. Benedict XVI, "The Role of Priests Is Irreplaceable," Vatican Information Service, September 21, 2009.

43. Benedict XVI, "The Role of Priests Is Irreplaceable."

44. Mary Bendyna, Tricia C. Bruce, Mary L. Gautier, "Listening to the Spirit: Bishops and Parish Life Coordinators," March 17, 2008, available at http://www. emergingmodels.org/article.cfm?id=42 (accessed March 12, 2010).

45. Congregation for the Clergy et al., "On Some Questions Concerning the Cooperation of the Lay Faithful," *Ecclesiae de mysterio* (August 15, 1997), also *Origins* 27, no. 24 (November 27, 1997): 403, 408.

46. Development of a National Title for Persons Appointed to Parishes in Accord with Canon 517§2: USCCB Implementation of Canon 517§2: Background Information, for the November 2000 meeting of the United States Conference of Catholic Bishops.

47. CARA *Special Report* (Summer 2005): 2.

48. See USCCB, *Co-Workers*, 67, in which the bishops indicate that the designation of a common title is beyond the scope of the document.

49. USCCB, *Co-Workers*, 14, 51.

50. USCCB, *Co-Workers*, 33–35.

51. DeLambo, *Lay Parish Ministers*, 79 and 149.

52. See Charles Zech and Robert Miller, study on "The Spiritual and Professional Development Needs of Catholic Parish Ministers," CARA *Report* (Spring 2006): 11.

53. USCCB, *Co-Workers*, 6.

Part III

MINING OUR SPIRITUAL TRADITION

8

Spirit Guides and Table Companions: Saints as Models for Lay Ecclesial Ministers

Regina Bechtle, S.C.

> You are glorified in your saints, for their glory is the crowning of your gifts. In their lives on earth you give us an example. In our communion with them, you give us their friendship. In their prayer for the Church you give us strength and protection. This great company of witnesses spurs us on to victory, to share their prize of everlasting glory, through Jesus Christ our Lord.[1]

Saints span centuries and cultures. They speak in a multitude of tongues and appear in both genders, all ages, and a variety of hues. In every century of the Christian era, in endlessly fascinating incarnations, they portray God's love, goodness, intelligence, compassion, openness, humility, integrity, and beauty. They make the gospel of Jesus Christ wondrously, puzzlingly, sometimes annoyingly concrete. They are martyrs, ascetics, pilgrims, warriors, mystics, theologians, artists, humanists, activists, outsiders—and more.[2] They are the saints, our sisters and brothers in Christ.

The canonized saints have long served the Christian community as models and paradigms. We think of them as our "dream team," our big-time winners. They prove that mere mortals *can* get it right; they cheer on the rest of us who plod our way toward the full vision of God that is our calling and our birthright. They remind us that Paul's salutation to the Christians of the church at Corinth—"You who have been sanctified in Christ Jesus, called to be holy"[3]—is addressed to us as well.

In our churches and our psyches, Catholics often enshrine the saints on pedestals, at a respectful and respectable distance from the mundane muck of our own lives. Yet we also address them with tender familiarity in times of anxiety, need, and joy. "Saint Joseph, help us sell our house." "Saint

Anthony, find my lost driver's license." "Saint Monica, bring my daughter back to the church." We tend to approach the saints with a unique mixture of reverence and confidence. It is as though we know viscerally that in God's family, we who are saints in the making do indeed qualify as "fellow citizens with the saints."

Baptized into Christ, we have been called by God to a new relationship with the Trinity and summoned to a new way of life with others in the world. Lest we lose our way, we need the wisdom of these trusted family elders who have walked the road before us. We can imagine ourselves sitting with them at the banquet table of God's abundance, members of a Spirit-contoured community where all are truly welcome.

But saints are more than our good buddies and "best friends forever." Viewed against the backdrop of their times, saints can shed light on the challenges of our own lives and illuminate the way forward. They can revive our flagging spirits in times of difficulty and keep us focused in hope on God's future, God's dream that we long for but do not yet see.[4] In the words of theologian Elizabeth Johnson, "Rich connection to the great historical company of the past functions as a source of religious energy for the struggle now and also as a pointer to a different future in view of the gospel promise, tested and witnessed to in so many lives."[5]

Among our contemporary struggles and challenges, the arena of the church's organizational life presents particularly thorny issues for lay ecclesial ministers. As they strive to be faithful disciples, they need to navigate shifting sands within a community of faith that is also and unmistakably an institutional reality. We all live as members and participants in a church that wounds and is wounded, in a world that divides and is divided, in communities that disappoint and are disappointed.

So too did the saints in the local and universal churches of their day. Figures like Francis and Clare of Assisi in thirteenth-century Umbria, Angela Merici in sixteenth-century Italy, Vincent de Paul and Louise de Marillac in seventeenth-century France, Elizabeth Seton in early nineteenth-century America, and Frederic Ozanam and Rosalie Rendu in mid-nineteenth-century France understood that following Christ involved more than cultivation of an interior life. Their Christian calling propelled them to express and embody their relationship with Christ in the world to which they, like Christ, were sent. Then and now, that world involved principalities and powers, bureaucracies and structures, meetings and agendas, buildings and money, disagreements and compromises, intrigue and corruption—and grace in it all.[6]

How does one uncover the face of grace? How does one discern the Spirit's leading? How does one distinguish social sin from social grace? How does one determine the concrete choices that lead persons and communities toward, not away from, God? How do we collaborate with God to create communities and institutions that look and act more like God's dream? And how do we do that in organizations that are anything but perfect, and with persons who are anything but ideal?

This chapter encourages lay ecclesial ministers to enlist the saints not merely as wisdom guides for personal piety, but also as companions and coaches for addressing these and similar questions for discerning the Spirit in organizational life. I will first explore the concept of community as a foundational pillar of Christian spirituality and note the connection of community to institutions. Then I will draw upon the wisdom of several organizationally savvy saints who understood how to find grace around the table of societal and ecclesial institutions. Lastly, the example of Mary, mother of Jesus, first among the saints, will remind us that these times of crucial challenge are not the first such time in the life of the church.

COMMUNAL FOUNDATIONS

Immersed as we are in the highly individualistic culture of the twenty-first-century developed world, we might need a reminder that community matters profoundly in our Judeo-Christian faith view, and why that is so.

In the section from Acts read on Pentecost Sunday we listen as the Spirit fills the assembled company of believers and sends them out speaking in foreign tongues. Just after this, Peter stands up to address the crowd. These preachers are not drunk, Peter says, and he quotes the prophet Joel to interpret the meaning of this strange happening. No, he says, this is a sign that God is doing something new in our midst. This is a sign that the Messiah, the Christ, God's anointed one, has come among us. God's promises have indeed been fulfilled. The time of God's *shalom* has come, the time of harmony, of justice, of right relationships, the time when all will share in God's abundance. Look, see, says Peter, as Joel did before him, God is pouring out the Spirit upon *all* people. God is creating a beloved community.[7]

The God of our Judeo-Christian belief has an undisguised bias for community. The story of God's relationship with us as revealed in scripture proclaims that salvation happens to us as a people. We are meant to live, grow, build a better world, and make our way to God together, not separately. Without a doubt that process can be messy, slow, and inefficient. It flies in the face of our deep-seated belief that if you want anything done right you have to do it yourself.

But that does not diminish the power of the word of God: "I will be your God, and you will be my *people*."[8] It does not negate the dream that Jesus called "the reign of God." That dream was all about a new way of being in relationship, a transformed community, a new kind of family, a way of connecting and collaborating at the deepest level imaginable. Jesus never tired of talking about it, showing us what it might look like, and demonstrating how we must live if that dream is ever to be realized. Jesus' dream images a community where everyone belongs—sick, prisoners, poor, immigrants, the forgotten, the powerless, those on the margins. Jesus' dream takes flesh in the community's life in time and space, especially in those quintessential servants of the Good News, the saints.

Community Begins with God's Own Life

At times, we *feel* the power of community. In the silence and song of a meaningful liturgy; when a group finally reaches consensus after wrestling with differing points of view; at a wedding, anniversary, or jubilee celebration; when an organization bids farewell to a valued employee or mobilizes to aid a colleague in crisis, we sense the presence of our God who loves community. In inexpressible but real ways, we feel ourselves drawn into the communal circle, which is the life of the triune God.

The famous icon of the Trinity by the fifteenth-century Russian artist Rublev[9] gives us a glimpse of a God who lives a life of profound intercommunion. At the very heart of God, in other words, we find community. We find a ceaseless, dynamic movement of giving and receiving, a total self-giving that does not diminish identity but rather enhances it. The Trinity offers us an example of what we might call "mindful mutuality" in community.

Community is another name for the energy of God's Spirit, moving in and around us, transforming and reshaping us. We live and move and have our being within this vast field of Spirit energy. In moments when we are in touch with our deep desires, we know that we long to be in harmony with this movement, to be a clear channel for the divine thrust toward community making that is God's preferred way with human beings.

Theologians who reflect on the New Testament's understanding of what it means to be a saint remind us that community is the soil where holiness grows: "The whole church is a communion of saints. Saints are all the living people who form the eschatological community, chosen and beloved, called, gifted, and sent by God. . . . An individual may be regarded as a saint or holy one, but only in virtue of belonging to the community."[10]

Community is more than a concept; it always needs to find concrete, tangible expression in institutions, organizations, structures, and groups. The age we live in profoundly distrusts institutions, often for quite valid reasons. Yet this attitude can diminish our sense of common life and purpose. The Catholic worldview, by contrast, orients us to view institutions, those often unlikely carriers of the Spirit—parishes, schools, teams, diocesan offices, health and social service agencies, government bureaucracies—as places of possibility, open to the action of grace as well as the influence of evil.

Many Levels of Community

Community describes places of belonging, places where God's loving compassion becomes visible. In a world starving for connection and communion, we are called to live a life of community on many levels. Beyond the family, our primary place of belonging, community finds many other incarnations.

There is the community that we find in our ministry—the colleagues who serve with us, the people whom we serve. There is the parish or church community where we worship; the civic community of our village, city, state, department, or country; the catholic/Catholic community of our church; the global community of which we are all members, especially in a world where we can communicate instantaneously, regardless of distance. And there is the fertile and fragile community of Earth, in which we humans are learning to find our place, interdependent with all forms of life. All of these kinds of communities serve as channels for the Spirit's creative power, and all of them necessarily find expression in concrete institutions and structures.

Some saints have a genius for creating community, building bridges of understanding and compassion. Other saints raise their prophetic voices, witnessing that spirituality has a public face and requires passionate action, pointing to places where church and society have fallen short of Jesus' inclusive dream of community. The symbol of the communion of saints glows with "prophetic luminosity," spurring us on "to a new life of transformed relationships among all the friends of God and prophets."[11]

We turn now to an exploration of several aspects of contemporary institutional life where the saints can offer wisdom and perspective, as together we sit at the common table where Jesus welcomes all seekers of wisdom.

BEYOND DUALISM: SAINTS AS GUIDES IN THE WAY OF "BOTH-AND"

Some saints have the gift of ferocious single-mindedness. Simon Stylites, perched on a pillar in the desert of fourth-century Syria, comes to mind, along with reformers and crusaders like Joan of Arc. Undistracted by shades of gray, their focus on a cause, a goal, a tenet of faith, or a course of action is clear. They live in a landscape of black and white, either-or.

It seems that fewer and fewer situations in today's church and society benefit from this kind of approach that entertains no alternative possibilities. I suggest that a "both-and" spirituality, deeply rooted in Catholic tradition, better fits life in a world and church where diversity is a given but is not always easy to negotiate in practical terms.

Among saints skilled in "both-and" living, consider Saint Francis of Assisi. Though unswerving in his mystical passion for God and his pursuit of radical poverty, Francis in the thirteenth century received an unforgettable answer to his own version of a dilemma as old as the Pharisee's question to Jesus: "Which commandment in the Law is the greatest?"[12] As the story goes, Francis worried that his love of creation and of his dear friend Clare and her sisters diminished his relationship with the God whom alone he was meant to love. When Francis asked for forgiveness, God is said to have replied with a smile, "O Francis, what can I forgive? I love the same things as you"[13].

The Sufi tradition tells a similar story. At the time of evening prayer, a group of Muslim pilgrims on their way to Mecca faced east, toward the holy city. Only the Sufi master with them turned west, toward God, he said. The others, upset, chided him. "Your feet are pointing toward God," they said—a sign of disrespect. "Sorry," he replied. "Help me to place my feet in a direction that does *not* face God"[14].

Saints teach us that all love is one. They embody Jesus' teaching that love of God and love of one's neighbor constitute one single great and integrated command. Both loves flow from one source: the Spirit of God's own love, poured into our hearts.

As we mature in life with God and others, spiritual sages tell us, we are invited to grow beyond a dualistic type of thinking that compartmentalizes people and ideas into "either-or," "us or them" categories. Many of Jesus' sayings and parables make us uncomfortable because they fly in the face of our "either-or" logic and challenge us to bring seeming opposites together. "Love your enemies" (Matt. 5:44) is perhaps the most striking example.[15] The "both-and" realm of mystery and paradox provides more hospitable soil for mercy and forgiveness to thrive.

In a world where divisiveness grows ever more toxic and civility is in short supply in both political and ecclesial discourse, a "both-and" spirituality that integrates love of God and love of neighbor, that seeks to create coalitions and build bridges, will surely better serve today's lay ecclesial ministers than a mindset wedded to rigid dichotomies and dualistic thinking.

Frédéric Ozanam (1813–1853) is another holy friend who followed a "both-and" path. His way to holiness joined head and heart, created personal and structural responses to poverty, and sought to break down walls between people rather than cement divisions. During a half century of radical social and political change in France, Ozanam not only brought his formidable intellect to bear on the injustices he saw in French society, but he also met the poor face to face and created effective organizations to meet their needs.

A student of law and history who later taught literature at the Sorbonne, Ozanam was shocked to learn that in the Paris of the 1830s, 65 percent of the population was poor. He analyzed the root of the problem as a clash between conflicting forces, the spirit of materialistic self-interest evident in the growing middle class and the Christian spirit of sacrifice for the common good of all. His solution was to build bridges of understanding amid the class struggle, "if not to prevent at least to soften the encounter," he wrote. Being young and middle class carried with it the obligation, he believed, to act "as mediators which our status as Christians renders compulsory."[16]

Not afraid to expose himself to different ways of thinking in his search for truth, Ozanam studied world religions, Hebrew, and Sanskrit. He was deeply loyal to the church, but wanted it to speak a language that touched people's hearts rather than turned them off. As a member of a student discussion club, he set out to present the radical message of the gospel persuasively and attractively to his companions.

One day a heckler accused the earnest intellectuals of being all talk and no action, when the poor were suffering all around them. Ozanam took the challenge to heart. On his twentieth birthday he and several friends founded the Conference of Charity to seek out the poor in their homes and to offer them material and spiritual help. An intrepid Daughter of Charity, Rosalie Rendu (1786–1856), introduced them to poor families whom she had been serving for decades in Paris. A bridge builder in her own right, Rosalie mentored the young men in providing respectful, nonjudgmental, direct service to those most in need. The movement that we now know as the Society of Saint Vincent de Paul spread like wildfire.[17]

Ozanam saw what was, knew it was not the way God wanted it to be, and accepted his responsibility to say and do something about it. He chose to move beyond sterile finger pointing to purposeful action for the common good, rooted in personal spirituality. His words ring as true in our world as in his own:

"We are not blessed with two separate lives," Ozanam wrote, "one for seeking the truth and the other for putting it into practice."[18] With the one life that was God's gift to him, he blended both intellectual acumen and practical charity. Without diluting Catholicism's message, he allowed its inherent truth and beauty to shine; he met his opponents with civility and without rancor or ridicule. He sought to bridge the gap between rich and poor in both theory and practice, to reconcile rather than to divide.

The spirit of "both-and" is difficult. It invites us to hold in creative tension the apparent opposites of rich and poor, head and heart, action and prayer, person and society, solitude and community, individual and institution, love of God and love of the neighbor, the now and the not yet. Today, as they confront the widening gap between rich and poor in our world, lay ecclesial ministers seek to present the church's social teaching, to strengthen channels of solidarity, and to enlist people for direct service to their needy sisters and brothers. As they grapple with personal and ecclesial challenges in their ministry they will find Ozanam and Rendu solid friends and guides along the path of "both-and."

BEYOND DISILLUSIONMENT:
SAINTS AS GUIDES IN TIMES OF INSTITUTIONAL COLLAPSE

As they serve the Spirit embodied in today's church, lay ecclesial ministers see all too clearly the deep cracks in its institutional façade. Indeed, as scandals surface, as mismanagement becomes manifest, as structures once deemed irreproachable are revealed as flawed and fallible, and as economic pressures or power politics push departments, programs, or agencies to shrink or close, profound disillusionment can set in.

Without minimizing the particularity of our pain in the contemporary church, history reveals many other eras when the all-too-human face of the *ecclesia semper reformanda* took center stage. Saints who lived through times like these can steer us through the unique minefield of our own moment in history. They offer us a feast of wisdom, integrity, and common sense at the tables of life, be they in the boardroom, the faculty lounge, the parish meeting room, or the church sanctuary.

In the church of the fourteenth century, Saint Catherine of Siena (1347–1380) spoke out vehemently against corruption, yet she tempered her prophetic words with Christ's own charity. She advised her contemporaries not just to despise the sins of those clerics who gave scandal, but also to lift the same clerics to God through prayer, without judgment, asking God to cover them with charity.

Closer to our own era, the lifetime of Saint Elizabeth Ann Bayley Seton (1774–1821) spanned the formative years of the new American republic and its expanding Catholic population. In turbulent times not unlike our own, Elizabeth experienced both the beauty and comfort of the church and its growing pains. She met virulent prejudice from unsympathetic family and friends and lived through an 1806 riot that nearly destroyed the only Catholic church in New York City. She knew of parishes split by governance conflicts between lay trustees and clerics and scandal brought about by poorly qualified or dissolute priests.

Elizabeth, a model for multitaskers, lay and religious, fulfilled several vocations: wife, mother of five, widow, convert, educator, and foundress of the Sisters of Charity, the first native religious community for women begun in the United States. Professing her faith as a Catholic, she claimed the church as her home, her place of belonging, her ark of refuge. Its sacraments fed her soul and strengthened her for the hard work of managing and motivating a group of women gathered in community for service.

The Sisters of Charity in America followed a new model of holiness in the world, different from nuns in a cloister. Often her advisors stepped on one another's toes—and hers, too—as they differed over questions of authority, governance, and mission. In the first month of the community's existence, one of her priest superiors almost destroyed the community by his heavy-handed directive that forbade correspondence with the sisters' favorite spiritual director. When another superior let it be known that he intended to remove Elizabeth as mother of the community and replace her with one of his own protégées, she did not hesitate to appeal to the higher authority of Archbishop John Carroll: "If my own happiness was only in question I should say how good is the cross for me; this is my opportunity to ground myself in patience and perseverance, . . . but as the good our Almighty God may intend to do by means of this community may be very much impeded by the present state of things it is absolutely necessary you . . . should be made acquainted with it before the evil is irreparable."[19]

Saints like Elizabeth Seton remind us that holiness does not require us to ignore ineptitude or to act like doormats before blatant injustice. She did not hesitate to speak her mind to authorities when she had a different perception of how to meet the needs before her, or when she believed the good of the community and the integrity of its mission was at stake.

Once, the sloppily prepared sermon of a young priest so disturbed her that she confronted him with a firm reprimand: "Do you remember a priest holds the honor of God on his lips? . . . If you will not study and prepare while young, what when you are old?"[20] Yet even as she held herself, others, and the church that she loved to a high standard, Elizabeth had the saving grace of a forgiving spirit. "Carry those who give you pain in your heart before God," she instructed her fellow sisters, "and think of their virtues instead of their faults."[21]

Sometimes being an agent of forgiveness means reaching across a hostile divide and extending mercy to those who have wronged us. In a small Amish town in Pennsylvania in the fall of 2006, a disturbed man burst into a schoolhouse, killed five young girls and shot five others, then killed himself. The world watched in wonder as the families forgave this man who took their daughters from them. Members of the Amish community went to his burial service. A year later, the whole community donated money to the killer's widow and her three young children. The painful scars still remain among the Amish, but they give profound witness to the power of a forgiving community.

Theologian Roberto Goizueta reflects on the paradox that those who are most sinned against, from whom we might expect the fiercest anger—the poor, the oppressed, victims of violence—are often the very ones who humble us with the depth of their hospitality and forgiveness. This mystery, he finds, is rooted in the logic-defying stance of reconciliation that Jesus Christ embodied in his very person. Jesus' church is called to be a forgiving community."

Sometimes being an agent of forgiveness means finding courage to befriend those who think or act differently, or who may not welcome us. Timothy Radcliffe warns that "a consequence of the conflicting fundamentalisms of our time is that those who are different easily become not just strangers but enemies with whom it is impossible to talk."[22] In 1996 the late Cardinal Joseph Bernardin of Chicago prophetically recognized that "unnecessarily polarizing differences among church leaders and members hinder efforts to build the church community and to carry out its mission." He initiated the Catholic Common Ground Initiative (CCGI) as a call to renewed and respectful dialogue within the church and offered a working framework for such dialogue.[23] To this day, hundreds of Catholics have adopted the CCGI process and others like it. They find that they grow in understanding of the humanity and goodness of those who hold positions opposed to their own and in commitment to seek out areas of common agreement as starting points for resolving differences. Among the lessons she learned from her life and ministry as a theologian, the late Monika Hellwig included the key principle that "conflict is part of growth and the shaping of tradition, but that hatred and rejection of those who differ need not be."[24]

In times of institutional collapse, the examples of the saints can steer us to claim courage to find our voice, speak our truth, and seek common ground, and to offer forgiveness to those who have hurt or wronged us. Then, at the table where we had tasted only disillusionment, we may be able to find room for renewed hope.

BEYOND COMPETITION:
SAINTS AS GUIDES TO CREATIVE COLLABORATION

In the human institutions of church and society, personalities clash, turf battles erupt, and egos get bruised as a matter of course. Church ministers, no strangers to the effects of original sin, yet aspire to a different standard of collaboration rooted in Jesus' commandment to love one another as he has loved us, and Paul's vision of the one body whose members display diverse gifts.[25] They seek to create tables where all are welcome and their diverse gifts are celebrated.

Among the saints are many who model ministerial partnerships. They learned how to respect and blend one another's unique gifts in service of the mission of Jesus. Two such partners are Vincent de Paul (1581–1660) and Louise de Marillac (1591–1660). When they first met, they were an unlikely pair. Louise was well born and highly educated; Vincent was from a peasant family in the south of France. At first, Louise was repulsed to think of receiving spiritual direction from him. Soon she grew to respect the ways that God's Spirit worked through him, and he came to value her as a partner and collaborator.

In 1617, in a rural parish in France, Vincent came face to face with the needs of the sick poor and was moved to action. He saw that plenty of kind-hearted persons were willing to assist, but their goodwill lacked organization. So he started lay, parish-based Confraternities of Charity. The structure spread quickly through the towns and villages, but after ten years, some local groups were falling apart, losing their zeal. In Louise, Vincent recognized a highly intelligent and perceptive woman, a natural organizer and leader. He sent her traveling throughout France as a kind of supervisor to meet with the local Charities, assess their status, and make recommendations. And so began a thirty-six-year partnership that bore immense fruit.

The two differed greatly in temperament. Vincent was a visionary dreamer, intuitive yet deliberate, given to waiting upon providence. Louise was a planner, rational, responsible, persuasive, outcome-oriented, given to control. One commentator notes that Louise usually had to push Vincent "to tend to details, keep on schedule, make decisions, and practice tolerance," while he in turn tried to keep her focused on God's goodness and provident care, instead of yielding to her tendency to see herself, others, and the work before her in a gloomy light.[26]

Honoring the unique gifts of one's colleagues is not always easy. A recent study found that 80 percent of the time and energy expended by U.S. companies is devoted to personnel concerns. Few situations put us in touch with limitations as does the effort to work side by side, day by day, with other people.

As one theologian noted, "God delights in diversity. Why do we humans have such a hard time with it?"[27] Collaborative leadership in ministry requires us to face the humbling reality of our own less-than-perfect selves. Then we can meet the flaws of others—the splinters in their eyes, to borrow a scriptural image—with compassion. Louise could supervise her sisters effectively and motivate them to even greater effort because she had first faced and accepted her own limits. She often tempered her critique of her followers' personal and ministerial shortcomings with a disarming admission of her own failings. As one who always had to monitor her workaholic temperament, Louise undoubtedly drew from personal experience when she advised the superioress of the motherhouse to "watch over herself so that her heavy workload does not cause her stress. This makes it difficult for the sisters to approach her and difficult for her to speak cordially with them."[28]

Open and direct communication makes all the difference in ministry. Vincent de Paul told the leadership council of the Daughters of Charity how important it was to have close and open communication with one another because it fostered their unity of heart. Vincent also championed the virtue of simplicity as a hallmark of the two communities of women and men that he founded. To act with simplicity, he advised them, was not to be swayed by "the spirit of duplicity" but to "tell both the good and the bad, just as they are."[29]

Straightforward communication with our colleagues and those whom we serve and an observable congruence between our words and our actions nurture collaboration. As we practice simplicity, we will gradually become less ensnared by human respect and find courage to raise our voices against individual and institutional hardness of heart wherever we meet it.

The discipline and blessing of creative collaboration extends also to those whom we serve. Who among us does not cherish a store of memorable lessons gleaned from students, clients, those whom we imagine to be the beneficiaries of our ministry? Ministers—lay, vowed religious, or clerical—who recognize that they do not have all the answers are wise indeed. People who are poor, sick, or otherwise on society's margins have much to teach us about things that really matter: trust in God, hope, generosity, caring, serenity. Louise sought to develop this ministerial awareness in her sisters. By staying close to the poor, bearing their pains with them, and providing whatever help they could, she told the sisters, they would keep their priorities straight and their hearts serene in the face of suffering that they could not relieve. Saints like Louise teach us that "living at the center" where we co-labor with God minimizes the "need to protect the circumference of feelings and needs."[30]

Saints like Vincent and Louise understood that effective ministry draws upon communal energy. Much as we admire the exploits of individual mendicants, missionaries, and martyrs, we know that Christian ministry is not about being a "Lone Ranger." Vincent and Louise bequeathed this conviction to the organizations they founded in seventeenth-century France. After the priests of Vincent's Congregation of the Mission touched hearts by their mission preaching, they needed the lay Confraternities of Charity to sustain their good work in the parishes. The works of charity needed the resources provided by the wealthy Ladies of Charity, who in turn needed the young, strong village girls of the Daughters of Charity to carry soup to the hovels of the poor. The Daughters of Charity, who did not have a script to follow for their new, challenging way of life outside the restrictions of cloister, needed one another. They needed one another's wisdom, humor, inspiration; they even needed the witness of one another's struggle to be faithful to the demands of their life.

Like administrators, supervisors, and planners of today who try to coordinate the gifts of all for the good of all, our saints recognized that the whole is more than the sum of its parts. Vincent de Paul exhorted the Daughters of Charity to work together as "one body in several persons, united with the same end in view for the love of God."[31] Sitting around the table in service of the mission requires a coordinated focus; personal and institutional limitations and differences in personality, work preference, or leadership style, though significant, ought not to throw roadblocks in the path of our common commitment.

BEYOND RIGIDITY:
HOLY STUBBORNNESS AND HOLY SUPPLENESS

The work of ecclesial ministry happens around tables of many shapes and sizes. The intimidatingly long, narrow, and oak-solid kind, the comfortable kitchen table, the polished and uncluttered corporate model, the round meeting-room variety that always seems to have room for yet another person, the makeshift plywood carton on the sidewalk, the folding table that can be moved in an instant, the weathered coffee table that holds everyone's stories—each table calls for different ministerial skills and stances. All the tables, like all the ministries, converge on the one central Eucharistic table where the community gathers in worship and communion.

Moving between and among these many tables of ministry demands more than a roadmap. "Keep your eyes on the prize," says the civil rights anthem of the 1950s. In Jesus' words, "Seek first—set your hearts on—the reign of God." For "where your treasure is, there will your heart be also."[32] Ministers need a firm fix on their ultimate mission, along with a spirit of adventurous adaptability. Many of the saints were virtuosos in this balancing act.

The Mission Belongs First to God

With graced wisdom, the saints understand both that Christ's mission calls for our highest and best efforts, and that the mission is ultimately God's, not ours. All of us are subsidiary co-workers, partners invited into God's own labor. Pope John XXIII was a master of wit and perspective who knew who he was, whose he was, and to whom the mission belonged. The story is told that, on his nightly visits to the chapel before retiring, he would simply stand for a moment in the middle aisle and point to the tabernacle, saying: "It's your Church. I'm going to bed." Always, the saints remind us that the work we do, the work that evokes our passion and pain, is first God's work.

This conviction is not simply a pious platitude; it is a foundational theological truth. In every arena where we minister, God is always already at work, waiting to meet us. Brian McDermott describes apostolic spirituality as that which arises from the experience of being sent and focuses us on a mission beyond our private enterprises. "All the projects and practices of the apostolic person seek to unite the person to God's project, the reign of God. This is the profound dream and desire God yearns to realize in the world and beyond it, but not without our creative cooperation."[33] Commenting on the difference between Christian ministers and secular welfare providers, law professor Susan Stabile notes that one sent to minister in Christ's name realizes that "what we are about is God's business, not ours. What we do, we do in cooperation with and in support of God's desire for the world, not our own."[34]

Fixed on the Goal, Flexible on the Means

Lay ecclesial ministers, focused on the mission that Jesus invites them to share, could well aspire to be charged with "holy stubbornness" in its pursuit. Yet, with change as the norm in today's church and world, ministers need to be flexible about strategies to reach their mission goal. Confronted with obstacles, they need to find alternatives, to stretch, to be supple in service of the Spirit.

"Love is inventive, even to infinity,"[35] as Vincent de Paul taught. His colleague Louise de Marillac offered realistic advice in the face of unsettling circumstances: "Do not be upset if things are not as you would want them to be for a long time to come."[36] There was no need to be anxious when the shape of the work changed, as it inevitably would: "As it wasn't then what it is now, there's reason to believe that it's still not what it will be when God has perfected it as He wants it."[37]

Another saint who personifies the virtue of adaptability is Angela Merici (1474–1540). Orphaned in Lombardy at the age of ten, she lived with an uncle for ten years and then became a third order Franciscan, a group then at the cutting edge of church reform. At a time when women were not allowed to teach and unmarried women did not act independently, she saw the need to teach girls the basics of their faith, and so she began a school in her home. As word spread, a group of other women like her gathered around this new work. They lived in their own homes and met for prayer and instruction. The success of their innovative approach to education so impressed Pope Clement VII that he invited her to take charge of a group of nursing sisters in Rome. She respectfully declined, believing that her call was to be an educator. She founded the Company of Saint Ursula (Ursulines), intending it to be an association of lay consecrated women who served those in need without the constraints of cloister. The Company of Saint Ursula was among the first groups of noncloistered apostolic women, even though after her death, it became formalized as a religious order.

The writings of this pioneer saint crackle with action words: "*Fate—movetive—credeti—sforzative—sperate—gridate allui co'l cor vostro—che sense dubio vedereti cose mirabile.*" In translation by one of her contemporary daughters, her epistle of apostolic adaptability speaks to us over the span of five centuries: "Do something. Get moving. Be confident. Risk new things. Stick with it. Get on your knees. Then be ready for big surprises."[38]

A contemporary theologian laments the miasma that has descended on many groups in today's religious world: "We are encumbered by old assumptions, burdened by memories that limit our horizons, and, therefore, unfree to see God coming to us from the future."[39] To meet the ministerial challenges of her own day with suppleness, Elizabeth Seton counseled, "We must be so careful to meet our grace."[40] Paying attention to the grace of the moment, meeting our grace, then and now, demands a letting go of fear, worry, and the need to control outcomes. It calls for a kind of institutional imagination, a trustful waiting in times of uncertainty, creative readiness to move when the Spirit whispers, "This way!" Such flexibility cuts through the mire of worn assumptions and limiting memories. Such suppleness frees us to recognize the God who is always coming to meet us.

MARY, FIRST AMONG THE SAINTS

As they prayed, the place where they were gathered shook, and they were all filled with the Holy Spirit and continued to speak the word of God with boldness. The community of believers was of one heart and mind, and no one claimed that any of his possessions was his own, but they had everything in common. With great power the apostles bore witness to the resurrection of the Lord Jesus, and great favor was accorded them all. There was no needy person among them, for those who owned property

or houses would sell them, bring the proceeds of the sale, and put them
at the feet of the apostles, and they were distributed to each according to
need.[41]

This passage from Acts gives us a glimpse of the post-Resurrection community,
still reeling from the impact of the Spirit of the risen Jesus. One in mind and
heart and possessions, they lived in a communion that overflowed into mission—an ideal picture, to be sure, that probably lasted all of five minutes!

An alternate image of the early church that especially nourishes my prayer
is one from a fourteenth-century illuminated manuscript.[42] The disciples are
gathered in a circle with Mary in the center. She is obviously the wisdom
figure to whom they turn.

The early church faced momentous questions to which today's ministers
can readily relate. Among them were questions of membership and inclusion:
"Who can be part of our company? Who is worthy to follow the Way? Can the
Gentiles belong to Christ if they don't follow Jewish laws and customs?"

The post-Resurrection community also puzzled over questions of mission
and motivation. No doubt some felt the urgency of preaching the Good News
more vehemently than others; some scored higher on commitment than on
clarity. Some needed to be prodded, while others needed to be tempered.
Their mission questions mirrored some of those we face in today's church:
How do we best present a clear, compelling, and consistent message? What
public venues are the most promising? When the message is ignored or re-
jected and the messenger is run out of town, is there a plan B? How might we
rethink our strategy so as to keep focused on the ultimate goal?

The nascent church grappled with resource management, with receiving
and administering money and property, with assessing and providing for the
diverse needs of all in a fair and orderly way. As ministers steward the material resources of their institutions, as they try to balance departmental priorities equitably, as they manage portfolios in a time of diminishing returns, as
they encourage sharing and look for deeper cuts in already-lean budgets, they
can draw strength (if not practical advice) from their ancient counterparts.

Can we not presume that the early community turned to Mary for prudent
pastoral counsel and motherly guidance?

- A mother knows how to build up her family, not to tear it down.
- A mother knows how to make room for all around the table, how to encourage more than chastise.
- A mother knows how to set limits that help her family to grow in responsible freedom, how to lead them beyond self-absorbed concerns into a
  discerning awareness of what is best for all.

- A mother does not muzzle her children, but knows how to encourage them to speak lovingly with freedom and boldness.
- A mother knows that the diverse gifts of her children are meant to enrich the whole family, meant to be welcomed and called forth and held in common.

When you are tempted to widen the divisions in your midst, our Mother Mary would say, find the *we* beyond the *us* and *them*. Deepen instead your desire to see as God sees.

The end of Vatican II's Constitution on the Church, *Lumen gentium*, calls on the "entire body of the faithful" to beg Mary, "who aided the beginnings of the Church by her prayers," to continue, from her heavenly place of glory, to bring our needs before her son. "May she do so until all the peoples of the human family . . . are happily gathered together in peace and harmony into the one People of God."

CONCLUSION

This chapter has invited lay ministers—indeed, all of us who sit around the tables of societal and ecclesial institutions—to enlist the help of the saints, not just as personal friends and protectors but as spirit guides and wise companions as we discern the Spirit's leading. They model the way of "both-and," showing us how to bridge dualisms and divisions. They shore up our fragile hope and hold out the possibility both of claiming our voice and cultivating a forgiving spirit during times of institutional crisis. They encourage us to build collaborative partnerships by accepting our own humanity and honoring the diverse gifts of our colleagues in ministry. And they impel us to keep focused on the mission that is God's, while we seek the suppleness to adapt our prized plans to ever-changing circumstances.

Gertrude Foley reminds us that the saints "lived at a particular historical moment, within specific life situations, among certain other men and women who affected and shaped their lives. All of these factors—historical setting, life situations, and other people—had both nurturing and limiting impacts on the saint's life, just as they do on ours."[43] Throughout their stories, the saints offer to all of us living lessons in dealing with the less-than-perfect nature of institutions (and the humans who shape them).

Around the tables of life and ministry, the saints support us with their example, friendship, strength, and protection. In our everyday efforts to remain faithful to Christ and his mission, they spur us on, eyes on the prize that he promised. Blessed are we in their company.

NOTES

1. Preface for Holy Men and Women, *Roman Missal* (ICEL, 1973).

2. Lawrence S. Cunningham uses these descriptors to identify "ideal types which have characterized certain eras of the church's life." See his *The Catholic Heritage* (New York: Crossroad, 1983), 2.

3. See 1 Cor. 1:2. Bible quotations are taken from the New American (NAB) version of the Bible.

4. Compare Rom. 8:23–25.

5. Elizabeth Johnson, "Community on Earth as in Heaven: A Holy People and a Sacred Earth Together," in *The Santa Clara Lectures* 5, no. 1 (Santa Clara, CA: Santa Clara University, 1998), 12.

6. Compare to: "Holiness is not limited to the sanctuary or to moments of private prayer . . . holiness is achieved in the midst of the world." "Economic Justice for All," U.S. Bishops' Pastoral Letter on the Economy, 1986. www.usccb@org/jphd/economiclife/pdf/economic_justice_for_all.pdf (accessed September 14, 2009).

7. Compare Acts 2; Joel 3:1.

8. Compare Jer. 31:1.

9. Also interpreted as depicting three angels visiting Abraham at the Oak of Mamre.

10. Elizabeth Johnson, *Friends of God and Prophets* (New York: Continuum, 1998), 60–61.

11. Johnson, *Friends of God*, 63.

12. Matt. 22:36.

13. Quoted without citation as "Poem of St. Francis of Assisi" by Richard Liddy, "'Hints and Guesses': Discerning Values, in Zeni Fox and Regina Bechtle, SC, eds., *Called & Chosen: Toward a Spirituality for Lay Leaders* (Lanham, MD: Rowman & Littlefield, 2005), 42, note 2.

14. Adopted from a story by the fictional Persian storyteller Nasruddin, www.nasruddin.org/pages/stories/whereisGotnot.html (accessed April 12, 2010).

15. Compare also Matt. 18:12–14, 20:1–16.

16. Ozanam to Louis Janmot, November 1836, quoted in Pierre Pierrard et al., *Ozanam: Husband and Father, Champion of Truth and Justice, Lover of the Poor, Founder of the Society of St. Vincent de Paul* (Strasbourg: Editions du Signe, 1997), 11.

17. The society currently numbers about 950,000 members, men and women, in over 130 countries worldwide.

18. Ozanam to Charles Hommais. 1852. Quoted in Pierce Fierrand et al., *Ozanami: Husband and Father, Champion of Truth and Justice, Lover of the Poor, Founder of the Society of St. Vincent de Paul* (Strasbourg, France: Editions du Signe, 1977), 20.

19. Seton to Carroll, January 25, 1810, in *Elizabeth Bayley Seton Collected Writings,* edited by Regina Bechtle and Judith Metz, 3 vols. (Hyde Park, NY: New City Press, 2000–2006), II:106, original in Archives of the Archdiocese of Baltimore (AAB). Hereafter cited as *Seton Writings*.

20. Seton to Reverend Simon Bruté, "Journal 1815," *Seton Writings,* II:323, original in Archives, Saint Joseph's Provincial House (ASJPH).

21. *Seton Writings* IIIa:386, original in ASJPH.

22. Timothy Radcliffe, "Rebuilding Our Human Communities," *The Pastoral Review*, December 1996 (excerpt), available at http://www.thepastoralreview.org/cgi-bin/archive_db.cgi?priestsppl-00054 (accessed March 12, 2010).

23. See http://www.nplc.org/commonground/initiative.htm (accessed September 29, 2009).

24. Monika Hellwig, quoted in Leo O'Donovan, "The Vocation of a Theologian: A Tribute to Monika Hellwig," *America* (November 28, 2005).

25. Compare John 15:12; 1 Cor. 12:4–7.

26. Margaret John Kelly, "The Relationship of Saint Vincent and Saint Louise from Her Perspective," *Vincentian Heritage* 11, no. 1 (1990): 84. Available at http://via.library.depaul.edu/vhj/vol11/iss1/6 (accessed April 12, 2010).

27. Colleen Mallon, personal conversation, October 2007.

28. A.91B, "Rule for the Motherhouse," Louise Sullivan, ed. and trans., *Spiritual Writings of Saint Louise de Marillac* (New York: New City Press, 1991), 754. (Hereinafter cited as *SWSL.*)

29. *Saint Vincent de Paul: Correspondence, Conferences, Documents*, vol. 10, newly translated, edited, and annotated from the 1923 edition of Pierre Coste, ed. Marie Poole, Julia Denton, Elinor Hartman, Ellen Van Zandt, trans. Marie Poole, annotated John W. Carven (Hyde Park, NY: New City Press, 2006), 78. (Hereinafter cited as *CCD*, with volume and publication date.)

30. Richard Rohr, *Everything Belongs* (New York: Crossroad, 1999, 2003), 24–26.

31. *CCD*, vol. 9, 2005, 81.

32. Matt. 6:33, 21.

33. Brian McDermott, "What Is Apostolic Spirituality?" *America* (November 11, 2002), available at http://www.americamagazine.org/content/article.cfm?article_id=2593 (accessed March 12, 2010).

34. Susan Stabile, "Christian (vs. Secular) Service of Others," July 12, 2009, available at http://susanjoan.wordpress.com/2009/07/12/christian-vs-secular-service-of-others/ (accessed March 12, 2010).

35. *CCD*, vol. 11, 2008, 131.

36. *SWSL*, L. 519, 614–15.

37. *CCD*, vol. 9, 2005, 194.

38. Words of Angela interpreted artistically by Terry Eppridge.

39. Constance FitzGerald, "From Impasse to Prophetic Hope: Crisis of Memory," *Proceedings of the Catholic Theological Society of America*, 2009, available at http://www.ctsa-online.org/0021-0042.pdf (accessed March 12, 2010), 22.

40. *Seton Writings* 11, 595, original in Les Archives des Ursulines de Quebec (AUQ).

41. Acts 4:31–35.

42. Stefano da Verona, *Initial A with the Pentecost: Cutting from an Antiphonary*, painting in tempera and gold on parchment, private collection. Image available at http://www.myriobiblos.gr/afieromata/pnevma/icons_en.html (accessed March 12, 2010).

43. Gertrude Foley, "Saint Louise de Marillac: Woman of Substance, Woman of God," *Vincentian Heritage* 21, no. 2 (2000): 22. http://via.library.depaul.edu/vhj/vol21/iss2/2 (accessed April 12, 2010).

9

Formation for Lay Ministry: Learnings from Religious Life

Juliana Casey, IHM

"**B**ehold, Ava Grace!" So proclaimed the celebrant at a recent Sunday liturgy as he concluded the baptism of three infants. Holding each child over his head, the celebrant presented them to the congregation as a great gift. The applause was loud and long for each. The joy—not only for parents and godparents, but for all present—was palpable.

Ava Grace, Thomas Michael, and Madeline Susan were welcomed into the community of the faithful, and thus began their life's journey into the Catholic faith, the gift of grace, and the life of God's Spirit. They also began their journey into proclaiming and acting within and for the reign of God in our midst. Baptism is the first fragile step into a call and a vocation to holiness that all the baptized share.

The great majority of the baptized will live their call as disciples within the many facets of their "secular" lives. For some, that call will manifest itself in a vocation to religious life or priestly life. For many, that call will realize itself in another face of ministry within and for the church: lay ministry. Perhaps that ministry will be one of committed service in a parish or a diocese. Perhaps it will take place within a Catholic institution, for example, in education or health care. In the latter cases, a "job" may be consciously and intentionally recognized and claimed as a ministry. It then becomes a means of proclaiming God's kingdom among the people. The task of eliciting and supporting this consciousness, or, in other words, the formation of laity for ministerial leadership in the context of Catholic institutions of health care, education, and social service is the particular focus of this chapter.

FORMATION FOR MINISTERIAL LEADERSHIP

A great deal has been written, discussed, worried about, clarified, and questioned about laypersons as ministers and their formal recognition by the institutional church. Some of that discussion has focused on their qualifications and preparation. If they have neither studied in the seminary nor been formed in religious life, how can they be prepared and qualified to carry out a ministry? In response to these discussions, many forms of preparation have been tried. Some have been very successful; others have been less so. This is a learning time for all involved in the "explosion of lay ministry" in the church.

Many years ago, as a formation program in our health care organization was introduced, a vice president responded with a rather sarcastic question: "Are you going to make us mini-novices now?" Although the question was meant to be sarcastic, it also contained a kernel of truth. The presence, leadership, and heritage of members of religious communities have profoundly affected how we understand the form and the function of lay ministry, particularly as that ministry is carried out in institutions that are not directly related to a ministry of the word and sacrament. Further, much of what we know about how laypersons are formed in and for ministry has come to us from the experience of vowed religious life. In a sense, that is all we have known.

Mini-Novices?

Vatican II, in its great wisdom, recognized the call of everyone to holiness, which is contained in the message and life of Jesus and initiated in baptism. Proclaiming this call has been and is essential to the mission of the church to realize the reign of God in our world. Further, the Council Fathers not only recognized but encouraged what was then called the "apostolate" of the laity. Volumes have been written on this. Volumes will continue to be written, for this invitation from the Council Fathers not only recalled and reinvigorated the gospel message, it initiated a veritable flood of debate, discussion, and experience of ministry within the church.

Much of the initial discussion, reflection, and struggle focused on ministry that was related to diocesan or parish life. Often this ministry was in some way connected to the sacramental life of the church. The discussions around the very use of the word ministry illustrate this. If ministry is connected to the sacramental (and thus priestly) life of the church, how can those who are not ordained be involved in ministry? Cardinal Avery Dulles's response to this question is pertinent here. He said, "I don't think the term 'ministry' is only used in the Catholic Church for the ordained. Unless it's qualified—like 'sacred ministry' or 'Petrine ministry' or something like that."[1]

Ministry is more than sacramental ministry, however. Thomas O'Meara's definition of ministry provides a more comprehensive understanding: "Christian ministry is the public activity of a baptized follower of Jesus Christ flowing from the Spirit's charism and the individual personality on behalf of a Christian community to witness to, serve and realize the kingdom of God."[2]

The church carries out its mission through persons and through the works that they do. Some of these works, particularly in education and health care, have developed into large, complex, influential Catholic institutions. What is important for us here is to recognize that, while laypersons were always present and involved, these Catholic institutions were founded by, grown by, governed by, and literally permeated by women and men religious. They did not think of themselves as "ministers," nor did they call their work "ministry." Their work was, rather, an extension of the inspiration of the founder in response to the needs of God's people, and in fidelity to the gospel call to serve.

Their way of serving, however, was a mirror image of their way of life, of their vocation to vowed religious life. One frequently entered a particular religious community because of the works they did. There were "teaching orders" or "nursing orders." If a young woman wanted to be a nurse, she did not enter a teaching order. If that same woman wanted to teach, she did not enter a religious congregation renowned for its health care work. For women and men religious, their lives as members of a religious congregation and their work (ministry) were one.

When, for various reasons, the leadership of these Catholic institutions was no longer dominated by those vowed religious, the model for the work either changed radically or explicitly imitated that of the sisters or brothers who began the work.

Changing the Model, Transferring the Model

What did these two alternatives look like? How were they implemented? If it changed radically, the institution became a business: a nonprofit corporation that did good work and was led by hard-working people who were committed to keeping the institution alive and—often—"doing what the sisters wanted." These new leaders did this from their observations of the sisters (or brothers or priests). They did not do it from their personal experience of the motivation, passion, or single-mindedness of vowed life.

At the same time, many Catholic institutions attempted to follow the model of the religious in whose history they walked. This model had several significant characteristics.

First, the work itself was begun in response to a need. Often that need was expressed through the request of a member of the clergy who invited sisters to respond to educational, health care, and/or social service needs. The need was primary; over time, the institution developed to further serve the need, but this was secondary.

Second, those first generations were marked by a single-mindedness that suffered all sorts of difficulties in order to do the work to which they had been called and to which they had been sent. Sisters worked all hours, lived in extremely difficult conditions, faced persecution, sometimes went hungry, and were frequently undervalued. They did this willingly because they were serving God and helping the people. It must also be said that obedience played a role in this single-mindedness. One was sent by a superior; one followed a rule that dictated every moment of the day.

Although obedience was influential in the lives of the religious, it was frequently creatively interpreted when it came to following the wishes, directions, even orders of authorities who differed with or did not understand the single-mindedness of these men and women. The stories of women and men who found creative ways to serve those in need and to further their ministries are legend. They are inspiring and have given a wonderful flavor of daring and freedom to these ministries.

Third, religious did this in community. They worked all hours, lived in difficult conditions, faced persecution, went hungry, and were undervalued or ignored *together*. The support, encouragement, shared motivation, and shared faith often enabled that which could never have been done by individuals working alone.

As the presence of vowed religious diminished, these characteristics and the model that was shaped by them were held up to new leaders as the goal. The experience, motivation, and some practices of religious life, including an expectation of a lifelong commitment to a ministry, were transferred to the new lay leaders as their model. As the gradual transformation of persons in key leadership roles in Catholic institutional ministries unfolded, from exclusively vowed religious to primarily religious to primarily laity to almost exclusively laity, it is important to note that initially the model for formation was *transferred* rather than *translated*. In other words, there were multiple attempts to adopt the model as it was. One example of this was a discussion of a "lifetime commitment" to a particular ministry (e.g., Catholic health care or Catholic education). Although such a commitment could be seen for a person who had made a permanent commitment through vows of poverty, celibacy, and obedience, it was difficult to envision for laypersons whose lifetime commitments were to marriage, family, or other meaningful roles.

In general, however, much of what the religious had lived and given to the ministry was seen as valid and valuable for the new leaders. Some examples were:

Recognition that this work was more than work. It was a ministry, that is, a public proclamation of the Good News of the gospel of Jesus Christ. What one did in this ministry was more than teaching Spanish or chemistry, more than performing successful surgery or setting broken bones, more than getting help for someone, finding counseling, giving aid. A ministry meant that it was a visible sign of God's love for the world. A ministry proclaims this is what it looks like when God's reign arrives: the sick are made well, the suffering are comforted, the vulnerable are strengthened, the ignored are seen. (See, for example, Matt. 11:2–6.) Lay leaders could be invited to see themselves as indeed involved in a ministry.

Recognition that this ministry was a ministry of the Catholic Church. Diocesan and parish ministry, as well as health care, education, and social service ministries, were all carried out in the name of and under the auspices of the Catholic Church. As such, these works proclaimed God's reign and inherited a long, complex tradition of that proclamation. Persons engaged in the work inherited that tradition with the grace of its strength and wisdom, and with the burden, at times, of its history and multiple interpretations of its law; they inherited the very identity of the institution as a ministry of the Catholic Church. Lay leaders could be invited to learn the tradition more fully and to see their work as part of the furthering of God's reign.

The importance of motivation. The ministry was designed to serve the people, especially the most vulnerable. For vowed religious, it was to be expected that the primary reason for serving in this ministry was not for advancement of a career, for huge salaries, for power or glory, but rather to serve. Lay leaders could be invited to embrace these values.

Motivation leads to a single-mindedness. Women and men religious understood their work as response to a call, and since they were called, they were to respond wholeheartedly, single-mindedly. The work they did was, for many religious, the way they achieved their sanctification. Lay leaders could be invited to reflect on stories of call, to explore their own call to their work, and to see their response as an aspect of their path to holiness.

Single-mindedness leads to sacrifice, even to self-sacrifice. Long hours, total giving, and willingness to suffer and to go without, all were part of vowed religious life. They came with the vocation. Glory was disdained, salary was nonexistent, and obedience was the norm. One did what one was asked. One did not question. One gave his or her all, because one had already given her or his all. What is the relevance of such self-sacrifice in the case of the highly educated, very intelligent, dedicated laypersons who had been hired because of their expertise and abilities and whose "all" included commitment to another, perhaps, or to a family or to another form of community? Was self-sacrifice to include sacrifice by family members as well?

Simply transferring the model of vowed men and women's service in the ministry would not work. Nothing had prepared laypersons for these aspects of their roles. After long discussions, intense reflection, false starts, and mistakes, the need for ministerial formation for lay leaders was recognized.

Formation for Ministry: Translating a Model

Perhaps the most significant element of this recognition was the need to translate, rather than transfer, the model. Any formation for lay leaders in any ministry within the Catholic Church needed to be grounded in the experience of the laypersons themselves. To transfer a model that worked within established vowed life to the lives of others who had not been called to live that life simply would not and did not work. This realization led to searching for the elements, the tone, the core of a formation for the ministry itself, rather than formation for religious life, of which ministry was a part.

So, what are those elements, what is the tone, where is the core? There are many elements, and experience always points to new ones. I will focus on six of these: formation itself, call and vocation, the meaning of ministry, the Catholic Church, the heritage of the founders/sponsors, and the Catholic social justice tradition. Each of these elements must always be placed within the context of what it means for the leader personally and what it means in his or her particular work.

Formation

For a long time, those who were responsible for the development of lay leadership in Catholic ministries resisted the use of the term "formation." There were good reasons for this. Formation sounded as if it came from the nuns. It sounded like something that sought to change people, to convert them. In some instances, it carried a pejorative overtone—we are not good just as we are, so "they" need to change us. As we began to see, however, preparation for leadership in ministry is about more than the transfer of knowledge. Lay ministry involves the whole person and calls for attention to spirit and to heart as well as to knowledge and skills. The need for true formation, with its attention to the whole person and to relationships, was recognized and named. Preparation for *ministry* requires knowledge and much, much more.

Vocation and Call

When we begin to listen to individuals who lead ministries, we soon hear phrases like: "I was called to do this"; "This is why I'm here"; "This is more than a job to me." Essential to formation for ministry is the recognition of a personal call, or vocation. Examination of this call in a person's life is crucial to her or his formation. This examination focuses on examples of call in the scriptures, in the lives of other persons, and in a person's own life. It leads to recognition that some One, some inspiration, some desire has led this person to this work and sustains him or her in it. What may have begun as a job, a step on the career ladder, is transformed into a purpose, a meaningful work that enriches the individual and others, as that person discovers the call to which he or she had already responded.

Ministry

A job becomes a ministry. That is, it is service to people in the name of the church.[3] There are times in my own ministry when I speak with new executives and have the desire to tell them that they have no idea what they are in for! Ministry demands a great deal from a person. In the first place, it touches into that passion, motivation, total commitment that women and men religious have long exhibited, and that laypersons enter into when they hear and respond to the call to ministry.

The perspective of ministry changes everything. Promotion means greater opportunity to serve. Success means more people are helped, more homeless persons are cared for, more teenagers are given hope for a better life, and more families are restored. Goals focus on caring, listening, and transforming. Financial success becomes a means to continue the ministry, a way to care for others. All one's skills and talents are placed at the service of the ministry and the people it serves. The ethics of ministry, the leadership style of ministry—these are based in service rather than expediency or control and command.

The perspective of ministry gives a great deal as well. To participate in a ministry is to recognize that one participates in something greater than oneself. It makes work meaningful and, at its best, sacred. The office, the classroom, the bedside, the counseling center, any place of work becomes a sacred place, made holy by the call, by need, by service. The sisters and brothers saw this. They knew it without putting words around it. Lay leaders need to grow in this. They need to realize ever more deeply that not only the sisters' and brothers' work but also theirs is holy and blessed.

The Catholic Church

The call to ministry, as we speak of it in this chapter, is situated within the context of the Catholic Church. That means that it lives within a tradition of centuries and a worldview that is global and local at the same time. When the Catholic Church allows an institution to use the name Catholic, it expects certain things from that institution. Among these is adherence to the Catholic tradition as it affects the particular ministry. The church asks that leaders know this tradition, know to whom they are accountable, and respond with fidelity.

Lay ministers are part of a church that understands itself as called to serve and to bring about the reign of God. Lay ministers are called to participate in that call and to work to bring about God's reign. They are part of, not separate from, the institutional church. As such, they act in accord with the church's norms and values. It is not enough to do what one instinctively thinks is right. One must always measure decisions and actions against the tradition and the community of the faithful.

Here again, the model of religious life is translated. As members of a religious community, brothers and sisters were clearly part of the Catholic Church. In many cases, they were the visible face of the church. Their identity as Catholic was neither a question nor an issue. Lay ministers are that presence now. They are not identifiable by their garb. They are identifiable by their actions.

Another important aspect of ministry within the Catholic Church is that of community. Vowed religious life is obviously built upon a foundation of community. Men and women religious worked together to achieve a common mission. The church itself is a community, a communion brought together in faith to achieve a common mission: the building up of the reign of God.

Ministry in the Catholic tradition is not primarily about personal sanctification; rather it is first about communal service to God's people. As a minister in this tradition, one is part of a communion, part of the people of God. There is a broad responsibility implied in this. We are our sisters' and brothers' keepers. We are one body, a community of diverse persons. Lay ministry does not imitate the life in common of vowed religious. It does translate that deep understanding of community into working together with, being supportive of, bearing the burdens of, rejoicing with co-workers in the vineyard.

Heritage of the Founders

The beginning of most Catholic ministries is characterized by a great and holy person who saw a need and responded to that need. Whether that person was Vincent de Paul, Catherine McAuley, Elizabeth Seton, or any of the many others who responded to God's call to serve, they left an indelible mark upon the religious communities that followed them. Members of these communities then carried that mark or character with them as they founded new works. They often gave these works their name; they always gave them their "flavor." The ministries begun by women and men religious carry with them a precious heritage of commitment to the gospel, love of God, service and care for people, attention to the most vulnerable, continued search for justice, and much more.

For members of the religious communities, this knowledge was in their bones. They learned it from day one of their life in their community. They *were* the living legacy of the founder. For the lay ministers who now lead Catholic ministries, the legacy must be learned. Ministry formation needs to include a great deal about the history and the heritage of founding religious communities. More important, it will need to find ways to inculcate the spirit of the founders into the lives and actions of today's lay ministers. For example, a laywoman was giving the history of her ministry: "The Sisters founded the hospital in 1878 to serve the immigrant community. It's a hundred and more years later, *and we're still here.*" The sisters' presence has become our presence—"and we're still here."

One fear that is frequently encountered among lay ministers is that they cannot adequately replace the sisters or brothers who have gone before them. Ministry formation needs to make it clear that they do not replace what has gone before. They are a new iteration of God's call to serve. Ministry formation also needs to help lay ministers understand and believe that with the help of the loving God, they can indeed minister to the people.

Social Justice Tradition

Catholic institutional ministries began as service to those in need. These ministries have consistently exhibited a priority for the needs of the most vulnerable. In so doing, they have both imitated and manifested Jesus' predilection for those who were least. Particularly in the United States, vowed religious communities shared in the poverty of those they served. Many of today's Catholic ministries originated among immigrant communities in the nineteenth century. They served as vehicles for integrating whole communities into the mainstream of U.S. culture. They also served as effective places for the maintenance of the Catholic faith. In most cases this was done almost unconsciously. Until the second half of the twentieth century, there was not a lot of discussion of the "Catholic social tradition."

This tradition, and deep knowledge of it, is necessary for authentic ministry in the church. It is a tradition that leads us back to the roots of our faith in the ministry of Jesus Christ. It is also a tradition that calls us to fidelity to that mission in the daily events of our lives, our work, and our organizations. It is this tradition that guides us in how to live in society, how to work with others, how to treat our employees, and how to act with justice.

Laymen and laywomen who have not experienced the "givens" of religious life are nonetheless called to continue that same sensitivity and dedication to the needs of the most vulnerable among us. The seduction of power, so prevalent in so many institutions, is contradicted in the call to justice.

Elements of vowed religious life, then, continue to be central elements of all ministry in the church. They serve as models—and inspiration—for the content and the way lay ministry is carried out today. The formation of women and men religious offers a rich example and direction for the formation of lay ministers.

Since formation addresses the whole person, the *tone* of any processes or programs is crucial. Again, religious life can serve as a model. An enormous amount of time and energy in formation in religious life is devoted to prayer and meditation. All new members learn to pray, to meditate, to reflect upon the scriptures, to engage in *lectio divina*. One's whole day is marked by prayer.

In many ways I believe this is the most important gift the model of religious life can offer lay ministry. The world of the lay minister whose service is within Catholic institutions is a hectic world. It is marked by crises, demands, the need for finely honed skills, speed, tension and conflict, and the expectation of quick decisions and snap judgments. These are the norm. Reflection is not at the top of the list.

Ministry, though, must be grounded in prayer and reflection. If not, it is not ministry. To carry on the work of Christ, to advance the mission of the church, it is absolutely essential that the minister be in touch with that ministry and that mission.

Leadership always involves decisions. All too often decisions are made without awareness of those affected by the decisions, how this particular decision echoes the faith tradition, or how it may contradict that tradition. Reflective decision making is vital to the ministry.

Reflective people are even more vital. Lay ministerial leaders must be at home with their own soul or they cannot serve others. Prayer, reflection, meditation—these are skills learned by vowed religious. They are ones that need to be learned by all. Experience in this area has shown that most leaders seek this learning. Most seek to be in touch with their deepest selves and with their God. Ministry formation needs to foster these skills.

Ministry formation is not school. It is growth in spirit. It is development of the whole person. Its goal is deepened commitment and ongoing service. Its "proof" is the opened spirit of its participants and their ability to touch into the riches of the Spirit present in their lives and in the Catholic tradition.

The *core* of ministry formation is ministry itself. It is not about skill development, training, making "mini-novices," or conversion. It is about preparing, equipping, and supporting committed persons who have been called to share in the ministry of the church. Women and men religious stand as inspiration and as model for this kind of formation. Perhaps the most significant model they offer is that of their consistent ability to change in response to the needs of the times. The Sister Formation movement led to radical changes in the way sisters were formed and prepared them for the even greater changes called for by Vatican II. This flexibility remains a model for us as we continue to develop our understanding of the meaning of and need for lay ministry in the church.

LEARNINGS

Intentional efforts in the formation of lay leaders in Catholic institutional ministries are still in the early stages. Such formation is still learning how to exist. It finds itself in that exciting and uncomfortable place of new beginnings. There are some things that have been learned, however, and glimpses of wisdom have emerged.

The *first* learning is that, while models (particularly those of religious life) are important for ministry formation, they cannot be adopted without a critical eye. Lay ministry formation is not about making clones of the good sisters or brothers. It is about the development and growth of committed laypersons who have been called, *as* laypersons, to serve the church through its ministries. It is their experience that must be the context for any formation.

Although religious life is frequently characterized as a single-minded devotion to holiness, to service, and to a ministry, the layperson's life is a reflection of multiple demands, multiple cares, and multiple loves. For many, their love of spouse and of family is primary in their lives. This reality is for them the ground of holiness and the primary sacred place of encounter with the divine.

For example, when a group of mission leaders was asked to reflect upon where and how they found moments or spaces of peace, one participant spoke of going home from work at the end of the day and holding his eighteen-month-old son in his arms as he rocked him in a favorite chair. Formation for ministry, if it is to be effective, will reverence this primary commitment, learn from it, name it as holy, and recognize the profound responsibility that it carries.

Laywomen and laymen are called to a ministry. Within that ministry, the demands of the work are multiple—stressful at times, and consuming at others. Whereas formation for religious life includes the gift of time for extended periods for education and reflection, lay ministry does not have that luxury. Designers of lay ministry formation processes have had to become very creative in their use of limited time. The necessity of adult education methods, the feasibility of weekend sessions, wise use of interactive and ongoing processes—including web-based ones—have proven essential. Creative methods of integrating a focus on spirituality into these processes have been developed and can, themselves, provide new models for a spirituality for laity.

Second, the privilege of participating in lay ministry formation makes abundantly clear to any facilitator that there is already present a deep commitment to ministry, to church, to service among the people. Beset by the complexities of multiple demands, often unsupported by the official church, sometimes unacknowledged by colleagues, thousands of men and women know themselves to be called by God, to be called to serve. And they have answered this call at great cost, with enormous generosity and with great grace. This learning teaches all of us about the multiple ways God works among us. In this case, lay ministry formation becomes a model for all other formation. It is witness to fidelity, to courage, and to sensitivity to the Spirit.

A *third* learning is that in lay ministry formation there is both continuity with and discontinuity from other forms of formation. Continuity appears in the content of this formation, its tone, and its core focus on the mission and ministry of Jesus Christ. Discontinuity can be seen in the methods of formation, the experience that grounds participation in formation, and the lives of those who do participate. What is important, I feel, is to recognize both continuity and discontinuity and to learn how each formation influences and enriches the other.

Yet another learning awaits those who have eyes to see. The gift of baptism, the riches of the Spirit, and the continuous presence of the loving God are abundantly present in the lives and dedication of men and women given to ministry in the church and in the world. For thousands of people, hearing the call of baptism and acting upon it has led to blessing and joy—not without difficulties. For hundreds of thousands of people, lay ministers have been inspiration, consolation, presence, and witness to God's love for them and the church's care for them. We have not been left orphans.

THE FUTURE

Ava Grace and her two companions in baptism will grow up surrounded by great numbers of people who will teach them about God's reign and their place in it. Some will be clergy, some will be members of a religious congregation, but the majority will be laypersons. All will minister; all will continue the mission of the church.

Ava Grace will be blessed because of this. As will all of us.

NOTES

1. Cited in J. Filtreau, "Bishops Approve Lay Ecclesial Ministry Guidelines," Catholic News Service, November 16, 2005. www.catholicnews.com/data/stories/cns/050b563.htm.

2. Thomas O'Meara, *Theology of Ministry* (Mahwah, NJ: Paulist, 1983), 142.

3. Compare O'Meara's definition, above.

Part IV

IMPLICATIONS FOR PASTORAL PRACTICE

10

The Call of *Co-Workers in the Vineyard of the Lord* for Cultural Diversity in Lay Ecclesial Ministry Formation Programs

William H. Johnston

The ranks of the church's ministers expanded in the United States in the years after the Second Vatican Council. Significant numbers of religious and laywomen as well as laymen generously devoted themselves to the work of the church, doing so even as a full-time career, a life's calling. In their 2005 document, *Co-Workers in the Vineyard of the Lord*, the U.S. Conference of Catholic Bishops (USCCB) speaks to this phenomenon, now called "lay ecclesial ministry." They affirm it as a work of the Spirit, offer benchmarks for assessing present practice, and point the way for future development.

One particular concern of the bishops is the formation of lay ecclesial ministers. In *Co-Workers* they propose content and methods for four dimensions of formation, call for integration of those four dimensions, encourage ongoing formation, and name the principal agents of formation. Each of these topics could benefit from further elaboration; although it is the longest part of the document, the formation section is nonetheless more brief and less detailed or informative than the formation material in church documents pertaining to priests and deacons.[1] Future research and writing might explore in more detail, for example, the meaning and purpose of each of the bullet-pointed elements of formation in *Co-Workers*, the best practices for making the most of the suggested methods of formation, the importance of the ecumenical dimension, and the multifaceted role of theological reflection throughout the process.

This chapter seeks to contribute to this task of elaboration by reflecting on one factor mentioned several times in *Co-Workers*, the dimension of cultural diversity. This topic is both important and urgent as we face the future of pastoral ministry and ministry formation in the United States. This chapter is written in the hope of moving cultural diversity toward the forefront of our collective attention. I particularly hope to encourage and assist directors and formators of academic, diocesan, or agency ministry formation programs who may have found it difficult to address this issue in a thoroughgoing and practical way. In what follows I propose a conceptual framework and offer practical suggestions for program review and reform, raise the question of whether a paradigm shift is needed in our basic model of formation, invite personal action steps, and provide some bibliographic resources in the notes.

CULTURAL DIVERSITY IN THE CHURCH

In the book of Revelation, John describes his vision of "a great multitude that no one could number, from every nation, from all tribes and peoples and languages, standing before the throne and before the Lamb" (Rev. 7:9),[2] ever offering praise to God. The worship of heaven, we are told, is rich in harmonious cultural diversity. Yet the church on earth, from the days when "the Hellenists murmured against the Hebrews" (Acts 6:1)[3] until now, is ever facing both challenges and difficulties in intercultural relations. In the United States these difficulties have their own particular shape and tenor, given our history of slavery, racism, and immigration. The Catholic Church here has always had the responsibility of being a church of many cultures, to be and genuinely feel like home as much for each new immigrant as for the lifelong resident. Meeting this responsibility concerns every member of the church, especially those who minister in its name, and doing so well requires commitment, effort, knowledge, and skills. Cultivating such traits and abilities among Catholic people is a work of catechesis; cultivating them among the church's ministers is the work of ministry formation, the topic of this chapter.

A TWOFOLD CALL TO CONVERSION

In *Co-Workers* the bishops issue a call and challenge to those responsible for ministry formation: "The increasing cultural diversity of the Church in our country calls for a similar diversity in the preparation of its lay ecclesial ministers."[4] To ponder the implications of this challenge, I suggest we look at *Co-Workers* in part through the lens of another U.S. Catholic Bishops' statement, *Welcoming the Stranger Among Us*.[5] This document is a response to the "'new' immigration to the United States" that can be dated from the 1965 Immigration Act, and was written to inform, guide, and invigorate the church's pastoral response to that phenomenon. Structuring its reflections around the calls to conversion, communion, and solidarity, the bishops challenge the church to more fully welcome and embrace people of diverse cultural backgrounds who come to this country, and to do so not in the mode of assimilation as traditionally understood, but "in ways that are respectful of their cultures and in ways that mutually enrich the immigrants and the receiving Church."[6]

It is important to note the significance of this challenge and the degree of critical self-refection it will demand from persons of the (still, though increasingly less) dominant culture of the United States. What it entails is suggested in the bishops' comment: "These immigrants, new to our shores, call us out of our unawareness to a conversion of mind and heart through which we are able to offer a genuine and suitable welcome."[7]

The key phrase is "our unawareness." The document recognizes that persons of a dominant culture—until they are invited or compelled beyond its framework, usually through encounter with persons of other cultures—are typically handicapped by an "unawareness" of the fact that their own culture is not simply "the way things are" (ethnocentrism), but is one culture among others, with its own distinctive and idiosyncratic characteristics.[8] Breaking out of such unawareness and beginning to recognize the features of one's own culture can be difficult to do—rather like trying to hear how your own accent sounds to others.

What it takes to deal with "our unawareness" is, as the bishops recognize, nothing less than a "conversion" that is both personal, in "mind and heart" and "spirit," and structural, "in our institutions."[9] This challenge echoes that of Pope John Paul II in his Message for World Migration Day in the Jubilee Year 2000; he spoke then of "the urgent need for a transformation of structures and a change of mentality."[10] Such a "change of mentality" or "conversion in spirit" would mark the beginning of the healing of "our unawareness." When we come thereby to see with new eyes and feel with new hearts, we will be more able to envision, desire, and work toward that "transformation of structures" (John Paul II) and "conversion . . . in our institutions" (U.S. Bishops) that are needed if the church in the United States is to be as culturally diverse as the people of the United States, and if the ministers of this church are to provide just and effective pastoral ministry for all its people. So let us explore this twofold challenge of personal conversion and institutional transformation in the context of ministry formation for lay ecclesial ministers.

Personal Conversion of Mind and Heart

Change of mentality, conversion in spirit, conversion of mind and heart—the phrases all suggest the magnitude of the challenge of awakening from "our unawareness" to the multivalent realities of cultural diversity in the world, in one's own cultural-societal context, and in oneself. The reason this pertains directly to lay ecclesial ministry formation programs is that a majority of students and a significant majority of faculty are members of the dominant white Euro-American culture, and thus most susceptible to this unawareness.[11] The problem of "unawareness," then, which particularly troubles the dominant culture, must be taken with all seriousness lest lay ecclesial ministry formation programs, even if unknowingly and unintentionally, fail to provide the multicultural-intercultural experience and formation ecclesial ministers need in order to lead and serve effectively in the contemporary church.[12]

Here is one concrete manifestation of the challenge. Mark A. Chesler of the University of Michigan found that students of color "often report demeaning and discouraging contacts with the faculty." Yet, as he also states, "many faculty, especially white faculty . . . profess good faith interest in the welfare and achievement of students of color"—as would faculty and administrators in lay ecclesial ministry formation programs. Yet Chesler's study goes on to say that such faculty "indicate that they often do not know what they may be doing in the classroom that is experienced as problematic by students of color."[13] Precisely. In a word: "unawareness." Calling for additional goodwill efforts to be "more sensitive" may well fall on deaf ears as faculty already seek to be, and believe they are, culturally sensitive. A different angle of vision is needed. One source of help here could be the field of social psychology and its analysis of contemporary forms of racism. In contrast to traditional, overt, "redneck" racism, for example, the term "aversive racism" is used by Gaertner and Dovidio to describe whites who believe in racial equality, genuinely embrace egalitarian values, see themselves as nonprejudiced, yet still hold negative attitudes and feelings about blacks, often unconsciously, and "discriminate in subtle, rationalizable ways."[14] Though more difficult to acknowledge[15] and change than overt racist attitudes, aversive racism can be ameliorated. Once they come to recognize their unconscious attitudes (that is the key), "the good intentions of aversive racists can be harnessed to produce self-initiated change in [those] unconscious biases with appropriate awareness, effort, and practice over time."[16] Gaertner and Dovidio offer their Common Ingroup Identity Model as one possible method for reducing bias. This model, grounded in the natural process of social categorization (e.g., the ingroup/outgroup distinction), uses such methods as decategorization, recategorization, and mutual intergroup differentiation to improve attitudes and relationships with "the other."[17]

Other analyses of this key topic describe "modern racism," "symbolic racism," and "new racism"; in his 2001 pastoral letter on racism, "Dwell in My Love," Cardinal Francis George of Chicago distinguishes spatial, institutional, internalized, and individual racism.[18] Within the extensive literature on this subject are resources offering perspectives and concrete methods useful for those who design and conduct formation programs for lay ecclesial ministers.[19]

Structural Transformation of Institutions and Programs

Personal conversion needs to be expressed in personal action to bring about actual structural change. This is what the bishops have in mind when they write in *Co-Workers* that "a multicultural emphasis should pervade the content, methods, goals, and design of formation programs."[20] This sentence is far-reaching in scope and calls for implementation measures both wide-ranging and profoundly transforming.

Notice first the strong words, "emphasis" and "pervade." It is not just that a multicultural *awareness* should *influence* formation programs, but that a multicultural *emphasis* should *pervade* them. The difference between "awareness" and "emphasis" is the difference between someone bringing up "the multicultural question" at a program planning, curriculum development, or new student admissions meeting, and someone not letting it drop, meeting after meeting, until the question is recognized and accepted by all as legitimate and essential, everyone naturally addresses it, and no one person needs to be its champion. The difference between "influence" and "pervade" is the difference between the dimension and experience of cultural diversity being available as compared with unavoidable in one's program; it is the difference between a program's optional components and its pervading or even defining character.

What would it look like if this were happening? What would it entail to make this real in those four areas the bishops mention: content, methods, goals, and design? Let us consider each area, beginning with goals. (The following is written in the language of the university setting but is meant to apply as well, with adaptations, to diocesan formation programs. "Courses," for example, can correlate with "workshops" or the topics of regularly scheduled program sessions, "faculty" with "presenters" or "facilitators," "students" with "participants," and so on.)

Goals

A. What goal do we hold for the way the diverse cultures in the United States should ideally relate? How should they relate in the church?
B. What kind of multicultural or intercultural community do we intend our formation program to be?
C. What competencies in knowledge, attitudes, and skills do we seek to build up in our students so they can minister effectively in culturally

diverse settings? Are these goals weighted comparably with the more traditional goals and topics of theological education?

There is more than one vision of how different cultural groups should ideally relate together, whether in the nation, diocese, parish, or formation program. Disagreements over such ideals go deep and can be contentious. All the same (or perhaps for that very reason), it is important for a community such as a formation program dealing with intercultural relations to explore openly how its members envision this goal. Figure 10.1, based on models developed by social psychologists, is offered as one way to sketch some options.

In Figure 10.1, the horizontal line represents the degree (low or high) to which a person values belonging to the dominant "American" culture of the United States. The vertical line represents the degree (low or high) to which a person values belonging to their own particular culture. The four resulting quadrants represent four general options or ideal types. Low personal culture + high U.S. culture (lower right quadrant) = assimilation, single identity. High

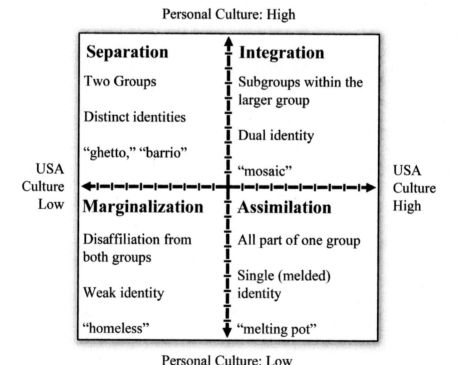

Figure 10.1.   Four forms of intergroup relations.[21]

personal culture + high U.S. culture (upper right quadrant) = integration, or "enlightened integration,"[22] maintaining dual identity within an overarching unity. High personal culture + low U.S. culture (upper left quadrant) = separation, distinct identities. Low personal culture + low U.S. culture (lower left quadrant) = marginalization, confused identity.

Since individuals may value each culture (personal, United States) to a greater or lesser extent, the number of potential positions on the graph, and thus the range of potential views held by persons in our formation programs, is limitless. A productive exercise for students and faculty each new program year would be to plot (a) themselves on the graph, and then their preferred/ideal positions for (b) the church in the United States, and (c) the formation program. Individuals then explain their own position and listen as others do the same; group discussion follows, in an environment of respectful, inquiring dialogue.[23] A helpful variation would be to plot positions on the graph as a line rather than a point, incorporating the dimension of time. Where on the graph, for example, would you think a new immigrant should be upon arrival in the country, and then ten years later; or where should our formation program (the particular constellation of people this year) be at the beginning of the year, and then at the end?

In *Welcoming the Stranger*, the bishops call the church in the United States to a position falling somewhere in the upper-right quadrant of integration: "Unity in diversity is the vision that we bishops, as pastors of the Church in the United States, offer to our people as they welcome the new immigrants and refugees who come to our shores."[24] Each new family or community is to be respected in its unique cultural identity, their gifts recognized and valued, their presence welcomed into the parish and diocese whose ministries are to accommodate them as fully as possible. Racism and the anti-immigrant position are explicitly denounced,[25] as are the expectation of quick, full assimilation, and the "nativism" whereby "established" Catholics "insist that there is just one way to worship . . . one way to organize a parish community, one language for all."[26] The bishops do speak of an "incorporation" of new immigrants into the life of the church and of parishes—opting against the upper left quadrant of separation—but they describe this "not [as] a call for 'assimilation' or the disappearance of one culture into another [that is, the lower right quadrant], but for continuing cooperation in pursuit of the common good and with proper respect for the good of each cultural tradition and community."[27] When they speak of "each [culture] changing at its own pace" they implicitly recognize and allow for a process of persons or cultures assimilating into the broader U.S. culture, but doing so at their choice and at their pace; the text does not propose such assimilation as the ultimate goal to be sought and eventually attained by all.[28]

What should happen in our formation programs? What kind of multicultural or intercultural places should they be? On Figure 10.1, where would you want to see your program, and why? Consider two possible approaches. In Option A, the task is to fashion the formation program to be a true welcoming space for all cultures in our national context, minority as well as mainstream. Persons of different cultures would find, in this learning environment, a place where they are truly welcomed and incorporated, where their input is valued, and where we can learn from them and they from us about what it means to be Catholic and American, so that everyone in the program is better prepared for ministry in this culturally diverse country.

There are certainly formation programs for which Option A would represent a reasonable goal and a positive step forward. Moreover, it seems to resonate with *Welcoming the Stranger*'s acceptance of "cultural pluralism" and its challenge to the church "to welcome these new immigrants and help them join our communities in ways that are respectful of their cultures and . . . mutually enrich the immigrants and the receiving Church."[29] And yet, in Option A the categories remain—there is a "we" who welcome a "them"; there is "mainstream" and "minority."

Option B is different; it sees the task as fashioning the formation program to be an intercultural space where no culture is dominant and people of every culture are equally at home—or, rather, where people of every culture, especially the dominant culture, may at first feel *not* at home, out of place, because this is not a space of "their" culture, but a genuinely intercultural space with everyone on an equal footing, namely, off-balance, until they find their balance together, with one another. As Irizarry defines it, "the term intercultural refers to a process by which culturally bounded selves share a common social space in order to forge a shared identity," something mutually built up by each and every member in a way that privileges none.[30] The process is not additive (I learn more about them, they learn more about me) but "*transformative* in that power is first disclosed, analyzed, shared, and constantly renegotiated among the diverse cultural groups in the community,"[31] yielding a new kind of space where no one culture is dominant. If there seems to be a certain artificiality or "hot-house" character to this vision (building an environment where many cultures relate in a way that is largely nonexistent in the wider society), Irizarry proposes seeing this instead pedagogically "as a form of micropolitics" where we offer students not only a vision, theory, sensitivity, and skill-set, but also at least a small taste of the lived experience of interculturality, to help them know how it feels and see how it might actually work in ministry contexts they will be called to serve.

Some variation on Option B is favored by many educators, including Irizarry and the other contributors to *Shaping Beloved Community*. Orlando

Espín, after describing and critiquing "multiculturality" (as similar to Option A), recommends "cultural diversity" (similar to Option B).[32] Greg Tanaka's book *The Intercultural Campus* explores Option B at length. Based on his research, and for the sake of actual practical effectiveness, he gives explicit attention to dealing with what might be called backlash against those of the current dominant culture.[33] Tanaka offers a variety of recommendations for building an intercultural campus, including social activities bridging cultural gaps, ethnic studies courses or ethnic studies content consistently incorporated in other courses, and workshops promoting racial-ethnic awareness.[34]

A or B—which option in our formation programs better prepares students for the culturally diverse church in the United States? Or is it first A, as a more manageable interim goal, then B? Does an Option C need to emerge? Are multiple models acceptable, or preferable? If B is deemed unrealistic, does it potentially serve the real world of ministry nonetheless, by drawing us to seek and find new and possible forms of intercultural relating we would not have discovered had we not striven in the direction of the perhaps impossible B? Or is the very commitment to strive in this direction the actual goal?[35] How we answer such questions will affect the shape of the programs we aim to provide for our students.

Finally, within the context of the total experience of our programs, what knowledge and skills do our students need in order to minister in a culturally diverse church characterized by "unity in diversity" and a variable mix of unawareness, prejudice, fear, uncertainty, goodwill, conversion, welcome, hospitality, and solidarity? This brings us to the related questions of content and method.

Content and Method

How would program content and method be different if an intercultural emphasis pervaded the formation program? Consider these points for self-assessment.

A. What theological subjects do students study? What leadership and ministry skills do they learn? How does this inform and equip them for ministry in a multicultural church?

B. What books and authors do faculty assign and read for their own research? What case studies are used in courses? What pastoral problems and whose issues are on the radar screen? What media are used, what voices heard, images seen, showing whom and what? Who is missing, invisible, overlooked?

C. What forms of popular piety, devotional practices, and traditions of spirituality do students learn about during intellectual formation? What prayer and devotional practices are students introduced to and given the opportunity to engage in as part of spiritual formation?

D. Does the program require and provide the opportunity to learn a second language, and its culture, for ministry? If not, why not?

E. What diverse, including culturally diverse, ways of learning and communication styles are recognized as valid and valuable—and then *used* in classroom or practicum/field settings, with whatever necessary faculty training it takes to do so? Are faculty willing to participate in such training and use such methods?

F. Where do our field trips go? What happens there? To what extent are immersion experiences in diverse cultures, locally or internationally, a feature of our program? What do we do to prepare for and debrief such experiences?

G. How does student assessment happen, and by what standards or criteria? What counts to show that students are learning and that they understand what is worth understanding?

What, in short, would we study in a formation program that was as culturally diverse as our country? And how would this content, encountered in diverse ways in classrooms and co-curricular program components, help to immerse participants in those many cultures, in such a way as to draw forth and make possible a "profound conversion" in the spirit and mentality of each person in the program and of the program itself as a formational entity?

Let us first recall what *Co-Workers* says. Cultural diversity plays a role in all four areas of formation. Human formation is to promote "appreciation and valuing of racial, ethnic, and cultural diversity."[36] Spiritual formation should "give expression to the rich range of ethnic or cultural prayer practices and popular devotions present among program participants or in their dioceses or regions of the country"; Marian devotion has a special place in the spiritual life of many cultural communities.[37] In intellectual formation, the "range, depth, discipline, and vigor of Catholic theology, past and present," is to be studied in "historical and cultural context."[38] Pastoral formation should take note of "the particular importance of family in different cultural communities," foster competence in "different cultural styles of communication," and include culture and language studies in the curriculum "so that language and cultural differences will not bar anyone from receiving the pastoral ministry of the Church."[39] Note also the mention of "immersion experiences (e.g., in other cultures)"[40]; recommended for ongoing formation, they are certainly, perhaps a fortiori, relevant for initial formation as well.

Welcoming the Stranger also offers strong support for formation of church ministers in skills needed for effective intercultural ministry, repeatedly calling for the study of languages and cultures[41] as well as intercultural communication theory and skills for everyone in church ministry.[42] Indeed, a considerable body of literature offers a wealth of theory for more fully understanding intercultural communication or conflict events and methods for improving behavior. Here are three brief examples.

First, social psychologists use some basic categories to describe features of human perception, valuing, or behaviors that are present in differing ways in different cultures. One such category is individualism-collectivism. In collectivist cultures, people tend to think of themselves as interdependent, prioritize group over personal goals, and prefer to behave in accord with group norms, which are strong; conflict is addressed in relational, process-oriented terms; uniqueness may be seen as deviance and conformity as harmony. In individualist cultures, on the other hand, people tend to think of themselves as autonomous individuals, prioritize personal over group goals, and prefer to behave according to self-chosen values and attitudes; conflict is addressed in more direct and outcome-oriented terms; uniqueness may be prized as creative and exciting and conformity viewed as dull or repressive.[43]

Coming to understand this and similar concepts can further two purposes. It can foster program participants' self-understanding; when they see themselves in some but not in other cultural qualities described, they can begin to understand that forms of thinking and behavior they take for granted and have assumed to be universal are in fact culture specific, characteristic of *their* culture and alien to others. It can also help explain and, one may hope, promote greater tolerance for behavior or values they previously considered oddly different, offensive, or incorrect.

Second, Geneva Gay describes communication styles she finds characteristic of different cultural groups—for example, passive-receptive (listen quietly and attentively) versus participatory-interactive (engage actively and simultaneously, speaking as the speaker is speaking, "amen-ing"); or topic-centered (linear, direct, focused on the single topic) versus topic-chaining (anecdotal, repetitive, bringing in other topics); or the conciliatory, ambivalent, diffuse modes of expression that may be used by Asian or other non-Western students.[44] Knowing these differences may help class or workshop participants to listen better to one another and may affect faculty criteria for grading students' oral or written communication.

Third, Janet M. Bennett and Milton J. Bennett's approach to intercultural diversity awareness and training could be fruitfully studied and applied in formation programs.[45] They address the task of how to foster the "*intercultural competence*" to communicate and relate effectively in diverse cultural contexts, and propose the "Developmental Model of Intercultural Sensitivity," a model focusing on development in "cognitive structure."[46] Six stages are involved, moving from the ethnocentric (where "one's own culture is experienced as central to reality in some way") to the increasingly ethnorelative (where "one's own culture is experienced in the context of other cultures").[47]

In a helpful article, Stephen S. Dudek illustrates how these six stages apply to parishes and other entities (such as formation programs) as their members encounter a new cultural group, tracing a journey from ethnocentrism toward the greater tolerance, welcome, and transformation of what he prefers to call ethnopluralism.[48] After concisely describing the six stages, Dudek then outlines an eight-step developmental process, giving practical guidance and suggestions to help communities experiencing diversity move toward increasing communion.[49] This information can be both useful content for students to know and apply in pastoral settings as well as a framework for understanding and improving the interculturality of the formation program.

Design

Finally, what about the "design" of a pervasively multicultural program?

A. Who—and for the sake of making an actual difference, this may be the most important question in the list—sits at the table where issues are raised, responses generated, proposals discussed, and decisions made?[50] And do they do so, not to review at a later stage plans others have already developed, but as full, contributing, decision-making participants involved from the beginning and throughout the process until the end?

B. What options are on the table when it comes to such foundational matters as curriculum goals, content, and methods; program marketing, student recruitment, admissions criteria, and orientation practices; financial aid; faculty hiring, development, assessment, tenure, and promotion?

C. What immersion or in-service opportunities (optional or required?) do faculty, administrators, and board members go through to give them a richer basis in personal experience for awareness and understanding of the realities of cultural diversity? Are there student- or faculty-exchange programs in place, with partner programs inside or outside the United States?

D. What help do students receive (within the program or from student services, campus ministry, etc.) to bridge cultural divides and build relationships and community both inside and outside the classroom?

E. What about the culture of the formation program itself? How is that culture formed? How and from whom (students, faculty, administrators, staff, families) do program "customs" emerge? What traditions should be cherished? Should any be altered?

F. Is there an alignment of functions between recruitment, admissions, financial aid, advising, faculty development, student services, fund raising, and so forth, so that everyone supports the shared vision (however conceived) of an intercultural formation program?

Whatever their particular role (e.g., program director, department chair, dean, president), administrators can impact formation programs in significant ways.[51] To take one simple example: if, in the process of designing orientation for new students, administrators attended to the social psychological validity and likely effects of such processes as "decategorization" and "personalization," they could build into their programs in a more intentional way planned opportunities and activities consciously designed to foster "repeated personalized interactions . . . over time"[52] among program participants as a whole and specifically those of differing cultural groups. This does not mean being manipulative, but simply recognizing the importance of the consistent steps they take to foster a positive, friendly social/interpersonal environment in their programs, doing so now aware that such steps can make their programs not only more pleasant to be in but also more effective in achieving their proper formational goal of creating a more interculturally enriching formation program environment to prepare participants for ministry in a culturally, ethnically diverse church and world.

REFORM OR PARADIGM CHANGE?

These reflections so far have dealt with reviewing and revising existing formational models. But another voice needs to be heard, one which questions the premises of existing models. Here are two succinct expressions of that voice. First, shortly after publication in 2003 of the *National Certification Standards for Lay Ecclesial Ministers*,[53] I was in conversation with the director of an archdiocesan multicultural ministry office; this person was not American-born. At the time I was on the board of the National Association for Lay Ministry, one of the national ministry organizations responsible for formulating the *Standards*. The director's overall assessment of the document was concisely put: "I don't see myself in your standards." Second, around the same time Allan Figueroa Deck urged that the national discussion about lay ecclesial ministry "needs to include the particular circumstances of the Hispanics who struggle to meet the often unrealistic requirements of existing educational protocols regarding lay ecclesial ministers."[54]

These two individuals expressed in short form a whole universe of discourse perhaps more spoken about among practitioners than written about in books and journals. Although pastoral and formational leaders in many ethnic communities would, I believe, understand and resonate with the point, their counterparts in white/Anglo communities sometimes find it harder to do so. And the dialogue needed to bridge the gap, between those for whom existing formational standards are unrealistic or inappropriate and those for whom they are obvious, reasonable, and necessary, has far to go. On one hand might be the question, "Why won't you accept and honor, as equally valid with yours, the ways of leadership discernment and formation that are recognized and effective in my community? Sometimes academic credentialing is just out of place or even counterproductive."[55] On the other hand one might hear, "You can't be a Catholic school teacher or hospital chaplain, or a priest or nurse in a Catholic parish, without the requisite academic formation and professional credentials; why should standards be lower for lay ecclesial ministers?" A further pivotal factor is the "disproportionately lower levels of socio-economic resources" available in some cultural communities.[56] We need thoughtful discussion as well as personal sharing on questions like these, and on the experiences and perspectives that underlie them, if we are to better understand the lay of the land and descry the way forward for ministry formation in the culturally diverse Catholic Church of the United States.

What might emerge from such discussion? A greater commitment to pursue advanced degree work by lay ecclesial ministers of every culture?[57] Or a recognition that we may need an entirely "different *model* of academy"[58]—that is, an educational-formational paradigm shift? The answer may be both/and, but what it looks like or how to achieve it has yet to emerge.

In the meantime, perhaps Figure 10.1 can help us plot a basic trajectory. At present it is too often true that formation is happening in different ways in different cultural communities, with insufficient respect across the cultural divide—that is, we are in the upper left quadrant of "separation." At the same time, formational leaders in nondominant cultural communities may fear they are expected to assimilate, to their detriment, to the dominant culture's model of ministry formation—that is to say, move to the lower right quadrant of "assimilation." Can this dilemma be resolved by our consciously choosing a place in the upper right quadrant of integration, where each culture maintains and strengthens its own distinctive formational visions, goals, and standards, while also cultivating understanding and respect for the visions, goals, and standards of others? What this might call for was expressed in a passage from the USCCB's October 2004 draft "Document on Lay Ecclesial Ministry":

> The dominant culture needs to recognize that the content, methods, goals, design, administration, and outcomes of truly intercultural [formation] programs are fully valid and equally legitimate with, even though they may differ from, the formation programs and patterns they are accustomed to. Their content and goals [in intercultural programs] are not diluted, but more culturally relevant; their methods and design are not less rigorous, but more culturally effective; the differences are not inherently inferior, but richly distinctive. Indeed [here follows a sentence that remains in *Co-Workers*, on page 36], formation programs operating from a single cultural model miss a dimension of richness available only through a living experience of many cultures.[59]

CONCLUSION

What can each of us do to make progress toward *Co-Workers*'s vision of a more richly intercultural ministry formation? Let us take a cue from Kim's matrix of interethnic communication[60] and pose the question for ourselves at three levels.

A. At the personal level: What will I do this year to become well informed about the ministry formation needs and circumstances of one cultural community other than my own? What will I do to imagine with more clarity the possibility of a new paradigm for ministry and ministry formation?

B. At the local level: What will I do this year in my own formational program or institutional setting to inaugurate, or to join and contribute to, conversations and projects aimed at enhancing intercultural awareness, communication, and understanding? How will I encourage and help my colleagues imagine a new formational paradigm?

C. At the regional or national level: What will I do this year in my professional membership organizations to promote dialogue and forward steps that will enrich the intercultural dimension of ministry formation?

Such efforts can contribute to a genuine "change of mentality" and "transformation of structures" (Pope John Paul II) in our ministry formation programs, making them better able to serve the richly diverse church we are. Progress toward this goal is an integral and urgently important dimension of the future to which the formation section of *Co-Workers* calls us.

NOTES

1. If we compare U.S. Conference of Catholic Bishops, *Co-Workers in the Vineyard of the Lord: A Resource for Guiding the Development of Lay Ecclesial Ministry* (Washington, DC: USCCB, 2005), with U.S. Conference of Catholic Bishops, *Program of Priestly Formation*, 5th ed. (Washington, DC: USCCB, 2006), and with U.S. Conference of Catholic Bishops, *National Directory for the Formation, Ministry, and Life of Permanent Deacons in the United States* (Washington, DC: USCCB, 2005), we find that the formation material in each document is, respectively, 21, 69, and 84 pages. As a percentage of each document, that material is respectively 31, 56, and 56 percent. Note also the U.S. Conference of Catholic Bishops' 113-page book on *The Basic Plan for the Ongoing Formation of Priests* (Washington, DC: USCCB, 2001); this topic covers one and one-half pages in *Co-Workers*.

2. Quote is from the New Revised Standard Version of the Bible.

3. Quote is from the Revised Standard Version of the Bible.

4. USCCB, *Co-Workers*, 36.

5. U.S. Conference of Catholic Bishops, *Welcoming the Stranger Among Us: Unity in Diversity* (Washington, DC: USCCB, 2000), 8.

6. USCCB, *Welcoming* 2; see also 33.

7. USCCB, *Welcoming*, 4; see 55.

8. Consider, for example, Robert T. Carter's comment, that "Whites generally do not see themselves as members of a racial group . . . [and consequently] do not understand or appreciate the role and significance of race and racism in the lives of People of Color (Sleeter, 1989)." Robert T. Carter, "Reimagining Race in Education: A New Paradigm from Psychology," *Teachers College Record* 102 (2000): 874, referring to C. E. Sleeter, "Multicultural Education as a Form of Resistance to Oppression," *Journal of Education* 171 (1989): 51–71.

9. USCCB, *Welcoming*, 4 and 30.

10. Cited in USCCB, *Welcoming*, 23. The editors of the ecumenical collection *Globalization of Theological Education*, in their introduction to the volume, recognize this same twofold challenge: "There is a consensus among contributors to this book that the new understanding demanded by the new global context requires nothing short of a conversion in the thinking of most who minister in North America, including theological educators, and calls for a transformation of the ethos and structure of the institutions through which they minister." In *Globalization of Theological Education*, edited by Alice Frazer Evans, Robert A. Evans, David A. Roozen (Maryknoll, NY: Orbis, 1993), 4.

11. According to CARA, in 2008–2009, participants in lay ecclesial ministry formation programs were 58 percent white/Anglo, 33 percent Hispanic/Latino, 3 percent black, 3 percent Asian, and 4 percent other; see Mary L. Gautier, "Catholic Ministry Formation Enrollments: Statistical Overview for 2008–2009," dated April 2009, available at http://cara.georgetown.edu/Overview200809.pdf (accessed March 13, 2010). Whites predominate even more in the ranks of faculty. In major seminaries in 2003–2004, 92.3 percent of faculty were white/Anglo; see Victor J. Klimoski, Kevin J. O'Neil, and Katarina M. Schuth, *Educating Leaders for Ministry: Issues and*

Responses (Collegeville, MN: Liturgical Press, 2005), 13, table 1. A survey in 2008 of member schools of the Association of Graduate Programs in Ministry (AGPIM) indicated that 84 percent of the faculty were white, 8 percent Hispanic, 5 percent African American, and 3 percent Asian; see "AGPIM Survey Results: February 2009" (report distributed at the AGPIM annual meeting, Tucson, AZ, February 2009).

12. Consider Espín's comment: "In the battlefront of pastoral care most ministries, ordained or not, might be discovering that they were trained for a church that does not and will not exist. Their ministerial training was probably based on premises that do not reflect the full and culturally complex reality of contemporary Catholicism in the United States." Orlando Espín, "A Multicultural Church? Theological Reflections from Below," in *The Multicultural Church: A New Landscape in U.S. Theologies*, edited by William Cenkner (New York: Paulist, 1996), 56.

13. Mark A. Chesler, "Perceptions of Faculty Behavior by Students of Color," Center for Research on Learning and Teaching, CRLT Occasional Papers, No. 7, 1997, University of Michigan, 1, available at http://www.crlt.umich.edu/publinks/CRLT_no7.pdf (accessed March 13, 2010).

14. Samuel L. Gaertner and John F. Dovidio, *Reducing Intergroup Bias: The Common Ingroup Identity Model* (Philadelphia: Psychology Press, 2000), 17. See also John F. Dovidio and Samuel L. Gaertner, "On the Nature of Contemporary Prejudice: The Causes, Consequences, and Challenges of Aversive Racism," in *Confronting Racism: The Problem and the Response*, edited by J. Eberhardt and S. T. Fiske (Newbury Park, CA: Sage, 1998), 3–32.

15. Because "aversive racists recognize that prejudice is bad, but they do not recognize [and are aversive to the suggestion] that they are prejudiced." Gaertner and Dovidio, *Reducing Intergroup Bias*, 14–15; also Dovidio and Gaertner, "Aversive Racism," 26.

16. Dovidio and Gaertner, "Aversive Racism," 29. Yet they also note aversive racists are prone to deny evidence of their racism, and the very denial "may then intensify racial conflict and distrust" (43).

17. Decategorization refers to re-envisioning a member of an outgroup (a group I do not belong to—perhaps, for an example, "mentally handicapped persons"), no longer simply in light of the characteristics or stereotypes of the outgroup, but now as an individual ("This is John, Frank and Mary's third son, who goes to school with my son, Pedro; John has Down syndrome"). Recategorization refers to re-envisioning two distinct groups (e.g., Anglos and Latinos) as united, in being members of the same superordinate group (as U.S citizens or human beings). Mutual intergroup differentiation refers to members of a shared superordinate group (e.g., U.S. citizens) simultaneously maintaining also a sense of their subgroup identity (as Korean American or Mexican American). These methods seek to break down barriers to understanding and positive relationships, or to recognize and harness the dynamics of social categorization (for example, recognizing the human tendency toward "ingroup favoritism" and applying it more widely, to members of other groups, by recategorizing them as members of one's ingroup). Such methods may be useful in the toolkit of a formation program administrator or teacher in fostering relationships in the program or classroom; they can help a lay ecclesial minister do the same in a pastoral ministry setting.

On the Common Ingroup Identity Model see, for example, Gaertner and Dovidio, *Reducing Intergroup Bias*; idem, "A Common Ingroup Identity: A Categorization-Based Approach for Reducing Intergroup Bias," in *Handbook of Prejudice, Stereotyping, and Discrimination*, edited by Todd D. Nelson (New York: Psychology Press, 2009), 489–505; John F. Dovidio, Samuel L. Gaertner, and Tamar Saguy, "Commonality and the Complexity of 'We': Social Attitudes and Social Change," *Personality and Social Psychology Review* 13 (2009): 3–20.

18. See J. B. McConahay, "Modern Racism, Ambivalence, and the Modern Racism Scale," in *Prejudice, Discrimination, and Racism*, edited by John F. Dovidio and Samuel L. Gaertner (Orlando, FL: Academic Press, 1986), 91–125; D. O. Sears, "Symbolic Racism," in *Eliminating Racism: Profiles in Controversy*, edited by P. A. Katz and D. A. Taylor (New York: Plenum, 1988), 53–84; Eberhardt and Fiske, *Confronting Racism*; Eduardo Bonilla-Silva, "'New Racism,' Color-Blind Racism, and the Future of Whiteness in America," in *White Out: The Continuing Significance of Racism*, edited by Ashley W. Doane and Eduardo Bonilla-Silva (New York: Routledge, 2003), 271–84. In Edwin I. Hernández and Kenneth G. Davis, *Reconstructing the Sacred Tower: Challenge and Promise of Latino/a Theological Education* (Scranton, PA: University of Scranton Press, 2003), see 53–57. Cardinal Francis George, "Dwell in My Love: A Pastoral Letter on Racism," available at http://www.archdiocese-chgo.org/cardinal/dwellinmylove/dwellinmylove.shtm (accessed March 13, 2010).

19. For example, for a proposed sketch of stages by which "whites" become more aware of their own racial identity, see Mark A. Chesler, Melissa Peet, and Todd Sevig, "Blinded by Whiteness: The Development of White College Students' Racial Awareness," in *White Out*, 215–30. For a helpful and detailed description of a method to foster this outcome—drawing on the literature of theological reflection and Kolb's learning cycle—see Carla A. Grosch-Miller, "Minding the Gap: White Theological Reflection on Racial Justice," *Journal of Adult Theological Education* 5, no. 2 (2008): 144–57. More generally, on the website of the University of Michigan's Center for Research on Learning and Teaching, see Shari Saunders and Diana Kardia, "Creating Inclusive College Classrooms," available at http://www.crlt.umich.edu/gsis/P3_1.php (accessed March 13, 2010); related resources are available at http://www.crlt.umich.edu/multiteaching/multiteaching.php (accessed March 13, 2010). Also useful are the works of Eric H. F. Law.

20. USCCB, *Co-Workers*, 36.

21. For the concept underlying this model, see John W. Berry, Uichol Kim, and Pawel Boski, "Psychological Acculturation of Immigrants," in *Cross-Cultural Adaptation: Current Approaches*, edited by Young Yun Kim and William B. Gudykunst (Newbury Park, CA: Sage Publications, 1987), 66, Figure 3.1. For adaptations of this model, see Stella Ting-Toomey, "Identity Negotiation Theory: Crossing Cultural Boundaries," in *Theorizing About Intercultural Communication*, edited by William B. Gudykunst (Thousand Oaks, CA: Sage Publications, 2005), 224, Figure 10.1; also John F. Dovidio, Samuel L. Gaertner, and Tamar Saguy, "Commonality and the Complexity of 'We'," 10, Figure 1.

22. The term "enlightened integration" comes from Fernando F. Segovia, "Two Places and No Place on Which to Stand: Mixture and Otherness in Hispanic American Theology," in *Mestizo Christianity: Theology from the Latino Perspective*, edited by Arturo J. Bañuelas (Maryknoll, NY: Orbis, 1995), 41, n. 16.

23. See William Isaacs, *Dialogue and the Art of Thinking Together* (New York: Doubleday, 1999).

24. USCCB, *Welcoming*, 1. See also U.S. Conference of Catholic Bishops, *Encuentro and Mission: A Renewed Pastoral Framework for Hispanic Ministry* (Washington, DC: USCCB, 2002), 37–38, and 57.(4).a.

25. USCCB, *Welcoming*, 2, 27.

26. USCCB, *Welcoming*, 24; see 33.

27. USCCB, *Welcoming*, 28, 36, 37, 44, 60; endnote 5.

28. USCCB, *Welcoming*, 60, endnote 5. By way of comparison, there is a more positive vision of assimilation expressed, for example, by Young Yun Kim, "*Unum and Pluribus*: Ideological Underpinnings of Interethnic Communication in the United States," in *Intercultural Communication: A Reader*, edited by Larry A. Samovar, Richard E. Porter, and Edwin R. McDaniel, 12th ed. (Boston: Wadsworth Cengage Learning, 2009), 185–97; also "Association and Dissociation: A Contextual Theory of Interethnic Communication," in Gudykunst, *Theorizing About Intercultural Communication*, 323–49.

29. USCCB, *Welcoming*, 1–2.

30. José R. Irizarry, "The Religious Educator as Cultural Spec-Actor: Researching Self in Intercultural Pedagogy," *Religious Education* 98 (2003): 365–81, at 371; he discusses interculturality especially in pages 371–75. For a more extended and relevant treatment, see his "Toward an Intercultural Approach to Theological Education for Ministry," in *Shaping Beloved Community: Multicultural Theological Education*, edited by David V. Esterline and Ogbu U. Kalu (Louisville, KY: Westminster John Knox Press, 2006), 28–42.

31. Irizarry, "Toward an Intercultural Approach," 30.

32. Espín, "A Multicultural Church?" 62–64.

33. In Greg Tanaka, *The Intercultural Campus: Transcending Culture and Power in American Higher Education* (New York: P. Lang, 2003), see, for example, 63–67, 101, 114–17, 144–46.

34. Tanaka, *The Intercultural Campus*, 98–120.

35. Tanaka speculates that "if there is going to be a new unity, it might very well be a *process* or *sentiment* and not a new structure at all." Tanaka, *The Intercultural Campus*, 43.

36. USCCB, *Co-Workers*, 37.

37. USCCB, *Co-Workers*, 42, 40.

38. USCCB, *Co-Worker*, 44.

39. USCCB, *Co-Worker*, 47, 48, 49.

40. USCCB, *Co-Worker*, 51.

41. USCCB, *Welcoming*, 2, 31, 36, 37, 39.

42. USCCB, *Welcoming*, 3, 31, 34–37, 39, 41.

43. See Harry Triandis, "Culture and Conflict," in Samovar, Porter, and McDaniel, *Intercultural Communication: A Reader*, 19 and 21; Gudykunst et al., "Theorizing About Intercultural Communication: An Introduction," in Gudykunst, *Theorizing About Intercultural Communication*, 10.

44. See Geneva Gay, *Culturally Responsive Teaching: Theory, Research, and Practice* (New York: Teachers College Press, 2000), 90–105.

45. See, for example, Janet M. Bennett and Milton J. Bennett, "Developing Intercultural Sensitivity: An Integrative Approach to Global and Domestic Diversity," in *Handbook of Intercultural Training*, 3rd ed., edited by Dan Landis, Janet M. Bennett, and Milton J. Bennett (eds.), *Handbook of Intercultural Training*, 3rd ed. (Thousand Oaks, CA: Sage, 2004), 147–65; also Milton J. Bennett, "Towards Ethnorelativism: A Developmental Model of Intercultural Sensitivity," in *Education for the Intercultural Experience*, edited by Michael R. Paige (Yarmouth, ME: Intercultural Press, 1993), 21–71.

46. Bennett and Bennett, "Developing Intercultural Sensitivity," 149 and 152.

47. Bennett and Bennett, "Developing Intercultural Sensitivity," 152–53. Ethnocentric stages are denial, defense, and minimization; ethnorelative stages are acceptance, adaptation, and integration (153–58). A self-assessment tool based on this theory has been developed: the "Intercultural Development Inventory," available at www.idiinventory.com/index.php (accessed March 13, 2010). This and other surveys and inventories are described in P. Christopher Earley and Soon Ang, *Cultural Intelligence: Individual Interactions Across Cultures* (Stanford, CA: Stanford University Press, 2003), 193–99, also 204–5.

48. Stephen S. Dudek, "Becoming Inclusive Communities of Faith: Biblical Reflection and Effective Frameworks," *New Theology Review* 21 (2008): 40–51, at 43–46. See also Robert Schreiter, "Just What Do We Want? Ministry in a Multicultural World," *New Theology Review* 13 (2000): 4–13, at 8.

49. Dudek, "Becoming Inclusive Communities of Faith," 46–50.

50. See U.S. Conference of Catholic Bishops, *Encuentro and Mission*, 51, explicitly endorsing "a vision that welcomes the many faces of the Church to the table where decisions are made."

51. See "Institutional Change and the Globalization of Theological Education" in *The Globalization of Theological Education*, 300–337; *Minorities on Campus: A Handbook for Enhancing Diversity*, edited by Madeleine F. Green (Washington, DC: American Council on Education, 1989); Hernández and Davis, *Reconstructing the Sacred Tower*, 72–76, 82–87.

52. Gaertner and Dovidio, *Reducing Intergroup Bias*, 43.

53. *National Certification Standards for Lay Ecclesial Ministers* (Washington, DC: NALM, NCCL, NFCYM, 2003).

54. Allan Figueroa Deck, "A Latino Practical Theology: Mapping the Road Ahead," *Theological Studies* 65 (2004): 287, n. 27. See also Mark M. Gray and Mary L. Gautier, "Latino/a Catholic Leaders in the United States," in Edwin I. Hernández, Milagros Peña, Kenneth G. Davis, and Elizabeth Station, *Emerging Voices, Urgent Choices: Essays on Latino/a Religious Leadership* (Leiden: Brill, 2006), esp. 70–75, and the reference to "issues related to formation requirements" on 89.

55. Recall, for example: "We learned that leadership is identified, developed, exercised, and accepted in different ways in different cultural groups. Charismatic rather than credentialed leadership is important in many minority communities." Subcommittee on Lay Ministry, *Lay Ecclesial Ministry: The State of the Questions* (Washington, DC: USCC, 1999), 56.

56. Gray and Gautier, "Latino/a Catholic Leaders," 75, also 88–89; Hernández and Davis, *Reconstructing the Sacred Tower*, 49–51.

57. For example, "Only by achieving academic credibility at the master's level and beyond can Hispanics gain better access to positions from which they can truly effect change." Hernández and Davis, *Reconstructing the Sacred Tower*, 47. See also Allan Figueroa Deck, "At the Crossroads: North American and Hispanic," in *We Are a People! Initiatives in Hispanic American Theology*, edited by Roberto S. Goizueta (Minneapolis: Fortress Press, 1992), 18–20.

58. Roberto S. Goizueta, "US Hispanic Mestizaje and Theological Method," in *Migrants and Refugees*, Concilium 1993/4, edited by Dietmar Mieth and Lisa Sowle Cahill (London: SCM Press, August 1993), 23; see also, Gary Riebe-Estrella, "Theological Education as *Convivencia*," in *From the Heart of Our People: Latino/a Explorations in Catholic Systematic Theology*, edited by Orlando O. Espín and Miguel H. Díaz (Maryknoll, NY: Orbis Books, 1999), 209–16.

59. The "Document on Lay Ecclesial Ministry," from which this passage is taken, was the 2004 draft version of *Co-Workers* that was made available to national ministry associations for purposes of consultation.

60. See Kim, "Association and Dissociation."

11

Adopting Effective Human Resource Development Strategies for the Catholic Church in the United States

Michael J. O'Loughlin with Michael J. Brough

Growing up in suburban Massachusetts, I was a parishioner at a vibrant, though seemingly unremarkable, Roman Catholic parish. Comprised of two thousand families, the church was served by a dedicated and charismatic pastor, a friendly parochial vicar, and a devoted troop of lay ecclesial ministers and volunteers. My earliest memories of Catholic life at this parish include the united effort to build a new church and rectory up the road on a beautiful patch of untouched farmland. Although not privy to the financial aspects of the building project at such a young age, I was awed by the efforts of the priests and families of the parish working together to realize the goal of building the new church. With my family, I attended various fundraisers, listened to homilies on the importance of giving, and, most importantly to me at the time, participated in social activities that gave us parishioners a sense of common purpose. Fairly quickly, the new buildings were finished, and the parish marched triumphantly in a parade of sorts from the old church to the new. The series of events that brought us a new spiritual home was possible because the pastor and his associates, both ordained and lay, tirelessly worked together toward a shared vision of what our parish could be.

As I grew older, I attended religious education classes taught by well-meaning, and often effective, volunteer teachers who reported to a lay director of religious education. The parochial vicar, a gregarious and dedicated man, led the youth group, and worked in tandem with lay ministers and parents to lead whitewater rafting trips to northern New England and plan casual social events for my peers and me to congregate in a safe space. The liturgies were reverent and meaningful, as the scores of lectors, cantors, acolytes, ushers, musicians, and lay ecclesial ministers labored with a sense of joy and purpose to create vibrant worship experiences for the parish. Whether one preferred lofty traditional hymns, the folk music that arose after Vatican II, or guitar-led praise music, there was a liturgy that appealed to each individual's sense of the divine. Eventually I was asked by the pastor to be a lector, to teach religious education, and to organize some events for the youth group. The place that had helped form my spiritual life was asking me to do the same for others, and after some prodding, I agreed. The life at the parish came together and was sustained through the blessing of the Spirit, of course, but also through the hard work and dedication of professional and volunteer ministers.

Soon after I left for college and said good-bye to my parish, a new pastor was appointed. Talking with my family and friends about parish life, it seemed that the vibrancy and excitement began to dwindle. Some attributed this to the fallout of the sex scandal that hit the Boston archdiocese particularly hard, others to the spate of parish closures that followed. This new reality left my parish with essentially a part-time pastor. But others saw no tangible reason for the dissipation of energy. On the occasions when I visited my parents and went to Mass, I, like others, felt that something was missing. The enthusiasm of the volunteers had dissipated; the liturgies no longer felt particularly inspiring; the youth group seemed to lack the vitality it once had. Of course, I am aware that nostalgia may have caused the life of the parish to seem diminished.

But as I began talking to those parishioners who were still involved in the parish while I was away, I realized that there had been a change in the culture at my church. The best lay ecclesial ministers and volunteers were no longer sought out, trained, and exhorted to continue their ministries. Instead, the parish bulletin passively asked those who were interested to sign up or call the parish office. Volunteer opportunities were no longer explicitly framed as participation in lay ministry. I was unable to pinpoint it then, but now it seems that the cause of this malaise was not abandonment by the Spirit, but a breakdown in human resource management and development at the parish. My parish had been blessed with a pastor who understood, perhaps instinctively, that best practices in human resource development would make parish life vibrant and life-giving, but the new pastor perhaps did not quite grasp this concept or simply did not have time to devote to the necessary tasks that follow. Whatever the reasons, the result was weakened parish life, with less spiritually nourishing liturgies, a dearth of programming for young people, a disinclination for members to see themselves as part of a people of God, and, eventually, a drop in attendance and donations. Once started, such a spiral is hard to control.

HUMAN RESOURCE DEVELOPMENT: AN OVERVIEW

Human resource development does not, at first glance, lend itself to passionate advocacy or emotional debate. It may appear to be a sterile subject, and the effort it takes to implement best practices must be constant, with results that are not quite quantitative. But as seen in the anecdote above, good human resource development in a parish has effects one can readily observe. The differing results between mediocre human resource development and best practices manifest themselves in myriad ways, from a spirit of vitality in the parish, to a sense of purpose among volunteers, to recruiting the best people for lay ministry positions.

In a 2007 address at the National Symposium on Lay Ecclesial Ministry in Collegeville, Minnesota, Michael Brough of the National Leadership Roundtable on Church Management highlighted the strides the church had made in implementing best practices in human resource development in parishes across the United States. He then challenged those present to "continue to raise our expectations concerning 'best organizational practices' if we are to continue to recruit, form, retain and reward the most qualified and gifted ministers for our Church."[1]

Although the church has already widely acknowledged the value of lay ministers, the way that these ministers are selected and formed is an underdeveloped area, both theologically and pragmatically. Effective human resource development is an area of church personnel management that has attracted the attention of Catholic bishops in the United States. *Co-Workers in the Vineyard of the Lord*, a document of the U.S. Conference of Catholic Bishops (USCCB), describes itself as "a pastoral and theological reflection on the reality of lay ecclesial ministry, as an affirmation of those who serve in this way, and as a synthesis of best thinking and practice." In it, the bishops articulate their "strong desire for the fruitful collaboration of ordained and lay ministers who, in distinct but complementary ways, continue in the Church the saving mission of Christ for the world, his vineyard."[2] The bishops make clear that lay ecclesial ministers are integral to further the mission of the church. Dioceses and parishes should follow this insight by recognizing that these individuals are valued employees, and in order to retain lay ministers with top talent and pastoral gifts, effective human resource development is essential. To that end, Brough offers several key factors identified in fostering employee engagement and enhanced human resource development at the parish level. Effective human resource development includes the purposeful selection of talent; meaningful work and clear impact of that work for lay ministry professionals; inspired leadership; continuous learning through professional development opportunities; a sense of community; and results-based recognition and rewards. He says that adopting these elements improves human resource development and suggests that they always be present whenever decisions are made about lay ecclesial ministers.

KEY ASPECTS OF HUMAN RESOURCE DEVELOPMENT

Recruitment and Selection

In *Co-Workers*, the bishops express their gratitude to those who serve as lay ecclesial ministers for service that is "unique and necessary for the life and growth of the Church."[3] With this recognition that lay ecclesial ministers are necessary to the life-giving mission of the church, it is essential that the best talent be recruited to serve in these roles. Bishops and pastors can take several basic steps toward this end. First, dioceses should build up the capacity and funding to provide central recruiting and formation services for parishes seeking lay ecclesial ministers. Having proper and adequate financial support in place is essential to ensuring that parishes are hiring the best talent as lay ecclesial ministers and that their positions are sustainable through the long term. Without this basic financial structure in place, the efficacy, sustainability, and impact of lay ecclesial ministers will be severely diminished. Although the demands on diocesan and parish budgets are already extraordinary, when parishioners understand the costs of supporting ministry, the money will follow.

Next, compulsory, comprehensive training should be provided for all those who interview and appoint lay ecclesial ministers. Research by Katarina Schuth indicates that almost a third of priests see themselves as either "not too effective" or "not at all effective" in the area of hiring and supervising professional staff.[4] Training would help them respond to that self-identified need, enabling them to seek out and retain the best candidates for lay ecclesial ministry positions. If those responsible for hiring in parishes do not feel that they can adequately find and hire talent, then it is unreasonable to expect that they will be successful in their searches. By equipping pastors and others who are charged with hiring with the skills to seek out top talent, parishes will benefit from an increase of talented and dedicated ministerial professionals.

Third, all parishes and dioceses should establish clear expectations for the qualifications, formation, and capabilities of potential lay ecclesial ministers. Just as priests are held to high professional standards, lay ecclesial ministers must be able to understand clearly what is expected of them and carry out their jobs skillfully and professionally. A pastor is not appointed because he is an affable fellow, but because he possesses the skills and knowledge necessary to carry out his job well. The same high standards must be utilized when hiring lay ecclesial ministers. One way to ensure that applicants possess the requisite skills is to create detailed and thorough job postings that clearly articulate what is expected of the incumbent and ways that success can be measured. Ten percent of full-time and 23 percent of part-time lay ecclesial ministers do not currently have job descriptions.[5] The church can and should improve on this number and also make sure that position descriptions are not a vague list of things needing to be done that have somehow fallen into the purview of lay ecclesial ministers, but rather a focused description of the essential functions of the position.

Finally, the diversity of the church and society should be reflected in those recruited to lay ecclesial ministry. The Catholic Church in the United States is changing, and hires should reflect this developing reality. Demographic data from the USCCB show that nearly 35 percent of Catholics in the United States are of Latino/Latina heritage; this cohort "contributed to 71% of the growth of the Catholic Church in the United States since 1960."[6] The future of the church in this country is one with a larger Hispanic presence than it has ever seen before; parishes and dioceses should acknowledge the current and future realities by hiring talented individuals who appreciate these realities.

Orientation and Support

The second area of a comprehensive personnel system identified in *Co-Workers* is the initial orientation and ongoing support for new lay ecclesial ministers. Once the church is successful in identifying and recruiting talented lay ecclesial ministers, it is then incumbent upon those churches to integrate these women and men into the life of the parish and diocese. The church can accomplish this through a well-organized and comprehensive orientation that is provided for all new lay ecclesial ministers in all parishes and dioceses. This orientation should utilize a personnel manual that is made available to all church employees and also include a review of the personnel policies and procedures of the organization.

As part of ongoing support, parishes need to make mentoring and leadership coaching available to lay ecclesial ministers in order to develop communication and leadership skills, for the sake of both personal and organizational development. To assist with this, continuing formation in the area of personnel development and management should be provided to human resource professionals by dioceses, national organizations, Catholic colleges and universities, and others.

Since 1970, the National Association of Church Personnel Administrators (NACPA) has been the premier organization promoting comprehensive church personnel systems that integrate Catholic social teaching and sound management principles. NACPA has professionalized human resource management in the church by strengthening working relationships among church leaders, ministers, and employees, and developing human resource skills and competence. From job descriptions to comprehensive compensation reviews, from self-audits to the overhaul of benefit programs, NACPA's work demonstrates that an investment in human resource development results in greater effectiveness in ministry.[7] The organization itself, and its various education programs and resources, can provide assistance to parishes and dioceses in offering effective orientation and support.

Finally, all church employees should be given professional development opportunities relative to their area of ministry to enable them to serve more effectively, especially as new challenges manifest themselves in the lives of the faithful. By implementing these goals, churches will better serve their lay ministers, who, in turn, will provide stronger and more stable ministry to parishioners.

Evaluation and Feedback

The *Co-Workers* document recognizes that self-reflection and formal performance appraisal provide valuable opportunities for the growth of individual lay ecclesial ministers. Unfortunately, formal evaluation has not been part of the culture of the church, and many do not appreciate the benefits, never having had a positive experience of the process themselves. The Villanova Center for the Study of Church Management sponsored a two-day national conference exploring this subject; this in-depth analysis made clear that there remains much more work to be done in this area.[8] Yet despite the dearth of formal study, the call in *Co-Workers* to integrate best organizational practices means that the issue of performance management deserves serious attention.

All those who work in the parish, both ordained and lay, should possess a shared understanding of what they are doing and why. With this in mind, all parishes and dioceses should have a clear mission statement that forms a shared statement of purpose for all those in the ministerial workplace. Parishes and dioceses should also develop a formal performance management system for all who minister in the church. An aspect of this would be that all lay ecclesial ministers receive a formal, annual performance appraisal. While the number receiving performance evaluations has grown, from 37.2 percent in 1990 to 44.2 percent in 2005,[9] more than half of all lay ecclesial ministers are still without the benefit of such a potentially fruitful and even transformative experience. Training should be provided for all lay ecclesial ministers and all supervisors to develop the skills that will make performance management processes a mutually beneficial experience for both the individual and the organization.

Some parishes have already profited from such an approach. Joseph Donnelly, pastor of Sacred Heart Church in Southbury, Connecticut, recalled how his parish successfully implemented an evaluation system for ordained and lay ministers, leading to a greater understanding of ministry as a team effort and closer adherence to the parish mission. Recognizing that ministers and other church professionals may recoil at the term "evaluation," Donnelly called the process a "Performance Perspective," and described it as "a way of helping people be accountable for the work they are doing based on their job description as well as on the unique gifts they brought."[10]

Donnelly's process involves creating an evaluation worksheet that asks a number of questions, including, "What do you perceive as this person's strengths? What do you perceive as their areas for growth? How would you describe their expertise in their own area of ministry? How is their ability to listen and work within a larger community?" Then, the individuals being evaluated are given several copies of this worksheet to distribute to those with whom they interact professionally. When the answer sheets are completed, the responses are collected and delivered to the employee being evaluated in a one-on-one conversation with the pastor or human resource professional. The pastor, who leads the evaluation in Donnelly's example, elicits response from the evaluated employee, and a conversation ensues around each comment. Every employee in the parish, including the pastor himself, is evaluated in this way. Donnelly says that a formal process such as the one outlined above allows all who are part of a parish team to hear the positive comments about their ministries, which can be quite uplifting and positive for development, as well as to consider weaknesses that can be corrected and improved.

Perhaps the most comprehensive performance development system involves a 360-degree assessment that provides feedback to both lay and ordained ministers on competencies of ministerial effectiveness. One such initiative has been developed in a joint effort of the National Leadership Roundtable on Church Management, the National Association of Church Personnel Administrators, and the National Federations of Priests' Councils. The leadership assessment tool was designed in collaboration with the world-leading Center for Creative Leadership (CCL) and has been customized for ordained and lay ministers in the Catholic Church. Reflecting the call in *Co-Workers* for a "formal opportunity for every individual minister to reflect on his or her own performance and get feedback from a supervisor and that may include the views of colleagues and those served,"[11] this 360-degree assessment draws upon the *National Certification Standards for Lay Ecclesial Ministers* to guide individual development plans aligned with diocesan or parish pastoral plans.[12] Those who minister in the name of the church are called to grow in the likeness of Jesus so that their ministry can more accurately reflect his life and communicate his message. Performance development systems formalize and enhance this growth.

Compensation

If performance management can be described as a sensitive matter worthy of further attention, one can imagine the challenge of addressing the complex issue of compensation for lay ecclesial ministry. When *Co-Workers* speaks of a desire to "achieve consistency where possible and to encourage diversity where appropriate,"[13] compensation is perhaps one of the most challenging areas in which to achieve this balance. Canon law speaks of the right of lay persons to "decent remuneration appropriate to their condition so that they are able to provide decently for their own needs and those of their family. They also have a right for their social provision, social security, and health benefits to be duly provided."[14] The USCCB speaks of the "need for renewal" within the church to ensure it is "exemplary" in its treatment of employees and meeting its obligations to provide a "sufficient livelihood for employees."[15]

In a presentation at the annual meeting of the Leadership Roundtable in 2007, Linda Bearie, chancellor of the diocese of San Jose, noted that her diocese seeks to achieve fair compensation practices by utilizing a five-to-one ratio. That is, the highest-paid employee in the diocese is not paid more than five times the lowest-paid employee.[16] Bearie said that her diocese is concerned with recruiting "the best and brightest to work for the Church and live their lives without having to worry about just scraping by." To achieve this, the diocese of San Jose has "a committee of ministers, business managers, pastors, and parochial vicars from [parishes] who contribute to the annual updating of compensation information."[17] Having formal guidelines in place regarding compensation enables those hiring lay ecclesial ministers to pay fair salaries to their employees and allows them to focus on the needs of the faithful. The alternative creates unhealthy work environments where ministry cannot flourish.

David DeLambo, associate director of the Office of Pastoral Planning for the diocese of Cleveland, has observed, "Those in ministry right now are those who can afford to be in ministry."[18] That is, only those who have the benefit of financial security can afford to serve in ministry in the church, not necessarily the most talented individuals. To rectify this, the church should strive to ensure that all parishes and dioceses undertake a comprehensive compensation survey and follow best practices already in place in some dioceses providing a compensation program "to administer the salaries of those working with them in an equitable and consistent manner."[19] Lay ecclesial ministers should be compensated fairly and with consistency at all times.

Student debt is one issue that the church must address if it is to be able to attract the most talented individuals to ministry and to offer compensation that meets the needs of lay ecclesial ministers.[20] One report on graduate theological students in church ministry paints a disturbing picture of students whose "level of debt is affecting their career choices, holding them back from purchasing homes, preventing them from saving for their children's education, limiting their retirement savings, causing them to delay health care needs, and creating stress in their personal and professional lives."[21] Ministry cannot flourish in this context, nor can many would-be talented and dedicated lay ministers choose to enter the field as a result.

As part of a comprehensive compensation program, parishes and dioceses should take both internal and external equity into account when establishing individual salaries and salary ranges for all lay ecclesial ministers. This involves reviewing the fairness of employment contracts or compensation programs when compared with other employees within the organization (internal equity) and between parishes or dioceses (external equity). Dioceses should also develop creative solutions to ensure health and other social benefits are provided for all lay ecclesial ministers. Presently, 19 percent of full-time lay parish ministers do not have medical insurance, while 45.8 percent do not receive annual retreat time.[22] Although working in ministry is certainly a vocational calling and should not be viewed as a lucrative field in which to build wealth, the church must offer salaries that are fair and competitive in order to attract top talent to care for the needs of the faithful. And finally, the portability of benefits, talked about by the bishops in *Co-Workers*, should become a reality for all who dedicate their lives to lay ecclesial ministry.

Transitions and Terminations

When transitions go well in the ministerial workplace, both individuals and the community of faith can grow from the experience. When transitions and terminations are not well handled, painful turmoil can result. *Co-Workers* states that dioceses can be helpful not just in "clarifying expectations,"[23] but also in providing guidance and protections for all those involved. In this area, written termination policies should be part of diocesan and parish personnel policies, and wherever possible all terminations should be referred to a human resource specialist. Exit interviews should be offered to all lay ecclesial ministers, and supervisors should reflect upon and learn from the findings. Outplacement assistance should be available for all lay ecclesial ministers who are leaving a church position. This can have immense benefits not only for the individual who is leaving but also for the morale of those staff members who remain. Finally, severance payments and a continuation of benefits should be offered for a transition period.

Grievance Procedures

A comprehensive personnel system, as identified by the bishops, includes the need for conflict management and dispute resolution. Fortunately, many tensions and conflicts in the ministerial workplace can be readily resolved with common sense and good pastoral judgment. However, a formal grievance procedure protects all parties and addresses situations where a lay ecclesial minister feels unfairly treated. To achieve this, all dioceses and parishes should have formal policies and procedures that are clear and fairly implemented. Access to qualified mediation services should be offered to lay ecclesial ministers and their supervisors as part of any grievance procedure, and all church employees should have access to canonical processes that are available and appropriate for particular grievance situations.

LESSONS FROM BUSINESS

To be clear, the Catholic Church is not a business. Rather, it is an institution with a unique, divinely mandated mission to proclaim the gospel to all people. As Linda Bearie noted in her presentation at the Leadership Roundtable meeting, "the mission we pursue in our Church is not the mission of many organizations. We have different values. . . . In the Church, our overriding value is that we take care of people. We take care of souls."[24] And as Mary Edward Spohrer, chancellor of the diocese of Paterson, New Jersey, said at the same meeting, employee formation is essential to lay ministers, as it is to employees in any organization, but this formation must take place in communities of faith. She states that "we must encourage the building of the faith community so that formation and integration can take place through relationships rooted in faith."[25] So the Catholic Church is not a business, and those who dedicate their lives and careers to the church are not simply working for a paycheck. But the church does have employees, and lessons from the business world certainly can benefit the church in this area. The Leadership Roundtable is doing just that, bringing exceptionally skillful businesspeople together to offer their wisdom and knowledge in service to the church.

Geno Fernandez, a partner at the leading consultancy firm McKinsey and Company, highlighted how major businesses handle the recruitment and retention of talent, and how the church might benefit from these methods and observations. From his experience at McKinsey, Fernandez says that there are four key elements in human resource development one must consider in order to achieve best practices. These are the development and training of talent, the importance of a successful value proposition, the time spent on training, and the importance of rigorous evaluation.[26] Fernandez noted that top performing companies are those that have a culture of seeking out top talent, that "focus their agendas on attracting, retaining, and developing the right people."[27] Relating this to the Catholic Church, he posed this question: "How often in diocesan councils and in parish life do we sit down and talk honestly about the people we work with, and whether we have the right people for the right jobs? It's a difficult conversation for many of us—but one that needs to take place."[28]

Every employee in an organization must be able to understand why she or he is there and what is distinctive about the work of the organization. This is called creating a successful value proposition, and again Fernandez relates this to the Catholic Church, saying that "the Church has perhaps the most exciting mission of all: proclaiming the good news of the Gospel." All employees of the church, including lay ecclesial ministers, should be able to understand their day-to-day work as part of advancing this mission, and the excitement of this mission must permeate all aspects of daily work. Fernandez highlights the spiritual rewards that ministry offers, but says that this is not necessarily enough, and exhorts the church "to look at its compensation system and see whether it's appropriate for attracting the kind of talent it needs in the dioceses and parishes."[29]

Another aspect to consider in effective human resource development is the amount of time employees spend training. At training events, at which McKinsey employees spend nearly six weeks each year, "the value proposition is enforced. The culture is inculcated. Excitement is built." Fernandez says that orientation workshops are essential, but that yearly training and continuing education must be integral to every successful organization. He offers two approaches that worked well at McKinsey: mentorship and coaching. While employees can certainly learn from books and classes, interaction with successful employees works best. And once an employee has mastered a role, it is her or his turn to teach others. Regarding coaching and feedback, Fernandez says that this is an area where the church could do better. He says, "Feedback is essential to giving people the motivation to do better. None of us likes to receive negative feedback. But if we could create a culture where people could turn around and get immediate, honest feedback from their co-workers on their performance and find out what they could be doing better, it would be quite helpful in changing behaviors."[30]

Finally, Fernandez says that a culture of evaluation is necessary for excellence in the human resources realm. He says that evaluations can be used most effectively when viewed in two dimensions: a look at how well people are executing their tasks, as well as "their potential, which brings into play questions such as whether they have the right intelligence, the right values, and the right gifts that can be used." Fernandez concluded his talk with the observation that "there are many dedicated and highly talented people out there who are willing to help the Church, even in these times of adversity. It's now up to the Church, and to us as its members, to take the lessons from high-performing organizations and apply them creatively in ways that both motivate and ensure the success of our people."[31]

ACHIEVING EXCELLENCE

One tool that the Leadership Roundtable has created to help parishes and dioceses adopt best practices in their temporal affairs is the *Catholic Standards for Excellence*, made up of several clear and concise codes that, if followed, will ensure that Catholic organizations are in compliance with best practices in human resource development and other aspects of church management. These codes were taken from the nonprofit sector, with leading ecclesial experts, including canon lawyers and other chancery professionals, adapting them to fit the needs of the Catholic Church in the United States. J. Donald Monan, chancellor of Boston College, spoke about the potential benefits of incorporating the *Standards for Excellence* when he said, "If our [the Leadership Roundtable's] whole purpose is to help the Church professionalize its institutions and fulfill its financial, managerial, and personnel obligations, then this document becomes a small miracle."[32]

The introduction to the human resources section of *Standards* states that "a diocese's [or parish's or Catholic nonprofit's] relationship to its ministerial personnel, both clergy and lay, paid and volunteer, is fundamental to its ability to achieve its mission."[33] The *Standards* calls for "human resources policies [that are] fair, establish clear expectations, and provide for meaningful and effective performance evaluation." The guide then goes on to offer six key provisions that should be followed in the realm of human resource development. Among the codes, parishes and dioceses should have "written personnel policies and procedures . . . governing the work and actions of all clergy, employees, and volunteers of the organization." Also, parishes and dioceses should have written job descriptions, systems for evaluation, orientation and ongoing training, and opportunities for formation. The *Standards* is able to convey the bulk of what has been treated in this chapter in easy-to-understand, concise codes that any parish or diocese can implement. Beginning with a self-assessment, the *Standards* program provides educational resources, templates, policy manuals, and other practical aids for successful implementation. In addition to human resources benchmarks, *Standards* has sections on mission and program, governance and advisory bodies, conflict of interest, financial and legal requirements, openness, fundraising, and public life and public policy, with specifically adapted versions for parishes, dioceses, and Catholic nonprofits.

CONCLUSION

Human resource development in the Catholic Church in the United States is an underdeveloped area that can easily be utilized to improve the temporal affairs of the church. Lay ecclesial ministers provide essential pastoral services to the faithful and work with ordained priests and deacons to serve a growing flock. To retain the best laypeople for these essential positions, the church must adopt the best practices in human resources. Laypeople in ministry face unique financial challenges, and if the church wishes to attract intelligent, articulate, compassionate people to serve as lay ministers, they must be fairly compensated, understand their work as contributing to the life-giving mission of the church, be offered professional development opportunities, and feel fulfilled in their work. Serving as co-workers in the Lord's vineyard, lay ecclesial ministers play an increasingly visible and essential pastoral role in the church, and if they are to flourish, the church must look more closely at human resource development and innovation.

NOTES

1. Michael Brough, "Raising Expectations in the Ministerial Workplace," *Origins* 37, no. 13 (September 6, 2007), 204.

2. U.S. Conference of Catholic Bishops, *Co-Workers in the Vineyard of the Lord: A Resource for Guiding the Development of Lay Ecclesial Ministry* (Washington, DC: USCCB, 2005), 5, 6.

3. USCCB, *Co-Workers*, 9.

4. Katarina Schuth, *Priestly Ministry in Multiple Parishes* (Collegeville, MN: Liturgical Press, 2006), 87.

5. David DeLambo, *Lay Parish Ministers: A Study of Emerging Leadership* (New York: NPLC, 2005), 101.

6. "Statistics on Hispanic/Latino(a) Catholics," available at http://www.usccb .org/hispanicaffairs/demo.shtml (accessed March 13, 2010).

7. A full list of resources and consulting services is available at http://www.nacpa .org.

8. Villanova University, Center for the Study of Church Management, available at http://www.villanova.edu/business/excellence/churchmgmt/ (accessed March 13, 2010). Proceedings to be published in 2010 by Lexington Press, ed. Charles Zech.

9. DeLambo, *Lay Parish Ministers*, 103–5.

10. Joseph Donnelly, in a section titled "Best Practices from Model Parishes," in the published proceedings of the 2008 annual meeting of the National Leadership Roundtable on Church Management, *Managerial Excellence: Engaging the Faith Community in Leadership in the Church Today*, 34–37; available at http://www.nlrcm .org/churchepedia.docs/Model%20Parishes(2008).pdf (accessed March 13, 2010).

11. USCCB, *Co-Workers*, 63.

12. More information on this 360-Degree Leadership Assessment Tool is available at http://www.leadership-tools.com/360-degree-feedback-leadership.html (accessed March 13, 2010).

13. USCCB, *Co-Workers*, 4.

14. *Code of Canon Law*. Libreria Editrice Vaticana, 1983. Canon 231§2.

15. *Economic Justice for All: Pastoral Letter on Catholic Social Teaching and the U.S. Economy* (Washington, DC: USCCB, 1986), 347–53.

16. Linda Bearie, in a section titled "The Economic Considerations of Recruiting, Retaining, and Motivating the Very Best for Church Service," in the published proceedings of the 2007 annual meeting of the National Leadership Roundtable on Church Management, *Give Us Your Best: A Look at Church Service for a New Generation*, 67–70; available at http://www.nlrcm.org/wharton/2007/report.pdf (accessed March 13, 2010).

17. Bearie, "Economic Considerations," 70.

18. DeLambo, *Lay Parish Ministers*, 127.

19. Parish Compensation Program. Diocese of San Jose, California, July 2007, 1.

20. Anthony Ruger et al., *The Gathering Storm* (New York: Auburn Theological Seminary, 2005). In reports in 1995 and again in 2005, researchers identified the significant problem of student debt for those training for ministry. Calling it "the gathering storm" the researchers note: "There is alarming news about the indebtedness of theological students. In the last decade, the percentage of students who have debt has increased, and the average amount of debt has increased dramatically. Some graduates have found the repayment difficult. The situation creates stress and may affect their persistence in ministry" (1). See also *Financial Assistance for Lay Persons Preparing for Lay Ecclesial Ministry*, USCCB Subcommittee on Lay Ministry, March, 2002, available at http://www.usccb.org/laity/laymin/finasst.shtml (accessed March 13, 2010). See also DeLambo, *Lay Parish Ministers*, 123–29.

21. Ruger, *The Gathering Storm*, 2.

22. DeLambo, *Lay Parish Ministers*, 128–29.

23. USCCB, *Co-Workers*, 44.

24. Bearie, "Economic Considerations," 68.

25. Mary Edward Spohrer, in a section titled "The Economic Considerations of Recruiting, Retaining, and Motivating the Very Best for Church Service," in the published proceedings of the 2007 annual meeting of the National Leadership Round-

table on Church Management, *Give Us Your Best*, 54–57, available at www.nlrcm .org/TLR/documents/Report.pdf (accessed March 13, 2010).

26. Geno Fernandez, in a section titled "The Economic Considerations of Recruiting, Retaining, and Motivating the Very Best for Church Service," in the published proceedings of the 2007 annual meeting of the National Leadership Roundtable on Church Management, *Give Us Your Best*, 50–54, available at www.nlrcm.org/TLR/ documents/Report.pdf (accessed March 13, 2010).

27. Fernandez, "Economic Considerations," 51.

28. Fernandez, "Economic Considerations," 51.

29. Fernandez, "Economic Considerations," 51–52.

30. Fernandez, "Economic Considerations," 53.

31. Fernandez, "Economic Considerations," 54.

32. J. Donald Monan, in appendix B, "Standards for Excellence: An Ethics and Accountability Code for the Catholic Sector," in the published proceedings of the 2007 annual meeting of the National Leadership Roundtable on Church Management, *Give Us Your Best*, 87, available at www.nlrcm.org/TLR/documents/Report.pdf (accessed March 13, 2010).

33. From *Catholic Standards for Excellence: An Ethics and Accountability Code for Catholic Dioceses* (Washington, DC: National Leadership Roundtable on Church Management, 2007), 6–8, available at www.catholicstandardsforexcellence.org (accessed March 13, 2010).

12

Strengthening Ministerial Leadership:
Perspectives from Systems Theory

Zeni Fox

"To live is to change, and to live long is to change often"; so says the old maxim. The church has undoubtedly lived long, and history shows that it has changed often. The last part of the twentieth and the beginning of the twenty-first centuries have brought significant change to the Roman Catholic Church in the United States, perhaps especially in her ministerial leadership. *Co-Workers in the Vineyard of the Lord*, approved by the U.S. Conference of Catholic Bishops (USCCB) in 2005, is an official recognition, and affirmation, of one of these changes, the emergence of lay ecclesial ministry.[1] This chapter will explore implications of this change and some challenges it presents to us, individually and collectively, to also change. What must we do to integrate lay ecclesial ministers more fully into the community of ministerial leadership?[2]

SYSTEMS THEORY

A Change in Ministerial Leadership

For most of our history, ministerial leadership in parishes in the United States has been primarily vested in ordained men. Certainly, religious brothers and sisters played important roles in developing many ministries, which eventually grew into significant institutions. They also provided leadership in the majority of parish schools. But Catholic institutional ministries, including parochial schools, existed in domains largely separate from leadership in the parish. However, trends that began in the 1960s and 1970s have changed this. On the one hand, the phenomenon we now name lay ecclesial ministry began to develop; on the other, the number of priests began to decline. (For many reasons, I hold that there is not a simple cause-and-effect relationship between these trends.[3])In the late 1990s the number of lay ecclesial ministers surpassed the number of priests engaged in parish ministry.[4] In *Co-Workers*, the bishops name the exercise of leadership in a particular area of ministry as a characteristic of those seen as lay ecclesial ministers,[5] recognizing this development in ministerial leadership. Certainly, this is significant change. However, many of the implications of this change remain to be explored, and many of the adaptations to it need to be further developed.

Systems

One way of reflecting on this change is with the lens of systems theory. Today it is virtually a truism to say everything is connected. Biologists have helped us to understand ecosystems, quantum physicists invite us to ponder elementary particles that are radically relational, social scientists ask us to think about our families as a network of relationships. We realize that each thing that is, is part of a system, a grouping of things that are interrelated. And each system exists in relation to other systems. A change in any part affects all of the other parts of a system, and of the larger systems of which it is a part.

Change in the System

A study of change from a systems perspective introduces useful language and concepts. Change creates disequilibrium; systems strive to restore the balance that had been effective and was comfortable, familiar. Change is often the result of adaptation to a different environment; systems that do not adapt die. Boundaries help parts of a system, and systems in relation to other systems, maintain cohesiveness. In the process of change, we both stay what we are and change. This process is true of all parts of the universe and of the church. And in systems that are considered self-conscious (a family, the church), these processes partake of intentionality and have both cognitive and emotive dimensions, indeed, subconscious and unconscious aspects as well.

The emergence of lay ecclesial ministers is a change that is impacting the church in the United States (and even the larger church) in many ways. It is not just that there is now a body of ministers who are different in some ways from others we are familiar with in recent centuries, but also that there are new relationships with other ministers, and therefore new boundary issues to resolve; new roles to develop and stabilize, in themselves, and in relation to others' roles; new patterns of interaction to engage and refine; new ways of differentiating one individual from another; new ways of explaining ourselves to ourselves in light of our tradition. A whole system is in flux.

Let us observe this dynamic reaction by noting some discrete aspects of the life of the church system, viewed from diverse angles.

INTERACTIONS

Changing Patterns of Authority

Not so long ago, the pattern of interaction in our community was rather sharply defined in terms of hierarchical roles, with a clear distinction between laity and clergy, and often between laity and vowed religious. Ordained men, and sometimes vowed religious, exercised authority, taking that function quite for granted. This authority was both formal, often canonically supported, and informal. Generally, laymen and laywomen accepted that authority. In addition, the hierarchy taught, the lay faithful were taught; hierarchy acted only downward, and dialogue was not envisioned by either group.

In the mid-1960s, numbers of laywomen and laymen were hired as directors of religious education (DREs). Often they had master's degrees in their field and significant prior experience in education. As part of their role, they developed guidelines (e.g., for consistent student attendance and parent participation in children's sacrament preparation programs). They assumed that this exercise of authority was appropriate. Privately, parents often said, "Who does she think she is?" or "What right does he think he has to tell me what to do?" The DREs said: "Parents don't understand the importance of their involvement in religious education and resist efforts to get them to take their proper role." Pastors noted that there were tensions and sometimes concluded that either the DREs did not have good people skills or that parents were not willing to accept the responsibility that was theirs. The complexity of significant change in the system whereby laypersons were exercising authority relative to other laypersons was generally not examined.

Furthermore, because priests talk to other priests, and to their bishops, sometimes an interpretation was made: "It is better not to hire people with degrees, from somewhere else, because it does not work out well. We should identify and train our own people." Questions about the impact on individuals of being role initiators (relative both to the role of DRE itself and to a layperson in a position of authority in a parish) and of the dearth of role models for lay leaders were largely unrecognized.

In more recent decades, the number of laypeople in professional roles on parish staffs has continued to expand and their roles have grown more diverse. Today pastoral associates, youth ministers, directors of liturgy, and a host of others serve in parishes. On the one hand, we can note that their contribution to parish life is assessed most positively by pastors and parishioners alike.[6] And yet the impact on and the implications for the parish system of lay staff exercising authority have not been studied. It is notable that at the symposium held at Saint John's University, Collegeville, Minnesota, in 2007, the question of authorization for ministry was identified as one of the principal areas in need of study. Certainly this is a theological and canonical question, but it also concerns the relational life of the community and its life as a system that is presently in disequilibrium. Using the lens of systems theory could help to explain why there is considerable "push back" by some priests relative to the acceptance of lay ecclesial ministers. It would also clarify why issues such as a lay ecclesial minister's participation as a member of the parish council or participant at vicariate meetings are both important and complex, not only for the lay ministers, but for the greater integrity of the whole system as it adjusts to the change in ministerial leadership.

Changing Patterns of Relationships

We can note a second relational shift between the new ministers and priests in the system of the parish. The new lay leaders tended to see themselves as co-workers with the parochial vicars and pastors in their parishes (and this was long before "co-workers" was used as a designation by the bishops). They sought opportunities to reflect together with the clergy on the work of the parish, for example, by having staff meetings. In rectories with more than one priest living together they were used to a more informal pattern of interaction, over meals, or in the common room. They did not have a felt need for formal meetings. In parishes with only a pastor, a pattern of simply making and executing decisions alone likewise mitigated against a felt need for meetings. The research on parish ministers indicates that there has been an expansion of staff meetings, but that lay ecclesial ministers continue to desire this more than their priest colleagues.[7] The special issue of the participation of pastoral life coordinators at clergy meetings is also relevant when we consider these relational changes in the system.

At times there has been significant tension between individual priests and lay ecclesial ministers. Of course, some of this is to be expected in the normal dynamic of human interaction. But some could be better understood if the challenge inherent in the shifting patterns of relating were explored. For example, when a newly ordained priest joins a staff with one or more credentialed and experienced lay leaders, he might draw upon the pattern of relating with laypersons known from his youth, expecting that his authority is primary, even in their area of competence and responsibility. At the same time, the lay leader might expect recognition of the parameters of her role or the authority of his expertise. Drawing on older paradigms of lay-clergy interaction, clergy sometimes assume that only they have a charism to teach and expect lay ecclesial ministers to accept their viewpoints as definitive. Confrontation between them may be subtle or overt, but often it does not engage a central part of the issue: The system has changed, and the interactions between the individuals within the system are under stress as a way to adapt is sought.

In some dioceses, laypersons have at times been appointed to the role of pastoral care of a parish without a resident priest, a provision of Canon 517§2. Research has shown that individuals who were publicly installed as the pastoral life coordinator were more readily accepted by parishioners than those who were not.[8] One interpretation of this is that the clear mandate from the bishop, publicly executed, influenced the interactions between the people and the new leader. Such a mandate enabled the individual to more quickly get beyond the challenge, "By what right does s/he do these things?" The system was better able to adjust to the change, and the life of the community, leader and parishioners together was better able to unfold in a vibrant way.

Fostering Relationships

Co-Workers implicitly recognizes a change in the system, emphasizing the importance of developing new patterns of relating, an "ordering of right relationships among those called to public ministries." First treated is relationship with the bishop; it is the bishop who "creates structures and venues for fostering communion" with the varied ministers, and people, of the diocese. Those dioceses that have created a lay ecclesial ministry council to serve as an advisory body to the bishop (including Oakland, the first, as well as Boise and San Jose) have developed one such structure for fostering communion with the bishop. The document also treats the importance of developing "collaboration that is mutually life-giving and respectful" between priests and lay ecclesial ministers, as well as between deacons and lay ecclesial ministers. The sense of the change in the system, which includes changes in interactions between individuals and groups, is summarized in the document: "By virtue of their call, lay ecclesial ministers take on a new relationship to the mission of the Church and to the other ministers who work to accomplish it."[9]

BOUNDARIES

Inclusion and Exclusion

Each social system is held together by an invisible boundary that defines it. Boundaries may be sharply defined, making quite clear who is and who is

not within, or they may be porous or indistinct. In families, at times we negotiate the question of our boundaries. Should the new girlfriend be invited
for Sunday dinner? To visit the summer house? For Christmas Eve? Should
the fiancé be asked to visit the sick grandfather in the hospital? To read at
the grandfather's funeral? Should the parents of the fiancé be invited to the
funeral repast? Questions such as these both recognize a change in the family
system and struggle with finding a response that both maintains the system
and adjusts to the change. Often there are incremental stretchings of the
boundary to include the new person more and more. Too rigid a boundary is
detrimental to the growth of the extended family; too loose a boundary means
that too little holds people together to draw support from one another and to
treasure family custom and ritual.

In the Catholic community, the clerical system has a sharply defined
boundary. For priests, the process of gradual inclusion into the clerical world
is long, with a shared life in seminary, and several "entrance" steps celebrated
with great pomp and ritual. The customs and ideas that keep the cohesiveness
strong include various gatherings (e.g., clergy days), rituals (e.g., the Chrism
Mass and the funerals of priests' mothers), and theology (priests are different
from laity in essence). This boundary is often described precisely as a division of the church into two groups: clergy and laity.

Fostering Inclusion

One consequence of this is considerable ambivalence about when to include
lay staff in gatherings with priests. In one diocese, with a tradition of inviting
nationally renowned speakers to address the clergy, the lay ecclesial ministers petitioned that they be included when the topic involved parish ministry.
The decision was not to include them because "the priests need time to be
together" (which, of course, is true). A separate lecture would henceforth be
given by these speakers for all interested laity. The professional needs of the
lay ecclesial ministers, relative to their ministry and to their relationship with
the priests and with the laity in general, were not recognized. The boundaries
were maintained, the changes in the system were not acknowledged, and the
anger of the lay ministers at their exclusion was not even recognized.

In other dioceses there was recognition of a change in the topography of
parish ministry and a response to the new reality. For example, Bishop Joseph
Delaney, in the diocese of Fort Worth, instituted a "ministerium," a gathering
once or twice a year of all parish ministerial leaders—priests, deacons, and laypersons—to consider topics of import for parish life today. (In addition, there
are separate gatherings of priests, of deacons, and of lay ecclesial ministers.)
These events draw strong and enthusiastic attendance. In this diocese, a more

permeable boundary has developed between lay ecclesial ministers and priests. Several other bishops have addressed the importance of "structures of communion," including Bishop Matthew Clark. In an address on the relationship of the bishop and lay ecclesial ministers, he said: "Many of my brother bishops also agree, as do I, that establishing a vital, ongoing relationship between us and lay ecclesial ministers is necessary to the very life and mission of the church of the future."[10] He described the experience of his diocese as assembling "all who are involved in pastoral ministry—priests, deacons, lay—to special ministry days where we work together on common pastoral strategies," and noted that these gatherings have helped "to break down the natural barriers between various types of ministers in order to concentrate together on the church's mission," "despite the discomfort it causes a few priests."[11]

Although his emphasis is on the relationship of clergy and laypeople as members of the People of God in the Body of Christ, Pope Benedict XVI recently made explicit reference to the need for pastoral structures to foster collaboration of priests and laity and to the change of mindset that is required, especially concerning laypeople: "They must no longer be viewed as 'collaborators' of the clergy but truly recognized as 'co-responsible' for the Church's being and action, thereby fostering the consolidation of a mature and committed laity."[12] Changes in the church system require new structures to foster, in systems language, the renegotiation of boundaries and the cohesion of the body. And changes in mindset are needed in order to make this possible.

A change has indeed occurred in the system, and Catholics are trying to adjust to it, seeking a new equilibrium. Certainly the debate about these questions is rational and to be expected. But the rational debate also has emotive and psychological aspects, which are generally not acknowledged. On the one hand, priests wonder: Will we lose our treasured comradeship if it is diluted with new members? Will these new members be like a Trojan horse, bringing those who are not like us into our company? What will the inclusion of women do to our group? If I do not stand solidly within this group, which is so much part of my identity, who will I be? On the other hand, lay ecclesial ministers wonder: Will my experience and expertise be accepted? Will I myself be accepted? Will I be able to maintain a sense of self, and of my own ministerial identity, in the face of the deeply held sense of priestly identity? Will I feel overwhelmed by the theological knowledge of the priests? Clearly, boundaries are not unimportant realities!

Boundaries and Lay Ecclesial Ministers

Although *Co-Workers* outlines characteristics of those who could be designated lay ecclesial ministers and the roles that might be called lay ecclesial ministry, the document also states that it is for each bishop to apply the term in his own diocese.[13] This has led to considerable confusion about the boundaries of lay ecclesial ministry. In the archdiocese of Chicago, Cardinal Francis George has determined that those who serve as directors of religious education or pastoral associates, and who have been certified and commissioned by him, are lay ecclesial ministers. Here the boundaries are clear. But in another diocese, a brochure advertising a day devoted to the topic of *Co-Workers* stated that lay ecclesial ministry is the new name for lay ministry, quite without a definition by the bishop of that local church. In many dioceses, laypersons working in parishes have simply claimed the name, certainly in part because *Co-Workers* presents a theology and vision of church and ministry that resonates with them. In these instances the issue has porous boundaries indeed. If *Co-Workers* is to have the desired impact on both the formation of those laypersons who serve in leadership roles in the community and the collaboration of all in ministerial leadership, greater clarity regarding who is a lay ecclesial minister is certainly needed.

One aspect of the question of the importance of boundaries is really quite clearly stated in *Co-Workers*. More than once the theological teaching that there is a difference "not simply in degree but in essence" between the participation in the priesthood of Christ of priests and that of laity is affirmed.[14] At the same time, there is insistence on essential unity:

> Ministry is diverse and, at the same time, profoundly relational. This is so because ministry has its source in the triune God and because it takes shape within the Church understood as a communion. Ministerial relationships are grounded first in what all members of Christ's Body have in common. Through their sacramental initiation all are established in a personal relationship with Christ and in a network of relationships within the communion of the People of God. The personal discipleship of each individual makes possible a community of disciples formed by and for the mission of Christ.[15]

Another boundary question that is operative in the debates about the place of lay ecclesial ministers in the life of the church is that between "the world" and "the church." It is true that Vatican II emphasized the role of the laity in the world. The *Decree on the Apostolate of the Laity* states: "The characteristic of the lay state being a life led in the midst of the world and of secular affairs, laymen are called by God to make of their apostolate, through the vigor of their Christian spirit, a leaven for the world."[16] However, the council acknowledged that laity also has a role in the church. In several documents, the Council Fathers speak of various roles, functions, and ministries filled by laypeople. Nonetheless, in the years since the council there has been a tendency for some to describe the laity's role as only in the world and to use that formulation to call into question the validity of lay ecclesial ministry. This unfortunate response follows the same path as that which created a dichotomy between laity and clergy in the first place, emphasizing a rigid boundary between these two groups in the church. In *State of the Questions*, the bishops creatively engage this tension, stating:

> One element of the unique character of the laity, within the one mission of the Church, is its secular character. Because of this secular character, the laity are the Church in the heart of the world and bring the world into the heart of the Church. . . . All of the laity are called to work toward the transformation of the secular world. Some do this by working in the secular realm; others do this by working in the Church and focusing on the building of ecclesial communion, which has as its purpose the transformation of the world.[17]

Transcending a Boundary

The existential reality of the men and women serving as lay ecclesial ministers poses a challenge to an inadequate theology of the laity. No longer should anyone maintain a conviction that the work of the church belongs simply to vowed and ordained persons. Nor can a layperson think that the invitation to holiness, to a personal relationship with God, is given only to those in ecclesiastical life. Lay ecclesial ministers are an embodiment of a commitment to both secular life, "in the world," and ministry in the church. Their ministry itself signals that participation in the mission of the church is the role of every baptized person. Their deep participation in the communion of the church is a sign of God's call to all the baptized. In this case, we are invited to transcend an artificial boundary and to contemplate the working of God's grace in and through God's church, and in and through all that is good in God's world.

DIFFERENTIATION

The Task

System theorists describe the growth of individuals within a corporate group as a process of differentiation, of growing to be more who each one is (or, speaking spiritually, who each one is called to be). Furthermore, they say that this process serves the greater vibrancy and effectiveness of the system itself. This process, whether of the mid-marriage couple exploring ways that each partner will become more fully an individual person, or a teenage boy seeking more autonomy within the family, is difficult. The task belongs first to the individual, but the whole system is affected: the marriage becomes stronger, the family more flexible. The individual changes and grows and so does the system. For leaders, the more effectively they negotiate their differentiation within the group, the more effective their leadership.

Differentiation of Church Leaders

An example of this has been unfolding in parish life; at times a congregation senses turf battles between different ministers—the liturgist and the religious educator, the youth minister and the pastoral associate, for example. In part these battles can be due to the effort the new ministers are making to differentiate themselves from one another in the system. If the conflict is constructively handled (conflict can, indeed, be constructive or destructive), it can contribute to both clearer work identities for the ministers and greater vibrancy in the ministry. Each minister can lead more effectively when the locus of his or her leadership is clear to the individual and the community, when the leader is constructively differentiated from other leaders and from the group.

An example of differentiation that is having considerable impact in ministry today is the identification of competencies needed for particular ministerial roles. The National Federation for Catholic Youth Ministry was the first to enter into a process of analysis and consultation with its members in an effort to say this is what we do, and what we need to know, and to *be*, to do it well. They were struggling to define themselves relative to the two other large groups of lay ministers, religious educators (the first and largest group) and pastoral associates (at the time, of growing influence and seemingly less marginalized than they were). Their process of differentiation positively impacted the system, causing other organizations, including most recently the National Federation of Priests' Councils, to follow similar paths. Several of the lay organizations subsequently worked toward a common statement of competencies needed for all arenas of lay ministry.[18]

These actions impacted differentiation and influenced leaders in ministry formation, diocesan and academic, to work with the common competencies in shaping their programs. The bishops have acknowledged that they made extensive use of the document *National Certification Standards for Lay Ecclesial Ministers* in developing the chapter "Formation of Lay Ecclesial Ministry" in *Co-Workers*.[19] The well-being of the entire system is influenced by the differentiation of individuals and groups within it.

Differentiation Relative to the Lay Faithful

There is a tension, however, regarding the differentiation of lay ecclesial ministers relative to the lay faithful in general. In developing *Co-Workers*, there was an ongoing concern about creating a new class in the church, about fostering an elitism that would be detrimental for the community. The document states, "The call to lay ecclesial ministry adds a particular focus to the Christian discipleship expected of all the baptized. Their call, however, should not foster an elitism that places lay ecclesial ministers above or outside the laity."[20] The question of how to think of lay ecclesial ministers as both part of the lay faithful (not above nor outside of) and yet having a different, a distinct role in the community, is not answered here. In acknowledging that a characteristic of lay ecclesial ministry is "leadership in a particular area of ministry," the bishops indicate that there is indeed *differentiation*.

In recent years, vowed religious have struggled with this issue, desiring to strengthen their bonds with their fellow laity and also to live ever more fully into their particular role in the church. *Co-Workers* states something of this particularity, saying, "Consecrated persons participate in ecclesial ministry by their own title, according to the nature of their institute. Their exercise of ecclesial ministry is imbued with the grace of their consecration."[21] However, in relation to lay ecclesial ministers, there is a reluctance to differentiate them more precisely from the lay faithful. In a community seeking to live more fully into the vision of the church as a community, in communion with our Trinitarian God and one another, this is understandable. But if indeed greater differentiation brings growth for individuals and systems, the risks inherent in the task need to be engaged. This is first the task of the individuals, but the whole system is involved. We have noted how the individual associations of lay ecclesial ministers initiated work on differentiation competencies, which then impacted the larger system in diverse ways. The further work of differentiation must also be initiated by the lay ecclesial ministers themselves. Even small steps at the parish level, such as developing job descriptions that are clear and specific, would help this process. Cooperative work at the vicariate and diocesan levels to develop role definitions would significantly impact differentiation.

THE ROLE OF RITUAL

Edwin Friedman, who has explored the relevance of family systems theory for congregational life, has analyzed the import of times of passage in human life—births, marriages, deaths. He notes that at these times, the system is in disequilibrium and therefore more open to the healing of old losses, wounds, and hurts and more open to the manifestation of the sacred in our midst.[22] A further insight from Friedman is that the rituals developed by the tradition for marking life passages are the locus for families, in time and place, of particularly powerful healing and of encounter with the sacred. For many Catholics, the experience of the Church's rituals, for example for funerals, substantiates this insight.

What application could be made to the question of how to better integrate lay ecclesial ministers into the community of ministerial leadership? One could say that in the church system, Catholics are in a time of birth of a new form of ministerial leadership and death of a rigid clerical/lay divide. (Note that it is the rigid divide that is posited as dying.) There is potential in this moment for healing old hurts and for a new awareness of God's presence with us on the journey, ever shepherding his people. Already, the incorporation of laypeople into roles at liturgy (lectors, cantors, etc.) signals that we are not simply clergy and laity, two separate groups with two entirely separate functions and places, but a diversity of ministers, carrying forward the mission of Jesus. We are reminded that God, ever active, is present in and through all persons in the community, in all places in the world.

Co-Workers recognizes the value of blessings and rituals: "At certain points in the authorization process, public prayer and ritual can be significant for the lay ecclesial minister and for the community, highlighting the new relationships that the person is beginning in the life of the community." For parish ministers, the bishops emphasize that the rite would provide opportunity for the lay ecclesial minister and the community to pray together. They conclude: "Since the Church deeply values ritual blessings and communal prayer, such a celebration would both instruct the community and spiritually strengthen the lay ecclesial minister."[23] In systems terms, the ritual would validate the change in the consciousness of both the lay ecclesial minister and the community, facilitating increased equilibrium. In Friedman's terms, it would open both the minister and the community to a fuller awareness of God's presence and assist in healing hurts from the past.

TOWARD THE FUTURE

This analysis suggests many areas of church life that need creative attention to assist the task of integrating the new lay ministers into the corpus of ministerial leadership. Some of these are structural, some attitudinal; some require growth in understanding, some changes in behavior.

Co-Workers itself offers much to assist growth in understanding of the theology of lay ecclesial ministry, indeed, of ministry in the church. Deepening understanding for all members of the community, but most especially the clergy, is a task for programs of ministry formation and for continuing education. However, since resistance to change is to be expected, this is not simply a matter of instruction; experience itself must teach. Therefore, opportunities for telling the stories of lay ecclesial ministers, for hearing them tell their own stories of call and service,[24] for interacting on an interpersonal level are all needed to assist the growth in understanding that is required.

The bishops' document calls for collaboration among ministerial leaders. The task of creating communion among these leaders requires an understanding of the theological basis of collaboration, but also of practical strategies to foster it. There are various published resources and many workshop leaders who can assist in this effort.[25] A deeper grasp of leadership theory, including an analysis of the function of authority, is invaluable for this purpose. Again, ministry preparation and continuing education should include such study. Here, too, interpersonal interaction is invaluable in enabling a spirit of collaboration to grow.

Structures of communion, from parish councils to diocesan advisory bodies, vicariate meetings to diocesan education days, need to be assessed to determine what changes are needed to incorporate the new ministerial leaders appropriately. Where necessary, new structures such as lay ecclesial ministry councils and "ministeriums" should be created and existing ones reformed. In many dioceses, there is no official way whereby the bishop is in relationship with lay ecclesial ministers; *Co-Workers* points to the importance of creating ways to foster this, an ordering of relationships.

The role of blessings and rituals for lay ecclesial ministers, in dioceses and parishes, should be analyzed.[26] Existing blessings and rituals should be used and others created as needed. As a deeply sacramental people, the use of symbol and ritual is central to identity as Catholics. Appropriate blessings and rituals for lay ecclesial ministers will be central to their identity as ministerial leaders and will facilitate the acceptance of their leadership by their communities.

Lay ecclesial ministers themselves need to continue to ponder their place in the church and to articulate, from their experience in ministry, the differentiation appropriate to themselves, not only in relation to the tasks they perform, but also as men and women responding to a call to serve the community.

DISCERNING THE WORK OF THE SPIRIT

Believing that Jesus is always with his church, and that the Spirit is always present in what is, what insights from systems theory help us discern God's action in our midst today?

The theorists say that change in one part of the system affects all other parts. Change in parishes affects the diocese, change in a diocese affects the church in the United States, change here affects the world church. Vatican II proposed an understanding of the church as first the People of God. Prior to all particularities of status, role, and function, we are one body, with a common call to holiness, a common call to sharing in the mission of the church.

The history of recent centuries that emphasized classes within the church and too often saw holiness as possible only within certain states of life and mission as the task only of some needs considerable unlearning if this vision is to be fulfilled. The influence of lay ecclesial ministry on the rigid boundaries between clergy and laity, and at times between laity and vowed religious, is itself a growth toward a less dichotomized church. The differentiation of individuals and groups within the church is a movement in our time toward a fuller sharing in the mission and ministry of Jesus by all his disciples, with their particular tasks and roles. An increase of interactions characterized by mutual respect and the granting of appropriate authority to the new ministerial leaders strengthens the church's own authority. The church is growing into a greater fullness of ministry as it draws lay ecclesial ministers into the body of those who lead the community, the *ministerium*.

The Lord has promised that in every age we will be invited toward the change needed for the vibrancy of the community and the efficacy of its mission. The emergence of lay ecclesial ministers is indeed a change, affirmed in *Co-Workers* as the work of the Spirit. The response to them by the entire church is further change, which we pray will follow the Spirit's promptings, ever embracing the promise of the Lord in the book of Revelation, "'Behold, I make all things new'" (21:5).

NOTES

1. U.S. Conference of Catholic Bishops, *Co-Workers in the Vineyard of the Lord: A Resource for Guiding the Development of Lay Ecclesial Ministry* (Washington, DC: USCCB, 2005).

2. Already in 1997, Fred Hofheinz, program director for religion at the Lilly Endowment, observed: "There is no more important issue facing the American Catholic Church than . . . the integration of the new ministers into the ongoing life of dioceses across the country." Telephone interview with the author, March 13, 1997.

3. A pastoral letter prepared by Cardinal Roger Mahony and the priests of the archdiocese of Los Angeles clearly separates these two developments, stating: "Even if seminaries were once again filled to overflowing and convents packed with Sisters, there would still remain the need for cultivating, developing, and sustaining the full flourishing of ministries that we have witnessed in the Church since the Second Vatican Council. In the wake of the Council, we have arrived at a clearer recognition that it is in the nature of the Church to be endowed with

many gifts, and that these gifts are the basis for the vocations to the priesthood, the diaconate, and the religious life, as well as for the many ministries rooted in the call of baptism." *As I Have Done for You* (Chicago: Liturgy Training Publications, 2000), 15–16.

4. "The Study of the Impact of Fewer Priests on the Pastoral Ministry," preparatory document for the spring general meeting of the USCCB, June 15–17, 2000, in Milwaukee, Wisconsin, iv, v, available at http://www.usccb.org/plm/studyifp.shtml (accessed March 13, 2010).

5. USCCB, *Co-Workers*, 10.

6. When comparing their research of 1992 and 1997, Philip Murnion and David DeLambo state: "The picture from all sides shows considerable contribution to parish life [by lay ministers]. . . . These parish ministers are reported by all [pastors and parishioners], in most categories, not only as continuing what was already present in the parishes, but enhancing parish life." *Parishes and Parish Ministers: A Study of Parish Lay Ministry* (New York: National Pastoral Life Center, 1999), 54.

7. Murnion reflected at length on the differing desires of lay ministers and pastors relative to staff meetings in his 1992 study. Philip J. Murnion, *New Parish Ministers: Laity and Religious on Parish Staffs* (New York: National Pastoral Life Center, 1992), 73–74. He also analyzed another variable, the varying needs/desires of men and women.

8. Ruth Wallace, *They Call Her Pastor: A New Role for Catholic Women* (Albany, NY: SUNY Press, 1992).

9. USCCB, *Co-Workers*, 21–26.

10. Matthew Clark, "The Relationship of the Bishop and Lay Ecclesial Minister," *Origins* 30, no. 42 (April 5, 2001): 677. See also "The Bishop and Lay Ecclesial Ministers," chapter 8 in Clark's foreword in *Hope: Saying AMEN to Lay Ecclesial Ministry* (Notre Dame, IN: Ave Maria Press, 2009), 77–88.

11. Clark, "Relationship of the Bishop and Lay Ecclesial Minister," 679.

12. Pope Benedict XVI, "Address Opening the Pastoral Convention of the Diocese of Rome on the theme 'Church Membership and Pastoral Co-Responsibility,'" May 26, 2009, http://www.vatican.va/holy_father/benedict_xvi/speeches/2009/may/documents/hf_ben-xvi_spe_20090526_convegno-diocesi-rm_en.html (accessed March 13, 2010).

13. USCCB, *Co-Workers*, 11.

14. USCCB, *Co-Workers*, 24.

15. USCCB, *Co-Workers*, 21.

16. Article 1. *Vatican II: The Conciliar and Post-Conciliar Documents*, edited by Austin Flannery (Northport, NY: Costello Publishing, 1984), 767.

17. *Lay Ecclesial Ministry: The State of the Questions*, A Report of the Subcommittee on Lay Ministry (Washington, DC: U.S. Catholic Conference, 1999), 15.

18. *Common Formation Goals for Ministry*, edited by Joseph T. Merkt (Washington, DC: National Association for Lay Ministry, National Federation of Catholic Youth Ministry, and National Conference for Catechetical Leadership, 2000).

19. USCCB, *Co-Workers*, footnote 69, 34.

20. USCCB, *Co-Workers*, 58.

21. USCCB, *Co-Workers*, 13.

22. *Generation to Generation: Family Process in Church and Synagogue* (New York: Guilford, 1985), 162–69.

23. USCCB, *Co-Workers*, 59.

24. A volume that presents many such stories is *Shaping Catholic Parishes: Pastoral Leaders in the 21st Century*, edited by Carole Ganim (Chicago: Loyola University Press, 2008).

25. Loughlan Sofield has long been a leader in bringing research and practical wisdom to bear on the issue of collaboration. See, for example, *Collaboration: Uniting Our Gifts in Ministry*, with Carroll Juliano (Notre Dame, IN: Ave Maria Press, 2000).

26. Catherine Vincie's chapter in this volume, "Lay Ecclesial Ministry and Ritual," explores this question in depth.

Index

Albany, diocese of: and public promotion of roles for lay ecclesial ministers, 12

Amish community: and power of forgiveness, 132

Ang, Soon: *Cultural Intelligence,* 178n46

apostles, three characteristics of: 35–36

Aquinas, Thomas, Saint: on time, 55

Ars, Curé of: and introspective spirituality of Vatican I, 58

"As I Have Done For You" (Mahony), 76, 210–11n3

Asad, Talal, 95

Association of Graduate Programs in Ministry (AGPIM), 174–75n11

baptism, 21–22; as call to mission for all baptized, 27–28; as call to participate in mission of church, 205; discipleship conferred by, 26; restored theology of in Vatican II documents, 54; as shared call to discipleship, 143; as source of gift of God's presence in lay ministers, 154; as source of inclusive definition of ministry, 34

baptized, ministry of the: decline of in feudal times, 55–56; deriving from priest's need for assistance rather than from the Spirit, 61–62; limited model of the *munera* as ministerial framework for, 61; opening up of theological study to, 58; passivity encouraged in under hierarchical model of church authority, 61; sixty percent of ministry in America in last century and a half done by, 58; stirring the modern church by, 58; vs. neo-Platonic perspective of lay ministry; and wider role in church, 54

Bearie, Linda (chancellor, diocese of San Jose), 188, 190

Bechtle, Regina, S.C., x–xi, 213

Bell, Catherine: *Ritual,* 89, 94, 99n4

Benedict XVI (pope): and call for new structures and change of mindset concerning laypeople, 203; call to encourage vocations by, 115; call to reflect on revision of canon law code by, 103; insistence on essential difference between priests and laity by, 114

Benedict, Rule of, 95–96

Bennett, Janet M. and Milton J., 169–70, 178n46

About the Contributors

Regina Bechtle, S.C., Ph.D., is director of charism resources for the Sisters of Charity of New York. She researches, writes about, and offers retreats and programs on Vincentian spirituality, religious life, and leadership. She has served on her congregation's leadership team, coauthored a resource manual for women religious new to leadership, and directed a center for leadership and spirituality at the College of Mount Saint Vincent in New York. Coeditor of a three-volume collection of Saint Elizabeth Seton's writings and of *Called and Chosen: Toward a Spirituality for Lay Leaders* (2005), she has also published essays and poetry in religious and theological journals.

Michael J. Brough is director of planning and programs for the National Leadership Roundtable on Church Management. He has worked with and trained lay ecclesial ministers in dioceses and parishes across the United States and in twelve different countries. In his role with the Leadership Roundtable, he has contributed toward the development of personnel policies and procedures that enhance the effectiveness of all those in church ministry.

Juliana Casey, IHM, executive vice president, mission integration, and member of the Catholic Health East Senior Management Team, holds a Ph.D. and an S.T.D., both from the Catholic University of Louvain, Belgium. Her work includes creating resources basic to the formation of leaders within Catholic health care, organizing workshops that focus on the theory and praxis of ministerial formation, and collaborating with other leaders in the field, providing theological bases for transforming health care in the United States. She is the author of three books, including *Food for the Journey: Theological Foundations of Catholic Healthcare*, and numerous articles.

Sharon A. Euart, RSM, is a member of the South Central Community of the Sisters of Mercy of the Americas. She holds a doctorate in canon law from the Catholic University of America. She served as associate general secretary of the U.S. Conference of Catholic Bishops from 1989 to 2001. Currently she is executive coordinator of the Canon Law Society of America and a visiting lecturer in the School of Canon Law at Catholic University. She also serves as a consultant to the USCCB Committee on Canonical Affairs and Church Governance and as vice chair of the board of directors of CARA and is a past president of the Canon Law Society of America.

Zeni Fox, professor of pastoral theology at Immaculate Conception Seminary, Seton Hall University, is the author of *New Ecclesial Ministry: Lay Professionals Serving the Church* (revised and expanded edition, 2002) and various articles; in addition, she was the coeditor of *Called and Chosen: Toward a Spirituality for Lay Leaders* (2005). From 1994 to 2005, she served as an advisor to the USCCB Subcommittee on Lay Ministry, which developed *Co-Workers in the Vineyard of the Lord*. She has a doctorate in systematic theology from Fordham University; she was awarded the *Gaudium et Spes* award by the National Association for Lay Ministry.

Richard R. Gaillardetz, Ph.D., is the Margaret and Thomas Murray and James J. Bacik Professor of Catholic Studies at the University of Toledo. He received his Ph.D. in systematic theology from the University of Notre Dame. He is the author of numerous books and articles, including *Ecclesiology for a Global Church: A People Called and Sent* (2008) and *The Church in the Making* (2006). He was an official delegate on the U.S. Catholic-Methodist Ecumenical Dialogue from 2001 to 2005 and served on the board of directors for the Catholic Theological Society of America from 2006 to 2008.

Edward P. Hahnenberg, Ph.D., is associate professor of theology at Xavier University, Cincinnati. He received his doctorate from the University of Notre Dame in 2002 and served as a theological consultant to the U.S. Conference of Bishops' Subcommittee on Lay Ministry in their preparation of the document *Co-Workers in the Vineyard of the Lord*. A popular speaker, he is the author of three books—*Ministries: A Relational Approach* (2003), *A Concise Guide to the Documents of Vatican II* (2007), and *Awakening Vocation* (2010)—and numerous articles in academic and pastoral journals. A native of northern Michigan, he and his family now live near Cincinnati, Ohio.

Amy Hoey, RSM, Ph.D., has been a Sister of Mercy (Northeast Community) for over fifty-seven years. After ministries in education (elementary, secondary, and undergraduate) and in elected leadership for her community, she served for ten years as staff to the USCCB Subcommittee that prepared *Co-Workers in the Vineyard of the Lord.* After the document was adopted, she served as a lecturer and consultant for lay ecclesial ministry with dioceses and associations throughout the country. Her current ministry includes companioning the dying and serving as a parish volunteer.

William H. Johnston, Ph.D., University of Notre Dame, is assistant professor in the Department of Religious Studies, University of Dayton, where he teaches courses in pastoral ministry. Previously he worked in church ministry in the (arch)dioceses of Grand Rapids, Richmond, and Baltimore. He has assisted with several projects of the USCCB, is a former member of NACARE (National Advisory Committee on Adult Religious Education), and is a past board chair of the National Association for Lay Ministry. He published "Lay Ecclesial Ministry in Theological and Relational Context: A Study of Ministry Formation Documents" in *Catholic Identity and the Laity* (Orbis, 2009) and is currently working on a book exploring different dimensions of Pope Benedict XVI's *motu proprio, Summorum Pontificum.*

H. Richard McCord, Jr. is executive director of the United States Conference of Catholic Bishops' Secretariat of Laity, Marriage, Family Life and Youth. In this capacity he directed the project that produced *Co-Workers in the Vineyard of the Lord.* He has served the church professionally in parish, diocesan, and national positions since 1974. He has a master's degree in Christian education (Princeton) and a doctorate in education (University of Maryland). His writings on church issues have appeared in several collections and religious publications. He and his wife, Denise, are parents of an adult son.

Michael J. O'Loughlin is communications and development officer for the National Leadership Roundtable on Church Management, which is dedicated to promoting excellence and best practices in the management, finances, and human resource development of the Catholic Church in the United States. He has worked for several media organizations, including *Spectrum* magazine, the *Saint Anselm Crier*, and *New Hampshire News Links.* He holds a B.A. from Saint Anselm College, 2007, and an M.A.R. from Yale Divinity School, 2009. Originally from New England, he now lives in Washington, D.C.

Thomas F. O'Meara, O.P., did his doctoral studies at the University of Munich with Heinrich Fries and Karl Rahner. From 1981 until 2002 he taught at the University of Notre Dame, where he is William K. Warren Professor Emeritus. Recently he has been a visiting professor in South Africa, at the University of San Diego, and at Boston College. Among his twelve books are *Theology of Ministry* (1983; revised and expanded edition, 1999); *Thomas Aquinas, Theologian*; and an introduction to Karl Rahner's theology, *God in the World* (2007).

Catherine Vincie, RSHM, Ph.D., is professor of sacramental and liturgical theology at the Aquinas Institute of Theology in St. Louis, Missouri, where she has taught for the past fifteen years. She is currently chair of a new degree program in sacred music in collaboration with Webster University and the archdiocese of St. Louis. Her publishing interests are in the area of Christian initiation, Eucharist, liturgy and justice, and the liturgical year. Recent publications include "The Challenge of the New Science to Liturgy," *Worship* 83, no. 1 (2009), and *Celebrating Divine Mystery: A Primer in Liturgical Theology* (2009).

Emil A. Wcela is a retired auxiliary bishop of the diocese of Rockville Centre, New York. A former seminary rector and professor of scripture and subsequently a pastor, he continues to teach, lecture, and lead retreats for clergy and parishes. Past president of the Catholic Biblical Association, he has authored introductory guides to Scripture as well as articles in journals such as the *Catholic Biblical Quarterly*. He served on the Subcommittee on Lay Ministry in its first several years, when they developed *Lay Ecclesial Ministry: The State of the Questions* (1999).